The
Reading
Book
of
Days

The History of
Reading Society

The Reading Book of Days is a collaborative effort by members and associates of the History of Reading Society, with John Dearing as Editor and Penelope Starr and Philip Vaughan as Assistant Editors. See February 3rd for full list of authors.

First published 2013

The History Press
The Mill, Brimscombe Port
Stroud, Gloucestershire, GL5 2QG
www.thehistorypress.co.uk

British Library Cataloguing in Publication Data.
A catalogue record for this book is available from the British Library.

ISBN 978 0 7524 6801 3

Typesetting and origination by The History Press
Printed in India

JANUARY 1ST

1822: On this day, William Ford Poulton was born, son of Cornelius and grandson of Charles Poulton, architect of the 1786 Reading Town Hall. William became one of the most important Nonconformist architects; with his partner William Henry Woodman, he designed over seventy churches and chapels, including his masterpiece, Westminster Chapel in London. Poulton also designed the drinking fountain at St Laurence's, 1 London Street, Reading, and Wokingham Town Hall. In 1850 he married Georgina Bagnall, whose sister married William Woodman, making the partners also brothers-in-law. Poulton left Reading in 1883 and settled in Great Malvern. His daughter Lily founded Malvern Girls College; his son, Sir Edward Poulton, was an eminent zoologist.

SG (Gold, S., *Dictionary of Architects at Reading*, 1999)

———•◆•———

1889: On this day, Eric Harold Neville, a geometrical mathematician (heavily fictionalised in the 2007 novel *The Indian Clerk*) was born in London. After graduating at Trinity College, Cambridge, where he became a Fellow, he was appointed to the chair of Mathematics at University College, Reading. Over the next few years, his work was largely responsible for Reading receiving its university charter in 1926, with power to award degrees. Of his many published papers, most were short pieces addressing concise, succinctly solved problems. Retiring from the university in 1954, he died at Reading in August 1961.

VC (*The Mathematical Gazette*, May 1964)

JANUARY 2ND

1904: On this day, the *Reading Standard* printed a letter from Joseph Mosdell addressed to William McIlroy, which he shared with the readers; he eulogised McIlroy's new shop premises and called them 'Reading's Crystal Palace' in an accompanying poem. Plans were first submitted in August 1899, but after the usual disapprovals and amendments they were redrawn and resubmitted. The new structure occupied the same site as an earlier McIlroy's building but boasted an enormous 464ft frontage with shops on the ground floor, boardroom on the first floor and warehouse in the basement. The second and third floors, with their vast array of glass, housed the offices and 150 bedrooms for the staff, who were provided with a dining-room, sitting-rooms and music-room. The front was faced in light-red majolica glazed bricks. The overall architects were the firm of Joseph Morris & Son, but its unusual style hints more at son, Francis, than his father. The building is still in use today as separate shops with apartments above, though some of the decorative brickwork has been reduced. It has much in common with the former Pearl Buildings (1902) in Station Road, designed by the same firm.

SG (*Reading Standard*)

JANUARY 3RD

1891: On this day, Ellen Hopkins, aged fifteen, died while skating on the River Kennet, close to Huntley & Palmers biscuit factory. The weather had been particularly cold and the river was frozen. Ellen, whose father George was blacksmith at the forge in Merchant's Place, joined four friends for some Saturday afternoon fun. The five youngsters, aged eight to fifteen, unaware that hot water pipes from the factory made that area unsafe, were enjoying their skating – then the ice gave way. Ellen and two of the boys fell in; the other two, attempting to help, also toppled into the freezing waters. Passers-by extended ladders over the ice and the four boys scrambled out. Benjamin Hamblin, a worker at the factory, came out and tried to save Ellen but she could not grasp the pole he held out and she disappeared into the river. Within fifteen minutes her body was retrieved from the water but she was dead. At the inquest, held on 5 January at the St Giles Coffee House, Mr Hopkins congratulated the survivors' parents. He felt that no blame should attach to anyone but thought that there should have been signs to warn of the dangers there.
JP (*Berkshire Chronicle*)

JANUARY 4TH

871: On this day, Reading lamented a bloody encounter between invading Danes and the peasant-soldiers of Wessex, led by King Ethelred and his brother Alfred (later famed as Alfred the Great, the only English king called 'Great'). By 870 Wessex stood alone against the 'Great Heathen Army' of the Danes (sometimes termed 'Vikings'). At year's end the Danes made a fortified camp in Reading (located probably at the top of today's Castle Hill). The *Anglo-Saxon Chronicle* account of these events is the first written reference to Reading town. The threat to Wessex was now severe. The Battle of Englefield saw the Danes defeated, but in January, when the Wessex army attacked the Danes at Reading, their losses were heavy. Wessex regrouped to fight further battles, in which neither side was decisively victorious. In April 871 Alfred became King of Wessex. He entered peace negotiations, and the Danes withdrew from their Reading camp. But Alfred's Danish troubles continued, despite campaigns and truces right across England. To oppose the invaders, he even created a navy, before he died in 899. Happily, it seems that Reading escaped more bloodshed at Danish hands for the next hundred years.

PV (*Anglo-Saxon Chronicle*)

JANUARY 5TH

1136: On this day, King Henry I was buried with great pomp before the High Altar of Reading Abbey, the huge, rich foundation he had established fifteen years before. Stephen, the new king, and all his archbishops, bishops and nobles, attended the funeral. After William the Conqueror won England's throne in 1066, his family kept its French possessions and connections. Thus Henry (William's fourth son) was in his Duchy of Normandy when he became fatally ill – reputedly after over-indulging in lampreys. Thanks to the intervention of Hugh, Archbishop of Rouen, a former Reading abbot, Henry's embalmed body was returned for interment at the Abbey. The tomb was embellished with Henry's life-size effigy; but like most of the Abbey's glories, this monument is long gone. After Henry VIII dissolved the monasteries, Reading Abbey was plundered of its roof-timbers, lead, tiles and stone. Believing that the remains of the founder, Henry I, lay in a silver coffin, the sixteenth-century demolition gang rifled the tomb, scattering its contents; a later historian lamented that the King's bones 'could not enjoy repose in his grave, but were thrown out to make room for a stable for horses'.

PV (Hurry, J., *Reading Abbey*, 1901)

January 6th

1634: On this day, a valuable charity was established for Reading's poor, when Sir Thomas Vachel (1560-1638) signed a deed donating a set of almshouses near the church in St Mary's Butts. The stone plaque that still survives succinctly tells the story: 'Sr. THOMAS VACHEL Kt. Erected these Alms-Houses Anno Dom. 1634, and endow'd them with Forty Pounds p. Annum for ever for the Maintenance of Six poor Men.' Vachel married three times but had no children. He was a scion of the Vachell (sic) family, owners of Coley Park since the thirteenth century. The 1634 endowment, secured on rents for a property called Great and Little Garstons at Shinfield, also granted each of the 'poor men' 2s a week and two loads of wood per year. In 1867 these 'St Mary's Almshouses' were demolished. The proceeds from selling the land were then applied to building the present Vachel Almshouses in Castle Street, designed by architect William Henry Woodman. These thirty-two pleasant two-storey dwellings, stepping down to the Holy Brook, are occupied to this day. They now enjoy English Heritage Grade II listing, with the original Vachel plaque proudly displayed.

PV (Coates, C., *History & Antiquities of Reading*, 1802)

JANUARY 7TH

1937: On this day, early in the morning, a policeman patrolling Friar Street raised the alarm on discovering that the back of the Royal County Theatre was ablaze. Unfortunately, the fire had already spread so far that the fire brigade could only contain it, to prevent it spreading to adjoining shops. Everything inside was completely destroyed. The fire occurred during a run of the pantomime *Robinson Crusoe.* Over 100 people – theatre staff and cast – lost their jobs. Also, the town lost a popular entertainment venue, when it became clear that rebuilding the theatre was impracticable. A.H. Bull bought the site for expanding their Broad Street department store. Existing until the mid-1950s, this store featured a much-appreciated facility – shoppers were able to walk under-cover between Friar Street and Broad Street. Strangely, previous theatres in Friar Street had had devastating fires. A chapel, opened on the site in 1871, was sold in about 1888 to become the Royal Assembly Rooms. This was then converted into the Princes Theatre in 1893, being renamed the New Royal County Theatre in 1895 (to replace another in Friar Street that had burned down in August 1894).
JRW (Phillips, D., *Reading Theatres, Cinemas and Other Entertainments 1788-1978*, 1978)

JANUARY 8TH

1811: On this day, the British School was officially opened. The idea for such a school originated when Joseph Lancaster visited Reading in August 1809 to lecture on his plan for the Education of Poor Children. Local gentry, educationists, businessmen and clergy quickly endorsed the idea, forming a committee to subscribe and lend support as the boys at this stage needed sponsoring. A site in Southampton Street was purchased with Richard Billing, architect and builder, providing the design. The opening preparations were ready by October 1810, but the first headmaster, Nathaniel Higgins, was awaited. The school was first called the Reading Lancastrian School, but by 1814 the Royal Lancastrian Society changed its name to the British and Foreign Society, with schools based on Lancaster's plan opening all over the world; hence most British schools were so named. From 1901-3 the Reading institution was called Southampton Street Board School and from 1903-7 Southampton Street Council School. It then closed, with pupils and staff transferred to a new school named after George Palmer, which opened on 3 October. For many years the building was used by the school meals service, also for community activities.
SG (Barnes-Phillips, D., *This is our School*, Corridor Press, 2011)

JANUARY 9TH

1960: On this day, a short run of *Babes in the Wood* ended and Reading's Palace Theatre, in Cheapside, closed its doors for ever. It died on its feet, so to speak, with no publicity – just when interest in live theatre was reviving. Had it simply been locked up, to await 'discovery' a few decades later, Reading would possess an outstanding jewel attracting theatregoers from near and far. But it was razed to the ground in 1961 and an office block rose in its place. Built of concrete and steel (with public safety very much in mind), the 'Palace' boasted immense Edwardian opulence. Designed to hold up to 1,460 patrons, it was described as architecturally stunning internally, with an elegantly decorated semi-circular dress circle. Opening in 1907, it survived over fifty years and two World Wars, inevitably with mixed fortunes. Although mainly a variety theatre, it also put on plays, musical comedies, orchestral and 'big band' evenings, and scores of famous names trod its boards. The growing popularity of cinema and then television took its toll, and latterly, opening only occasionally, its offerings degenerated to 'seedy'. Such a sad loss for Reading.

JRW (Phillips, D., *Reading Theatres, Cinemas and Other Entertainments 1788-1978*, 1978)

January 10th

1705: On this day, Thomas Juyce died. In 1662 he was turned out of his Church of England parish of St Nicholas, Worcester for his refusal to use the revised liturgy prescribed by the Act of Uniformity from that year. Edmund Calamy, biographer of the ejected clergy, described him as 'a sober, grave, serious, peaceable, blameless, able minister'. The ejected clergy also included Christopher Fowler, vicar of St Mary's, Reading, who then held meetings in his house, earning the description by the borough's JP of 'author of most of the evil in the town'. Coming to Reading in about 1665, Juyce took up the independent ministry begun by Fowler but also encountered opposition. Local magistrates sought to put him in prison and he was forced into hiding for some time in a bark rick, being fed by the wife of the miller who owned it. His ministry of thirty-three years was one of the longest in the history of the Broad Street Congregational Church in Reading. In 1690 the congregation was put at 'four or five hundred hearers, ye people considerably rich'. The church, rebuilt in 1800, is now a Waterstones bookstore.

VC/JBD (Summers, W., *History of the Berkshire etc. Congregational Churches*, 1905)

JANUARY 11TH

1866: On this day, at a meeting of the Guardians of the Reading Poor Law Union, the plans submitted by local architects for the site of a new workhouse and infirmary at Oxford Road, Reading, were considered and a short list of two drawn up, comprising those of W. & J.T. Brown and William H. Woodman. A week later the Guardians picked that by Woodman. There was much local criticism of the Guardians' choice by those who preferred the plan submitted by Messrs Brown. Nevertheless, the Guardians submitted Woodman's plans to the Poor Law Board and they received final approval after criticism by the Board was addressed. By late 1867, the workhouse was nearing completion at a final cost of £14,000 and the first paupers moved in. An observer described the new buildings as looking more like a large public school than a Poor Law institution. A valuable source of income was the farm, inmates who were fit enough providing the labour. In 1915, the workhouse was requisitioned as a military hospital; the military departed in 1920. It survived as a hospital under the NHS until the rising cost of running two large hospitals in the town was considered prohibitive; Battle Hospital, as it was later known, closed in 2005.

SD (Railton, M. & Barr, M., *Battle Workhouse and Hospital*, Berkshire Medical Heritage Centre, 2005)

January 12th

1878: On this day, a notice was placed in the *Reading Observer* regarding a meeting of the Alphabetical Society, to be held the following night at the Athenaeum. This was to be the opening meeting of the Society, which was for men only. The first paper to be read before the Society was presented by the Revd G.S. Reaney, then minister of Trinity Congregational Chapel: 'That the Occupation of Constantinople by the Russians ought not be Opposed by England' – a hot topic of the day. The following edition of the newspaper reported that there was a large attendance. There seems to have been lively debate of the issue at hand, with strong arguments for and against the Russians expelling the Turks from Constantinople, and England's non-opposition to this happening – the majority of arguments being in favour of the proposal by Mr Reaney. Figures were given that 200,000 lives and £200 million had been spent on keeping the Turks there, and the question was raised whether this was worth so great a sacrifice. A show of hands being taken at the end of the evening indicated that there was a large majority for the affirmative.

AS/VC (*Reading Observer*)

JANUARY 13TH

1903: On this day came the long awaited visit of the American composer and conductor John Philip Sousa (1854-1932), with his band, to the Royal County Theatre, Reading. The 'early doors' were besieged two hours before the announced time and many would-be patrons failed to gain admission. Sousa, sometimes known as the March King, had been in England before, and had visited London and the major cities with sell-out performances. On his current tour, some of the smaller towns such as Reading were fortunate to engage this famous band. The newspaper reviewer said that it was difficult to speak about the concert without using a series of superlatives. The composition of the band was different from that of the military bands of this country, with the woodwind and the brass about equally divided. This provided a marvellous tone which the writer compared to the ponderous wood reed of an organ pedal. The programme consisted of many favourites, including 'Washington Post', 'Stars and Stripes', 'William Tell', 'Soldiers of the King', excerpts from *H.M.S. Pinafore* and a new march, 'Imperial Edward', dedicated to the King. There were also vocal and instrumental solos. A brilliant and electrifying evening!
SG (*Berkshire Chronicle*)

JANUARY 14TH

1440: On this day, the 1439-40 Parliament met at Reading Abbey, to complete its unfinished business. Parliament's removal from Westminster was due partly to plague in London (because of it, knights were to be excused the Kiss of Homage!) and partly to the desire of the court to remove Parliament from the influence of Londoners. Parliament was to be summoned at the Abbey on future occasions in the 1400s.

VC (Dodwell, B., Lambert, M.D., Slade C.F., *Parliament through Seven Centuries*, Cassell, 1962)

———— ◆ ————

1933: On this day, Reading's third round FA Cup-tie at Millwall was abandoned during the second half. When a heavy blanket of Thames fog enveloped the pitch with the Biscuitmen losing 2–0, the referee called off the game. The Reading players, relieved that they had been let off the hook by the abandonment, left the field. However, on reaching the dressing-room, they found that their goalkeeper, Dick Mellors, was missing. Quickly searching the ground, they discovered Mellors still guarding his goal – unaware of the referee's decision to stop the match! At the replay, Reading drew 1–1 but lost 0–2 at home at Elm Park in the third and final encounter.

NS (Local press reports)

JANUARY 15TH

1878: On this day, Matilda Stanley died. Born in Reading about 1821, the daughter of Ephraim Joles, she received the honorific title 'Queen of the Gypsies', with her husband, Levi, titled the 'King'. These titles simply indicated their people's love and trust, and nothing more. In 1856 Matilda, Levi and their families emigrated to the United States, with others of their people, settling near Troy, Ohio. Shortly after, they chose Dayton, Ohio, as their home during summer months, and it became a centre for Gypsies in America. Matilda was said to have had wonderful fortune-telling abilities and powers as a mesmerist. The press described her as a 'plain, hardy-looking woman, with a manner indicative of a strong and pronounced character'. After an illness lasting two years, Matilda, the Gypsy Queen, died in Vicksburg, Mississippi. Her embalmed body was placed in the Woodland receiving vault in Dayton; every day her family brought fresh flowers to strew over her. Matilda's funeral was held eight months later, giving time for word to spread and her people to travel to Dayton. Twenty thousand came from England, America and Canada to pay their respects.

VC (*New York Times*)

JANUARY 16TH

1902: On this day, a small group of nuns of the Order of Blessed Marie Madeleine Postel opened a school for Catholic girls in Castle Street, Reading. For the French sisters this was the happy culmination of eight years' poverty and hard work since their arrival at Southampton as refugees, bedraggled from a storm-tossed Channel crossing. Like many French nuns and priests of that time, they had fled the violent anti-clericalism that beset France after the fall of the Third Empire. They were destitute, their convent having been ransacked and pulled apart around them. The nuns' vocation was teaching, and this brought them a meagre living, first in Bracknell, later in Wokingham. Their excellent work came to the attention of Professor Rey of Reading College (forerunner of Reading University), who invited them to Reading, leasing for them two houses in Castle Hill which had been part of an inn, the King's Arms. (Over a century before, this hostelry had been a refuge for French priests fleeing the French Revolution.) From just eight pupils initially, the school's numbers grew steadily; by 1908, Reverend Mother was seeking more spacious premises.

PMS (The Sisters of St Joseph's Convent, *From Acorn to Oak, 1959/South Western Catholic History No.2, 1984*)

January 17th

1922: On this day occurred the death of ninety-two-year-old Right Revd Dr James Leslie Randall, first Bishop of Reading from 1889 to 1908. Suffragan bishops, assisting the diocesan bishop, were first permitted only for towns that were named under an Act of 1534, but in 1888 the Suffragans Nomination Act permitted the extension of the practice to other towns as required. Randall was one of the first bishops appointed under this new legislation. He was the son of the equally long-lived James Randall, Archdeacon of Berkshire from 1855-69; his brother, Richard, became Dean of Chichester. The future bishop was educated at Winchester and New College, Oxford. Ordained in 1853, he served as Rector of Newbury from 1857 to 1878. From 1880 to 1902 he was successively Archdeacon of Buckingham and Oxford, holding these posts concurrently with his bishopric. After Randall's resignation, the see of Reading was suspended for many years until revived in 1942. Mostly, it has been a 'dead end' job for its occupants, but the last two Reading bishops, Dominic Walker (1997-2003) and Stephen Cottrell (2004-10), have become diocesan bishops, of Monmouth and Chelmsford respectively.

JBD (Pugh, R. & M. (Eds), *The Diocese Books of Samuel Wilberforce*, Berkshire Record Society, 2008)

January 18th

1707: On this day, it is believed the beautiful Frances Kendrick dressed up as a man and challenged a young lawyer, Benjamin Childs, to a duel at Calcot Woods, south-west of Reading. Just as the confrontation was about to take place, Miss Kendrick threw down her cloak and mask, giving Childs the choice of a fight or marriage. He chose the latter and they were married a few months later.

NS (Hylton, S., *Reading Places, Reading People,* Berkshire Books, 1992)

———◆———

1944: On this day, two officers – one British and one American – stepped from a car outside Reading station. One of them was immediately recognised as General Montgomery, who was accompanying US General, John Lee, on visits to American camps in the south. The Mayor, Alderman Lovell, greeting the visitors, asked Montgomery how he kept in such excellent health after arduous campaigns in the desert, Sicily and Italy. He replied that his secret was not to undertake business after 9 p.m., then to go immediately to bed and sleep well. When the Mayor suggested he must worry if a battle was not going well, the great man replied that he never started a battle until he was quite ready, thus ensuring a successful outcome.

NS (*Berkshire Chronicle*)

January 19th

1966: On this day, the Reading Transport Society noted:

Severe winter weather brought 'load shedding' which affected the trolleybuses, while freezing rain in the morning peak-hour of 20th January brought all road transport in the Reading area into chaos. Motor and trolleybus services were badly hit, but the department managed to keep services going. We had reports of a trolleybus taking 1 1/2 hours from Tilehurst to Broad Street, and two collisions involving 141 and 177. And a dewirement occurred, resulting in a short-circuit which burnt through the overhead in King Street.

A History of Reading Society member recalls that day – sliding all over in his Morris Minor when driving to work, very cautiously, from Caversham Heights to London Road. At lunchtime it was still very raw, and he remembers a trolleybus returning to depot along Duke Street around 1 p.m., the overhead line festooned in ice. As the cobbles and old tarred-in tramlines over High Bridge were still coated with ice, the trolleybus had huge difficulty going up the incline of the bridge with both trolleyheads arcing magnificently, creating a brown smoke that looked like bromine!
JRS (Reading Transport Society records)

JANUARY 20TH

1802: On this day, Governor Joseph Wall, found guilty of the murder of Benjamin Armstrong, was sentenced to death at the Old Bailey. Although the crime was committed far from Reading, the town played an important part in the events leading to that end. Wall had been Acting Governor of Senegambia, West Africa, and was in charge of the garrison at Goree. In 1782, the troops protested when they learned that he and his paymaster, Dearing, were about to return to England; the men had been on short rations and were owed pay in lieu. Wall concluded that Armstrong was the ringleader of a mutiny, and without even the semblance of a court-martial ordered him to receive 800 lashes, as a result of which he died. Two years later, when Wall was being conveyed from Bath to London to stand trial, his escorts stopped for refreshment in Reading at the Bear Inn. Wall escaped through a window and, despite the offer of a £200 reward, he successfully reached safety on the Continent. Wall slipped back to England unnoticed in 1797 but, seemingly troubled by a guilty conscience, finally allowed himself to be brought to justice.

JBD (Birkenhead, Lord, *More Famous Trials*, Hutchinson, 1938)

January 21st

1843: On this day, the *Berkshire Chronicle* published an announcement that:

MR JOHN WHITE son-in-law and pupil of the lamented Mr Burt Begs to inform the Public that now having been established in His native town as a TEACHER OF DRAWING &c upwards of 7 years, he is far from wishing to be mistaken for his namesake in the Market Place, as an advertisement … [in last week's Chronicle] would insinuate. Mr. J W, satisfied with his own character, does not wish to assume that of any other person, and feels quite convinced that should any disreputable proceeding be reported of a John White, nobody would think … of carrying it to the door of John White, Southampton Street.

This came in response to a notice carried the previous week:

Caution to Parents and Heads of Establishments. Mr. J White (pupil of the celebrated Mr. Burgess) Teacher of Perspective and Drawing from nature respectfully informs his numerous and distinguished patrons, that as another person bearing the same name is offering services as a drawing master, Mr. J W Begs them to address Artist's Repository, 25 Market Place, where only his specimens may be seen and terms known.

SG (*Berkshire Chronicle*)

JANUARY 22ND

1751: On this day, William Bromley Cadogan was born in Bruton Street, London, second son of Lord Charles Sloane Cadogan and Hon. Frances Bromley. At six, he entered Westminster School, proceeding thence to Christ Church, Oxford. At Oxford Cadogan formed strong religious convictions, although it was not until 1780 that he experienced an evangelical conversion. In 1774, prior to his ordination the following year, he was presented to the living of St Giles-in-Reading, not far from the family seat in Caversham. He was also appointed rector of St Luke's, Chelsea, but St Giles' engaged much of his time. A hugely popular evangelical preacher, he drew large congregations to his sermons twice on Sundays and twice in the week. When not studying the Scriptures or visiting the sick and poor, he founded and led four Sunday schools that together instructed over 120 poor children. In 1782 he married Jane Bradshaw, but died suddenly at Reading on 18 January 1797, aged forty-six, from an inflammation of the bowels. The appointment of his successor, Joseph Eyre, caused controversy that led to the foundation of St Mary's, Castle Street in 1798.
VC (Doran, J., *The History and Antiquities of the Town and Borough of Reading in Berkshire*, 1835)

January 23rd

1625: On this day, Reading Corporation held a meeting, with Mayor Roger Knight leading the deliberations, aided by eight burgesses. The agenda was typical of municipal concerns of the day, such as action against outsiders breaking the local guilds' monopoly. In one dispute, six cloth-drawers complained that 'a stranger', Nathaniel Molson, was working at cloth-drawing in Reading. Six freemen smiths brought another case, deposing that another 'stranger', Billingselye, was dwelling and working with William Lowgey, smith, who employed him as a journeyman for wages of eighteen pence a week. Lowgey also illegally employed another 'stranger', a spurrier. Lowgey was heavily fined (£4) for permitting this. Other business included the Corporation agreeing (with a £20 grant) 'to ayde Henry Bell esquire, His Majesties Servant and Captayne of a Foote Company, and releive him in his journey to Court, from Plymmouth where he hath byn longe sicke'. This important person was active in 'state affairs' in Germany for James I and then Charles I. The Counter-Reformation in Germany ordered the burning of all Protestant books, but Bell acquired a hidden copy of Luther's *Colloquia Mensalia*, which he translated during ten years in prison. Archbishop Laud admired Bell's work and rewarded him. Bell published *The Table-Talk* of Martin Luther in 1646.

PV (Guilding, J., *Reading Records: Diary of the Corporation*, 1895)

JANUARY 24TH

1843: On this day died Charles Fyshe Palmer of Luckley House, Wokingham, one of Reading's MPs between 1818 and 1841. In Parliament, he advocated reform principles: Roman Catholic emancipation, Parliamentary reform and the abolition of slavery. He was born about 1770, the son of Henry Fyshe, who assumed the name Palmer on inheriting property. Richardson's *Recollections* portray him as:

> ... a man of remarkable appearance; in height six feet three, upright and by no means overburdened with flesh or fat; his limbs, loosely joined without elegance or muscular development; his features relieved from insipidity by positive ugliness; his costume that of bygone days, but smart and well-appointed; his manners those of a gentleman of the old school ...

Mary Mitford thus described him in 1818: 'vastly like a mop-stick, a tall hop-pole or an extremely long fishing-rod, or anything that is all length and no substance.' Despite these physical handicaps Palmer married a wealthy widow, Lady Madelina Sinclair, who was daughter of the Duke of Gordon, and this connection gave him contact with many noble families. The Museum of Reading has a watercolour portrait of Palmer by Henry Wellington Burt.

SG (Fisher D. (Ed.), *The History of Parliament: The House of Commons, 1820-1832,* CUP, 2009/Richardson, J., *Recollections,* 1856)

JANUARY 25TH

1827: On this day the canal was frozen over, and in some places the ice was nearly a foot thick. The Kennet and Avon Canal Company sent a large boat with a high gallery, the sides defended by iron, and towed by three horses, to break the ice. **AS** (*Reading Mercury*)

———•———

1990: On this day, as on several days in February, severe winds struck Reading, up to 90mph (144kph), exceeding those of the 1987 'hurricane'. Unlike 1987, the 1990 storms came during the working day. They were well forecast but even so the *Reading Post* reported 'chaos' on roads and railways. The Reading to Newbury line was blocked when a factory roof landed on the tracks! Several were killed as falling trees struck cars, and lorries skidded or overturned. A chimney crashed in Kendrick Road and garden sheds fell victim to the winds. Some 200 people were treated at the Royal Berkshire Hospital. Insurance firms cheerfully warned Reading residents that not all policies covered wind and falling-tree damage to fences, hedges and gates. Of course, power cables went down, adding to the deprivations. The National Rivers Authority issued warnings about the dramatically rising river levels. **JRS** (*Reading Post*/Murray, D., *Storm Force,* Archive Publications, 1990)

JANUARY 26TH

1850: On this day, the *London Illustrated News* and *The Lady's Newspaper* reported a great fire at Caversham Park, retirement home of William Crawshay II, the Welsh 'Iron King'. The blaze had started in the building's east wing, on the morning of Friday 18 January; the family were fortunately away from home, and the fire was blamed on preparations being made for their return. The household staff strove determinedly to save furniture and other property, and messengers were quickly sent to Reading to bring the fire brigade and police to the site. By the time the fire engines arrived, the blaze had firm hold. However, the firemen could draw water only from nearby wells and were unable to prevent the fire from spreading. Soon, fanned by a strong breeze, the flames enveloped the west side of the mansion, and all hope of saving it was lost. By twelve o'clock the building was ruined, with only walls still standing, but even so the fire continued to burn. Much of the furniture and belongings were saved, but the contents of the 'best rooms' were lost. Crawshay, uninsured, bore losses of thousands of pounds.

VC (*Reading Mercury/London Illustrated News/The Lady's Newspaper*)

JANUARY 27TH

1940: On this day, a few months before the Blitz of the Second World War, a less spiteful but horribly damaging 'ice storm' hit Reading and the whole country, during the coldest January since 1838. Temperatures as low as minus 18 degrees Celsius (0 degrees Fahrenheit) caused the Thames to freeze at Caversham Bridge; skaters populated Whiteknights Lake, and Prospect Park became a tobogganers' paradise. The night of 27 January delivered the real damage when rain, in warm air from the Atlantic, fell through the icy Siberian air already covering much of Britain. The resulting 'ice storm' saw the chilled rain freeze on contact with roads, roofs, trees and pylons. Its huge weight brought down power cables and trees, and made driving, even walking, almost impossible. The *Reading Chronicle* later carried many photographs and stories reporting that houses in Kings Road had been without mains water for almost a fortnight. Only the plumbers benefitted from the freeze! It was only on Friday 2 February, as the thaw set in, that the first newspaper reports about frozen Britain appeared. Not letting Hitler know that Britain had been literally frozen solid had been no more than prudent!
JRS (*Reading Chronicle*/'The Weather', Royal Meteorological Society, September 2010)

JANUARY 28TH

1825: On this day, the *Berkshire Chronicle* carried the following message: 'Notice is hereby given that unless the GIG now standing in the yard of Mr John Wheeler, stonemason, St Mary's Butts, Reading, be taken away within ten days from the date hereof, the same will be sold to pay for the expense of standing and for this advertisement.'
SG (*Berkshire Chronicle*)

1888: On this day, Samuel Isaacs was arrested in his lodgings in London, accused of 'burgulariously [sic] breaking and entering' the premises of Mr Sydney Baxter, jeweller in Minster Street, Reading, on 18 January. Baxter's assistant had left the premises at 9.25 p.m., leaving everything locked, but on his return found doors smashed and empty jewellery boxes scattered. More empty boxes were discovered around nearby Twyford station, and indicated a criminal hailing from London; however, little progress was made in Reading itself. Instead it was noted in a pawn shop in Whitechapel that valuable watches were being pawned. The owner of the articles, Isaacs, a man with a previous conviction for theft, was tracked down and arrested; he was later sentenced to five years' penal servitude.
JP (*Reading Observer*)

JANUARY 29TH

1869: On this day, ferryman Piper's house on Caversham Bridge was relocated in its entirety preparatory to the bridge's rebuilding. The *Reading Chronicle* reported:

> Under the direction of Mr Woodman, borough surveyor, the house occupied by the Piper family was moved. For some time past, workers have been engaged in removing the lower portion of the side walls, which were in a very rotten state ... After the house had been underpinned, a new cill was framed all round resting on three pairs of roller plates, protected by narrow strips of iron. The inner walls were strutted and stayed in such a manner as to make it almost impossible for the house to fall asunder during the removal. At an early hour, the workmen commenced removing the house, with the aid of hydraulic and screw jacks ... placed at the ends of the top roller plates nearest the bridge. In about three hours the ... process of removal was completed, the building having been shifted back eight feet, during which not the slightest hitch occurred; ... the movement ... was hardly perceptible and so steady that not a timber was strained nor a pane of glass broken.

VC (North, L., *Royal Reading's Colourful Past*, Cressrelles, 1979)

JANUARY 30TH

1649: On this day, King Charles I was beheaded, with consequences for two men of Reading who had signed his Death Warrant the day before. After Parliament had triumphed in the Civil War, the King was imprisoned but remained defiant. Step forward Daniel Blagrave of Southcote (1603-68), lawyer son of a noted local family. He had served as Reading's Recorder, then its MP, and was prominent among Parliamentarians baying for the King's head. After Charles was found guilty of treason, Blagrave was one of the Commissioners putting their names to the Warrant. In 1660, with the monarchy restored, regicides such as Blagrave feared for their lives; escaping abroad, he died at Aachen in 1668. Co-signatory with Blagrave was Henry Marten (1602-80) of Oxford who became MP for Berkshire. Parliament appointed him Governor of Reading early in the Civil War. Later he raised a Berkshire regiment supporting the radical Levellers, who marched 'for the people's freedom against all tyrants whatsoever'. Like Blagrave, Marten strongly favoured abolishing the House of Lords. When the Interregnum ended, Marten was condemned to death, but this was commuted to life imprisonment; he lived another twenty years, dying in Chepstow Castle in 1680.

PV (*Dictionary of National Biography 1885-1900*)

January 31st

1947: On this day, Redingensians shivered in a severe wintry spell; the Loddon, Thames and Kennet were frozen over, and skating on Whiteknights Lake was a popular way of warming up! In the aftermath of the war, people were facing a coal shortage and power cuts; food rationing continued and many commodities were in short supply. The need for cheering entertainment was critical – and Reading rose to this challenge, as this day's local newspaper amply demonstrates. Nine cinemas served film-fans: Central, Glendale (Caversham), Granby, Odeon, Pavilion, Regal (Caversham), Rex, Savoy and Vaudeville. Films ran for 'six days only' (no Sunday opening then); some would become classics that we still treasure: *The Jolson Story, Blue Skies* (Bing Crosby, Fred Astaire), *Monsieur Beaucaire* (Bob Hope) and *Night and Day* (Alexis Smith, Cary Grant); these were in 'glorious Technicolor'. The popularity of dancing is evident from the newspaper advertisements, for the Central Ballroom, Majestic Ballroom, Olympia Dancing, Oxford Dancing and Reading Town Hall (here, in concession to the 'plebs', it was 'evening dress optional'). Plentiful other attractions included Bamford's Skating Rink (so, icy inside as well as out!), the Palace Theatre, concerts, amateur theatre and whist-drives.

PV (*Berkshire Chronicle*)

FEBRUARY IST

1905: On this day, the Mayoress of Reading, Mrs Sutton, opened Elm Park (Wesleyan Methodist) Mission Hall. The *Reading Standard* reported:

> The hall, which has an imposing interior, occupies a splendid site and frontage on the Oxford Road. It is one of the results of the great extension scheme entered upon with such enthusiasm by the local Wesleyan body in May 1903. The south-facing building has striking large windows with circular arches, measuring 20 feet by 30 feet. It is built in the Renaissance style and consists of a hall with seating for 1000 people. The gallery has 'tip-up' seats, whilst the main floor uses ordinary chairs. There is an organ chamber and choir gallery. Below this hall, on the ground floor, are the school and five classrooms capable of accommodating 600 scholars, while in addition there is a ministers' vestry, stewards' vestry, and various offices. The entrance is by a wide semi-circular door giving access to a crush hall or lounge, upon which the stairs from the main hall and the school and class rooms converge. A considerable crowd gathered for the opening ceremony, including a great number of important church representatives.

In 1907 inclement weather caused the opening of Battle Library to be transferred to the Mission Hall.
VC (*Reading Standard*)

FEBRUARY 2ND

1910: On this day occurred the death of James Boorne, Reading-born ironmonger and tin-box manufacturer. Born in 1824, he was the son of James Boorne, a pawnbroker, who had moved from Deptford to Cadogan House, Mill Lane, Reading. The family were originally Baptists, but from an early age James junior attended Quaker meetings. As a young man he joined the firm of Richard and John Billing, architects and surveyors, leaving them in 1846 when he formed a partnership with Joseph Huntley. Later, Samuel Stevens joined the firm as a partner. The tin-box company of Huntley, Boorne & Stevens for many years supplied the decorative tins which carried Huntley & Palmers biscuits all over the world. The company continued in Reading until 1985 when it was sold to Lin-pac. Highly cultured, Boorne had a collection of paintings and china, and bred fancy poultry. He entered local politics in 1855 and, as Mayor of Reading in 1861, formally opened the Forbury Recreation Grounds and Drinking Fountain. After forty-seven years in the firm, he retired in 1893 to Cheltenham where he enjoyed a long retirement.

SG (Milligan, E.H., *British Quakers in Commerce and Industry*, William Sessions, 2007)

FEBRUARY 3RD

1978: On this day, a meeting was held at Reading Museum and Art Gallery to form a new society to be called The History of Reading Society. The previous week, the *Reading Chronicle* had reported that 'the intention is to allow members to discover more about the town through lectures, discussions, films and visits linked with historical items'. The first meeting would 'form a constitution, plan future meetings and have, on display, objects depicting Reading's history'. In addition, subscriptions were collected at £1 each. The first talk given to the Society was by founding Chairman, Peter Southerton, on *The History of Reading's Penal Establishments* and appropriately took place in St Mary's Church in Castle Street, built on the site of the former County Gaol. Thirty-five years later the Society is still flourishing and a group of its members and associates has banded together to write *The Reading Book of Days*. These are: Ken Brown (KCB); Vicki Chesterman (VC); Mike Cooper (MC); John Dearing (JBD); Joan Dils (JoD); Sean Duggan (SD); Sidney Gold (SG); Keith Jerrome (KJ); Joy Pibworth (JP); Chris Skidmore (CJS); Pat Smart (PSm); Adam Sowan (AS); John Starr (JRS); Penelope Starr (PMS); Nigel Sutcliffe (NS); Philip Vaughan (PV); and John Whitehead (JRW).
JBD (Records of The History of Reading Society)

FEBRUARY 4TH

1807: On this day, John Engelbert Liebenrood handed over the office of High Sheriff of Berkshire to William Blane of Wingfield Park. Liebenrood was born about 1756. At some time before 1813 he bought the estate formerly known as 'Dils', which remained in the hands of the Liebenrood family until 1902, when it was sold by Major Engelbert Liebenrood to Reading Corporation for use as a public park. Today the estate is known as Prospect Park, while the family name lives on in Liebenrood Road, which runs alongside the park. The Liebenrood family also gave land in Victoria Road, on which Tilehurst Village Hall was built in 1893/4. It was here, in 1894, that the first election of Tilehurst Parish Council was held. George Engelbert Liebenrood stood as a candidate, but was not returned. John Engelbert (died 1823) and his wife Lucy (died 1829) are both buried at nearby Purley. Lucy was described as a great friend of the poor. Her epitaph reads: 'although elevated in marriage to a rank of life far beyond her pretensions and expectations, by undeviating good and virtuous conduct she gained the love and esteem of all who knew her'.

VC (Babbage, T., *Tylehurst Described: An Historical Account*, Berkshire County Library, 1976)

FEBRUARY 5TH

1832: On this day, Mr Batty presented the first Grand Equestrian Performance of his Circus Royal in Oxford Road, Reading. His advertisement promised:

> such variety of entertainments as never witnessed in this part of the county before. The Circus is conveniently fitted-up and will be kept comfortably warm [critical, this, in February!] and the amusements such as all parties can partake of. Entertainments commence with 'L'Action des Voltigeurs' by the whole company – 'Grand Horse-Pyramids, or the Ruins of Troy', on the backs of three horses – 'Sailor's Return, or the Home-bound Indiaman', by Mr Hickie – 'Corde Crescent' – 'Grand Cavalry Entrée' – 'The Young Chinese Nondescripts – Still Vaulting' (including 'Brown the Clown') – Miss Smith will appear on the Tight-Rope – Mr Batty in 'The Huntsman's Glory, or Hounds in Full Cry', on the backs of two flying coursers. Boxes 2s. Pit 1s. Gallery 6d. Fires constantly kept and the Circus brilliantly illuminated. Ladies and Gentlemen taught the Polite Art of Riding, attended by Mr Batty. Horses broken for road or field.

The following week, the *Chronicle* commented favourably. Batty advertised another Monday performance, together with a Saturday morning session. Such were our ancestors' innocent entertainments.

PV (*Berkshire Chronicle*)

FEBRUARY 6TH

1903: On this day, the Music Master of Reading School, Dr William Boggis, an Old Redingensian, gave a recital in a packed School Chapel to mark the 'opening' of a new organ, built by Nicholson of Worcester, which replaced the one installed shortly after the chapel was built in 1873. The programme, which was very well received, concluded with his own composition: *Hora Data Quieti*, which may be translated as 'an hour granted for rest'. The new instrument was too large for the recess that had housed its predecessor, and so was installed in the gallery which had been enlarged and strengthened for the purpose. To protect the organ from the heat of gas lighting, electric light made its first appearance in the chapel. The old recess became an enlarged vestry, new mats were placed in the aisle and the chapel interior appeared quite altered to the eyes of Old Boys visiting that day. The organ cost £235. The eminent authority Sir John Stainer considered the price of an organ should be £100 for every 100 persons a building could hold. By that formula the outlay was about right. Ninety years later, after many modifications and two re-builds, 'Beelzebub's Bagpipes', as one master dubbed it, was itself replaced by the present Hill organ.

KCB (Reading School Archives)

FEBRUARY 7TH

1912: On this day, the *Berkshire Chronicle* reported the following story:

> No more tragic scene has ever been witnessed in Reading than that which surrounded the last moments of Mr Charles Smith, the senior magistrate of the borough, who was stricken down on Tuesday [6 February] morning as he was about to take his seat at the police court, expiring almost immediately. Truly if ever a man died at the post of duty it was he! Although in his eightieth year, Mr Smith enjoyed a physical and mental vigour that are the possession of few men of fourscore years, and his attendances at the Bench were a marvel of regularity and punctuality. It was, therefore, a part of the established order of things that on Tuesday morning, despite the cold and snow, Mr Smith should arrive at the police court a few minutes before half past ten, ready to preside over the proceedings of the court.

Smith was one of the most prolific architects at Reading, later in partnership with his son, Charles Steward Smith. Among their best-known works are St John's School, Wilson School, Tilehurst Congregational and Methodist churches, Prospect Park Hospital and Reading University College buildings. He was also twice Mayor of Reading.

SG (Gold, S., *Biographical Dictionary of Architects at Reading*, 1999)

FEBRUARY 8TH

1832: On this day, a coppersmith was incarcerated in 'The Hole' in Market Place, part of Blagrave's Piazza that once adjoined St Laurence's Church. 'Not liking his lodging … he loosened the nuts [of the lock] … and sallied forth to admire the beauties of nature. He was re-captured and the Law had its due course.' While clearly approving of his enterprise, the *Berkshire Chronicle* is silent about his retribution. Market Place's history abounds with tales of punishment in many forms. As well as 'The Hole', the whipping-post and 'le stokks' stood here, as did the 'Compter' or abbot's prison, which became the town prison, relocating to the ruined Greyfriars Church in 1590. In 1633, Lodowick Bowyer (*see* December 21st) had his ears nailed to the pillory in the Market Place. Another case saw burgess John Sawnders pilloried, and his ears cut off for 'speaking seditious words against the King's Council'. In 1652 the Corporation 'agreed that the cucking-stool be sett in the markett-place, and chayned to the pillory'. Market-trading continued regardless, till 1973, when – despite a 12,000-strong petition protesting against the move – the weekly market was relocated to Hosier Street, opposite St Mary's Church.

PV (*Berkshire Chronicle*/Guilding, J., *Reading Records: Diary of the Corporation*, 1895)

FEBRUARY 9TH

1782: On this day, William Havell was born in Vastern Road, Reading. One of fourteen children of Luke Havell, a drawing master at Reading School, William soon showed artistic ability and developed his skills under his father's tutelage. Deciding to become a professional artist, he set off, armed with brush and palette, to win fame and fortune as a landscape artist. At the age of twenty-two, his mastery at watercolour was displayed in an exhibition at the Royal Academy. Together with other artists of good repute, Havell assisted in founding the Society of Painters in Water-Colours. When the Society's first exhibition was held in London in 1805, Havell was the youngest artist displayed. Soon afterwards he travelled through Wales, and later Westmorland, sketching the scenery. Havell also painted a series of scenes around the Thames, which are now exhibited in various collections worldwide. Later he spent some years travelling and painting around India, but disaster struck when the ship carrying his work back to England sank. His remaining years were blighted by bad luck, ill health and reduced demand for his work. Havell died in Kensington, London on 16 December 1857, aged seventy-five.

VC (Cooper, J., *Some Worthies of Reading*, 1923)

FEBRUARY 10TH

1943: On this day, Reading experienced its darkest day of the Second World War. Fortunately, it was a Wednesday, early closing day, so that the town centre was less busy than usual. It was also dull and drizzly. Around 4.30 p.m., a solitary Dornier Do217 twin-engined bomber approached along the Kennet Valley, looped, and then commenced a bombing run, lining up St Giles' spire with St Laurence's tower. It dropped four 500kg bombs. Two fell in the Minster Street area killing three people but mercifully missing the bus garage and telephone exchange; the others fell either side of St Laurence's, one on a restaurant, the other on a solicitor's office. Thirty-eight people were killed and 151 injured, forty-nine seriously. Building damage in all four cases was extensive and the bomb-sites in Minster Street and at the site of the restaurant remained as stark reminders well into the 1950s. Turrets at the corners of the church tower were deemed unstable and removed. It remains unclear why the raid took place; possibly the target was a BBC radio booster station, located in Market Arcade, which, it is thought, may have hindered Luftwaffe navigation. On the seventieth anniversary a memorial was erected at the site to commemorate the victims of the raid.

JRW (*Berkshire Chronicle*)

FEBRUARY 11TH

1800: On this day, William Henry Fox Talbot, polymath and photography pioneer, was born. After education at Harrow and Cambridge, Henry turned to scientific pursuits, becoming a Fellow of the Royal Society in 1832. From 1834, at his family seat, Lacock Abbey, Wiltshire, he investigated the 'art of photogenic drawing', researching methods of 'fixing' images with light-sensitive paper. In 1841 Fox Talbot patented the Calotype system, whereby one negative could produce multiple prints. To realise Calotype's practical value in publishing, and judging Wiltshire too remote from potential London customers, in early 1844 he rented premises in Reading for a combined photographic studio and photo-printing works; the building still stands, in Baker Street. Fox Talbot's early photographs include an 1845 view of London Street; also photographed were some local residents, such as Mary Mitford, the writer. Under the management of Nicolaas Henneman (formerly Fox Talbot's valet), the business achieved some success, notably producing *Pencil of Nature*, the first commercially published book with photographic illustrations. Concluding that the Reading establishment was unfortunately not commercially viable, Fox Talbot moved Henneman to London in 1847. Reading's chapter in the history of photography came to an end.

PV ('Correspondence of W.H. Fox Talbot', De Montfort University, online project)

FEBRUARY 12TH

1898: On this day, Edgar Louis Granville, later Lord Granville of Eye, was born in Reading. Educated in High Wycombe and Melbourne, Australia, he joined the Australian Light Horse at the outbreak of the First World War, serving in Gallipoli, Egypt and France. After the war he established his own manufacturing business, and acquired directorships in pharmaceutical and armaments companies. In 1929, standing for the Liberals, he won the constituency of Eye in Suffolk. Granville would be associated with the seat for the next thirty years (twenty-two of them as MP), fighting his last election there in 1959 as a Labour candidate. Never quite achieving a ministerial rôle, he was successively Parliamentary Private Secretary to Sir Herbert Samuel (Home Secretary) and to Sir John Simon (Foreign Secretary) from 1931 to 1936. In the Second World War he served with the Royal Artillery. Granville had spells with all the major political parties as well as sitting as an independent. Made a life peer in 1967, he entered the House of Lords as Baron Granville of Eye. He lived to be the oldest member of the House of Lords, and one of the very few surviving members of the 1929 parliamentary intake. He died two days after his 100th birthday. **VC** (*The Independent*)

FEBRUARY 13TH

1817: On this day, Father Longuet, priest at the Roman Catholic Chapel of the Resurrection, was robbed and murdered in Reading. The possible weapons have been variously reported as clubs, bayonets and knives. His body, with several mortal wounds and the head nearly severed, was found in the early hours on the south side of Oxford Road (just beyond where the Territorial Army barracks now stand), a short distance from the old turnpike. His horse was found in a narrow lane leading to the River Thames. Father Longuet had been to Wallingford to give lessons, and, having received payment for his services up to the preceding Christmas, was on his way home. It was thought that his attacker was aware of this, as his money was missing. There was a person suspected of the murder, but he died by his own efforts, without being brought to justice; he was the 'black sheep' of a respectable and long-standing Reading family. A local paper of the time criticised those who knew the guilty man for not speaking out about his supposed guilt before his death. The offer of a £250 reward could not persuade anyone to name the culprit.

VC (Phillips, D. (Ed.), *Reminiscences of Reading by An Octogenarian*, Countryside Books, 1985/*Hereford Journal*)

FEBRUARY 14TH

1870: On this day, a public meeting was held at the Town Hall to launch a fundraising campaign for a public library in Reading. The initial impetus to establish a public library in the town had come from the Hon. Auberon Herbert, brother of Lord Carnarvon of Highclere Castle, near Newbury. Herbert had offered money to several Berkshire towns to establish libraries; Reading was offered £250 on condition that an equal sum was raised locally. Unfortunately the public meeting was unsuccessful; however, the audience included William Isaac Palmer, a local biscuit manufacturer. Palmer decided to take the matter into his own hands, establishing a public library at his own expense in a red-brick building in West Street. These premises, known as 'West Street Hall', had previously been occupied by a working men's club and institute which had failed, whereupon Palmer had purchased it for £450. At its peak, Palmer's new library had 400 readers paying only a few pence per quarter. Palmer also organised lectures and an evening college, and offered space for the staging of major art exhibitions. In 1883, when the Town Hall Library finally opened, Palmer donated West Street's 3,500 volumes to it.
SD (Cliffe, D., *Roots & Branches*, Two Rivers, 2007)

FEBRUARY 15TH

1971: On this day, currency decimalisation was adopted in Reading and throughout the UK and Ireland. Following 'Decimal Day', Britain ended its centuries-old system of pounds, shillings and pence (symbolised by £.*s.d.*) in which £1 consisted of twenty shillings, each shilling containing twelve pence, thus totalling 240 pence per pound. The new decimal system (£.p.) comprised 100 'new pence' to the pound, and a complete range of decimal coins was accordingly introduced. In Reading, the currency change caused some problems and delays on the Corporation buses. Services ran ten to fifteen minutes late; with every fare affected by the changeover, the transition was stressful, especially for buses manned by a single conductor-driver. Shops reported a slow start to trading. At Hardy's newsagents in Market Way, employee Judith McDougall, who came in on her day off, said, 'All has gone smoothly. We haven't had any trouble and the customers have been very helpful. We were all keyed up about working with decimal money. My tummy was turning over, but people have just accepted the fact that today is D-Day.' At KBD, the Market Place greengrocer's, manager Ernest Roberts said, 'We are with it. The till and scales have been converted and we are giving out only the new currency.'
VC (*Evening Post*)

FEBRUARY 16TH

1909: On this day died Arthur Hill, Freeman of Reading, Mayor 1883-87, and philanthropist worthy of his half-sister Octavia Hill. Born in Wisbech, Cambridgeshire, in 1829, Hill first worked for Morgan Peto (builder of GWR line sections around Reading, the station building and the Great Western Hotel). In 1852, Hill moved to Reading, where he purchased John Marshall's Great Western Coal Company, remaining its owner throughout his life. He also acquired Marshall's emigration contracting business, operating a depot in Plymouth for emigrants to Australia and other colonies. Hill's management skills gradually brought him to public affairs. While living briefly at Crowthorne, he helped establish its parish church (1868). Returning to Reading, he entered local government as councillor for Church Ward. His many achievements included upgrading Reading's out-dated sewerage system and radically reforming municipal finances. His four-term Mayoralty culminated in the 1887 Borough Extension Act, consolidating Reading's growth in area and powers. In retirement, he remained Alderman, JP and benefactor to many causes, including Reading's new University College.
PV (*Berkshire Chronicle*)

———◆———

1944: On this day, Reading Council's highest honour was bestowed on one of the town's leading citizens. Deputy Mayor William McIlroy was made an Honorary Freeman of the Borough. He had been Mayor for five consecutive years, four times during the war.
NS (*Reading Standard*)

FEBRUARY 17TH

1926: On this day, the foundation stone of Reading's new Kendrick Girls' School was laid on the corner of Sidmouth Street and London Road, next to Mary Russell Mitford's one-time home. At the founding of the two Kendrick Schools in 1877, the girls' establishment was installed in nearby Watlington House, but after fifty years a more spacious building was needed. The stone plinth originally above the front door of Watlington House was moved to the outer wall of the school where it can now been seen (in Sidmouth Street). The move to the new site in 1927 was billed as a major achievement of Reading Corporation, as it had taken years of negotiation with the Board of Education to accomplish. During the First World War, Kendrick Boys' School, originally located in Queens Road, was combined with Reading School and ceased to be a separate entity. The Kendrick Schools were established with a legacy from the celebrated Reading clothier, John Kendrick, to provide education for children of the middle classes. Most of his bequest was grossly mismanaged, but the small portion remaining sufficed to establish the two schools in his name. Kendrick Girls' is now a selective girls' grammar secondary foundation, and in 2010 became an academy.

VC (Phillips, D., *The Story of Reading,* Countryside Books, 1999)

FEBRUARY 18TH

1820: On this day, Mary Russell Mitford wrote about Reading's preparations for the parliamentary election:

> Reading is very gay with bell-ringing and canvassing just now, though I do not believe there will be any opposition; in fact, the ministerials are canvassing for a candidate, which desirable and gullible person they are not at all likely to procure. It is not every man who has an abstract taste for spending eight or ten thousand (pounds) for being beaten.

The political divide in Reading was between the Blues (or Tory Party) and the Whig Party, the latter being backed by tradesmen and craftsmen, whose political roots lay in the religious dissent movement which had flourished in the town for many years. About a quarter of adult males had the right to vote and turnout was usually high but electoral corruption was rife amongst all parties, hence the cost referred to by Miss Mitford. Polling lasted for six days, yet the majority of the 769 men who voted this time had done so within three. This election caused exceptional bitterness between supporters, splitting families and friends. John Berkeley Monck of Coley Park and Charles Fyshe Palmer, both landowners, won the election on behalf of the Whig Party.

JP (Online: 'The History of Parliament')

FEBRUARY 19TH

1835: On this day, Robert Lovegrove's stables in Reading, at the corner of London Road and Red Lane, were burnt to the ground overnight. Reading was a convenient spot for changing horses, and Lovegrove's stables were used by the Bath and Bristol stagecoaches. The fire was blamed on two men in charge of 'The Age', a stagecoach that left Reading for London before dawn. The coachmen claimed that they had carefully extinguished the stable light; nevertheless its spark had probably started the fire. Four coaches arriving from London found the stables still burning, and had to continue to Woolhampton to find new horses. The collapse of the thatched roof frustrated attempts to rescue thirty-five horses within. Only one horse survived the fire; appropriately renamed 'Miraculous', it continued to work the Reading to Bristol mail-run for many years.
NS (*Berkshire Chronicle*)

———— • ◆ • ————

1902: On this day, Reading enjoyed a Physical Culture display. It included C.B. Vansittart, 'the most muscular man on earth', who, with his bare hands, broke horseshoes, tore packs of cards, ripped tennis balls apart and created initial letters from iron bars; also Milo, who balanced a piano and pianist on his head, while a lady pedalled a bicycle on his chin!
VC (*Reading Mercury*)

February 20th

1861: On this day, a violent gale caused much of Reading Abbey Gateway to collapse. The gateway had been in a dangerous state, and the council had already accepted recommendations by Sir George Gilbert Scott to survey it, costed at about £1,000. As £500 was immediately forthcoming, the rest would be raised by public subscription. Within a few hours of this decision, the catastrophic storm struck, making restoration imperative and urgent. Scott sent his assistant, John Burlison, to oversee the project. Because expenditure was exceeding the sum subscribed, some of Scott's planned decorations were omitted. Almost forty years later, in 1900, benefactors led by Dr Jamieson Hurry had the task completed with thirteen more decorative heads, sculpted by Andrew Ohlson. Carved heads on the west face, inserted in Scott's time, served as the prototype.
SG (Slade, C., *The Town of Reading and its Abbey*, MRM, 2001/Hurry, J., *Reading Abbey*, 1901)

1994: On this day, Reading Rugby Club scored the highest-ever total in competitive rugby in Berkshire. In the County Cup, away to Tadley at their Red Lane ground, they amassed a record 132 points without reply. Notable performers were Belshaw (two tries, sixteen conversions), Hutson (five tries) and MacGeever (four tries).
NS (*Reading Evening Post*)

FEBRUARY 21ST

1836: On this day, the constables of Reading Borough Police Force began their duties, taking over stewardship of the peace from the watchmen appointed by the Commissioners for Paving. An 1835 Act of Parliament let local authorities determine their policing needs and Reading's Watch Committee decided that no fewer than twenty-one constables were needed to maintain the peace. Initially, the service suffered from ill-discipline but standards gradually improved and the force grew in numbers. The first police station was in Friar Street, but in 1912 the police took over the old British Dairy Institute building in Valpy Street. They remained there until 1976, when they moved to a purpose-built station in Castle Street. Reading Police was absorbed into the newly created Thames Valley Constabulary in 1968.
SD (Wykes, A., *The Queen's Peace: A History of the Reading Borough Police*, 1968)

———— • ◆ • ————

1872: On this day, at the Recreation Ground on Kings Meadow, Reading Football Club played their first-ever match. Reading School was the opposing team. A newspaper report commented: 'The ground was in good order and the weather exceedingly favourable and a large concourse of people were present. Play commenced at half past two and ended at four and resulted in a "draw", neither party gaining a goal.'
NS (*Reading Mercury*)

FEBRUARY 22ND

1937: On this day, Bill Ball from Caversham died, aged twenty-one, in the Battle of Jarama in the Spanish Civil War. A former pupil of Reading School, Bill volunteered to join the British Battalion of the XV International Brigade in support of the Republican government against the Fascist rebellion. He was mortally wounded while serving as a machine-gunner in the struggle to prevent Fascist forces taking Madrid. Others from Reading killed in this war were Julian Bell and Archibald 'Josh' Francis. Reading also sent medical volunteers, including Thora Silverthorne (who had come to Reading as a nanny for Somerville Hastings MP). Trained as a nurse in Oxford, she joined a medical aid unit and travelled to Spain during the early years of the war. On her return she raised funds and campaigned for aid for Basque refugee children. Later, Thora helped establish the National Association of Nurses, becoming General Secretary and participating in talks that helped shape the NHS. Elected an official in the Civil Service Association, she worked for the Union until she was seventy. In 1990 she attended the unveiling of Reading's monument to the Spanish Civil War, and died in 1999, aged eighty-eight.

MC (Cooper, M. & Parkes, R., *We Cannot Park on Both Sides: Reading Volunteers in the Spanish Civil War*, 2000)

FEBRUARY 23RD

1898: On this day, the Reading Early Closing Association held their Annual Dinner. Among the fifty members present were Alderman Monck, Mr Langston and Mr Bull. Sir John Lubbock MP, Alderman Hill and Alderman Heelas sent apologies for their absence. Members talked of the groundswell of opinion in favour of reducing the working-hours of shop staff. Although a Bill presented to Parliament by Sir John Lubbock had unfortunately not achieved a national reform, in Reading a voluntary code had been well received, and Arthur Hill's campaign had resulted in traders closing at 2 p.m. on Wednesdays. The additional hours of leisure had benefitted both health and education. It was said that already, for about ten years, shops had been closing also at the early hour of 5 p.m. on Thursdays. Thus the Association decided to put pressure on businesses to reduce working hours on Fridays, when many shops remained open until 9 p.m., and on Saturdays, when shop staff could expect to leave work only by 10.30 p.m. According to Mr Bull, such late opening only put money into the coffers of the gas and electricity companies, while Mr Brain maintained he had long felt that shops would close earlier only if ladies forced the issue by not shopping late.

JP (*Berkshire Chronicle*)

FEBRUARY 24TH

1939: On this day, William Giles, the well-known Reading-born artist and printmaker, died. The son of William Giles of 68 London Street, Reading, carver, gilder, frame maker and restorer, he was born on 19 November 1872. Educated at Reading School and a student at Reading School of Art, he won many prizes; he gained his Art Master's Certificate in 1891, and became a prominent member of the Vacation Sketching Club. He continued his training in Paris. On returning to Reading, he researched the Japanese method of wood-block printing, together with John Batten, Allen Seaby and Frank Morley Fletcher. In 1907 he married Ada Shrimpton, a former student of Reading School of Art and of Reading University Extension College (later the University of Reading). Giles exhibited regularly at the Royal Academy from 1899-1933; he was also president of the Society of Graver-Printers in Colour. In later life he settled at Newport, Essex, where he died. His funeral was held at St Luke's Church, Reading, and he is buried at Caversham Cemetery beside his wife. Giles bequeathed prints to the V & A Museum along with a bequest of £3,000 for encouraging the art of colour printing.

SG (*Oxford Dictionary of National Biography*, OUP, 2004)

FEBRUARY 25TH

1835: On this day, Mary Russell Mitford (1787-1855), best known as the authoress of *Our Village*, published in two volumes a companion series of town-based sketches entitled *Belford Regis or Sketches of a Country Town*. She explains in her preface that a critic of *Our Village*, set in the village of Three Mile Cross, just outside Reading's present boundaries, had 'recommended, since I had taken leave of rural life, that I should engage lodgings in the next country town, and commence a series of sketches of the inhabitants'. The resulting work would have been called *Our Market Town* but another writer had published a book with a similar name, so Reading was obliged to acquire a pseudonym. Mitford had no need to engage lodgings in Reading for she had lived there as a girl, and, as *Belford Regis* indicates, had an intimate knowledge of the town and its people: '... what can surpass the High Bridge on a sunshiny-day? The bright river, crowded with barges and small craft; the streets, and wharfs, and quays, all alive with the busy and stirring population of the country and the town – a combination of light and motion.' It is a fine work that deserves to be better known.

JBD (Mitford, M., *Belford Regis*, 1835)

FEBRUARY 26TH

1947: On this day, with the help of an interest-free loan from the government, the University of Reading purchased Whiteknights Park, an estate dating from before the Norman Conquest. It had passed to the Englefield family in 1606 and remained with them until the late 1780s when it was leased to William Byam Martin, just returned from India with a fortune to spend on improvements. In 1798 Whiteknights was sold to the Marquis of Blandford (later 5th Duke of Marlborough). A flamboyant and eccentric character, Blandford expended immense sums on converting the park into ornamental gardens full of exotic trees and plants, with rustic pavilions, fountains and grottoes. Whiteknights became a showplace, attracting many admiring visitors. His extravagant expenditure bankrupted the Marquis, forcing him to sell all the contents of the house, gardens and conservatories and he moved to Blenheim. Whiteknights mansion house was pulled down in 1840. Later, a Waterhouse-designed house on the site became home to Isaac Lyon Goldsmid, financier and philanthropist, who was the first Jewish baronet. The Goldsmid family supported Reading's Jewish community, and Goldsmid Road in west Reading is named in their honour. It was from them that the university bought the property which became the Whiteknights campus.

VC (Phillips, D., *The Story of Reading*, Countryside Books, 1999)

FEBRUARY 27TH

1926: On this day, Peter Frank Hannibal Emery, Reading's MP from 1959 to 1966, was born. The son of a small London manufacturer, he was an MP for forty-two years in all. Evacuated to the USA during the Second World War, he returned in 1944 in time for wartime service with the RAF, and later graduated at Oxford. He began his political career as a councillor in Hornsey, North London, and first hit the headlines in 1959 when he won the seat of Reading from the Labour left-winger Ian Mikardo. Emery later represented Honiton for thirty years, and the new constituency of Devon East for four. Mainly a backbencher, he also served as a junior minister in the early 1970s. In his last parliament he was treasurer of the Tory MPs' 1922 Committee; by this time he was among the few surviving Conservative entrants to the House of Commons from Harold Macmillan's 'You never had it so good' era. In his final Commons appearance in 2001, he stood beside Labour Health Secretary Alan Milburn on the Bill to ban tobacco advertising, speaking against Tory health spokesman Liam Fox. Not always taken seriously, he earned himself the nickname of 'the amiable blunderbuss'. He died in 2004.

VC (*The Guardian*)

FEBRUARY 28TH

1926: On this day, George Foxell died, six months before his 100th birthday. In December 1925 the *Reading Standard* published an article celebrating George's 100th Christmas. Hailing him as the oldest parish clerk in England, the article related that George had held that rôle at Holy Trinity for ten years, followed by almost fifty at St Laurence's, and was still in office! The account said that he:

> continues to enjoy good health, and possesses a good appetite, while he is very fond of his pipe of tobacco, which affords him much enjoyment. Mr Foxell's hearing is also quite good, and he has a remarkable memory, taking delight in recalling events of his boyhood days. He still possesses his faculties, and can converse on most subjects, a good deal of his time being spent in smoking and talking.

Born in Great Bedwyn, Wiltshire, on 28 June 1826, he was twenty-eight when he married Leah Rogers in Andover, where they had three children. Between 1858 and 1860 the family moved to Reading where ten more children were born. George and his family lived in the vicinity of Friar Street in the town centre, where he worked as a tailor. He was buried in London Road Cemetery on 5 March.
VC (*Reading Standard*)

February 29th

1840: On this day, the *Reading Mercury* published the following notice:

> Mr J C MILES of the Royal Academy of Painting, London, respectfully informs those ladies and gentlemen of Reading and its neighbourhood who may wish their PORTRAITS taken that he can adduce, as proof of his ability as a portrait painter, commendations from several of the most eminent painters of this present day – Howard RA, – Hilton RA and Sir David Wilkie RA besides the unanimous approval of the numerous parties who have sat to him for portraits, particularly at Bath where he has had the honor of painting persons of distinction. Mr Miles has no hesitation in affirming that the friends of any parties who may honor him with a sitting will acknowledge the faithfulness of the likeness. Several of his paintings in oil may be seen at Mr Sims', London Street and at 143 Friar Street.

John Clements Miles was christened at St Laurence's, Reading in 1816, the son of Charles Miles and Mary Ann Clements. He became a student of the Royal Academy Schools in 1830. He died at Bath in 1880, where he had established himself as an accomplished artist and where examples of his work may be seen at the Victoria Art Gallery.

SG (*Reading Mercury*/Family Research website)

MARCH 1ST

1954: On this day, Reading's Accident & Emergency facilities were enhanced by the commissioning of an up-to-date department at Battle Hospital. Casualty, as it was known in those days, had developed from a wartime First Aid Post in the Outpatients Department of the Royal Berkshire Hospital. After establishment of the NHS in 1948, Mr C.M. Squires was appointed Accident and Orthopaedic Surgeon in June 1949. He submitted a detailed scheme to transfer Casualty to Battle, which was more far-reaching than the Hospital Planning Committee had envisaged. A phased building alteration scheme was developed but full funding proved unavailable and only a piecemeal transfer was deemed possible. Work eventually started in November 1952 and completion of the transfer from RBH was marked by a ceremonial opening on 12 July 1954. During the 1950s and 1960s, the population in the Reading district mushroomed, with a knock-on effect on an under-staffed Casualty with inadequate facilities and accommodation. After regular pleas from Mr Squires, the design for a new, much larger, custom-built facility was incorporated in Phase III (South Wing) at the RBH, due to open in 1971. It was not ready until summer 1980!

JRW (Railton, M. & Barr, M., *Battle Workhouse and Hospital*, Berkshire Medical Heritage Centre, 2005)

MARCH 2ND

1944: On this day, a general meeting was held at the premises of McIlroy's Department Store, Oxford Road, Reading, to discuss the idea of forming a symphony orchestra, possibly under the title of the Reading Symphony Orchestra. Many of those at the meeting had been members of the Berkshire Symphony Orchestra, which had disbanded at the outbreak of war in 1939. The new orchestra had two distinguished vice-presidents: the composer, Dr Ralph Vaughan Williams, and the conductor, Mr (later Sir) John Barbirolli. The orchestra's rehearsals were held on Thursday evenings at the Jacobean Restaurant in McIlroy's. William E. McIlroy had been a vice president of Berkshire Symphony Orchestra and was a keen supporter of the new orchestra. John Fry, who had been professor of violin at Trinity College of Music in London, was engaged to be its first conductor. The first concert was given at the Town Hall in Reading in July 1944. The programme opened with the National Anthem and then continued with Mendelssohn's overture *Fingal's Cave* and Beethoven's *Emperor* piano concerto with Dennis Matthews as the soloist, concluding with Mendelssohn's *Italian Symphony*. In 1994, the Reading Symphony Orchestra celebrated its 50th anniversary. **SD** (Jones, F., *Reading Symphony Orchestra, The First Fifty Years*, 1994)

MARCH 3RD

1968: On this day, a Sunday, trolleybuses operated for the last time on Route 18 (Armour Hill–Liverpool Road), the penultimate route to be converted in the run-down of the trolleybus system in favour of motorbuses. Originally scheduled to take place a fortnight later, the date was advanced to coincide with the conversion to one-man and single-deck operation of another former trolleybus route, Route 15 (Stations–Northumberland Avenue). As a result, the double-deck buses could be used on Route 18. Trolleybus operation to Kentwood had been introduced in July 1944, mainly in the interests of operational efficiency, including the wartime saving of 20,000 gallons of petrol or 9,500 gallons of diesel per annum. The route served extensive 1930s housing bounding the south side of Oxford Road between Norcot and Kentwood, now more usually referred to as Lower Tilehurst, and including the Rodway Road estate. The trolleybuses had turned at a convenient existing roundabout at Kentwood so that the section of the former motorbus route to the borough boundary at the Roebuck became unserved, which raised considerable protest. On 4 August 1958, the trolleybus route was extended, not to the Roebuck but up Kentwood Hill, to a terminus just short of its junction with Armour Hill.

JRW (Hall, D., *Reading Trolleybuses,* Trolleybooks, 1991)

MARCH 4TH

1839: On this day, there was much anticipation in the town concerning a public debate to take place at the Town Hall between Robert Owen, a socialist with a philanthropic scheme at New Lanark and advocate of a new Moral World, and William Legg, minister of the Broad Street Chapel and a native of Aberdeenshire. Owen had previously visited the town to give a lecture in December 1838 but was denied use of the Town Hall and had to speak at a theatre instead. Legg had taken up his challenge to the clergy of the town after they had preached against attending Owen's lecture. On that occasion a correspondent from Aberdeen had written a virulently hostile letter to the local press attacking the idea of Owen visiting Reading, although he received support subsequently from the Philanthropic Society. On the next two evenings in March, townsfolk crowded to the Town Hall entrance, their interest being keenly aroused. Students from Oxford offered aged females a guinea for their shilling tickets, to no avail. It was noticeable how ably conducted the meetings were, firmly chaired by Dr Cowan with great impartiality. The press reported on the patient forbearance of the meeting, and the Christian demeanour of Mr Legg was recorded in glowing terms.
PSm (*Reading Mercury*)

MARCH 5TH

1913: On this day, Joseph Morris died; by the close of the nineteenth century, he had become one of Reading's most eminent architects. One of his earliest commissions was for a new parish church at Highmoor, Oxfordshire, in 1858. In the 1860s, he designed flanking wings for the Royal Berkshire Hospital in a neo-classical style to blend with the existing building, highly unusual at a time when neo-Gothic was the fashion. From 1872, he was surveyor of Berkshire's bridges, a post he held for thirty-three years. In Reading, his firm, Morris & Son, designed many board schools, also an iconic department store in Oxford Road for William McIlroy, and numerous terrace houses in Newtown for biscuit factory workers. In 1884, he came under the influence of the Agapemonites, a religious sect, for which, in 1893, he designed the Church of the Ark of the Covenant in London in an extraordinary neo-Gothic style. Towards the end of his career, he embraced the ideas of the Arts & Crafts movement, and with his daughter, Violet, designed many houses in that style around Reading and Wokingham. In 1905, he retired and moved to the Agapemonites' establishment at Spaxton, Somerset, where he died.

SD (Arnold, G. & Gold, S., *Morris of Reading*, Ancient Monuments Society, 1989)

MARCH 6TH

1453: On this day, Reading was once again the venue for England's Parliament. In the years before the nation became London-centric, various towns hosted Parliament, when it so suited sovereign and court. The Refectory at Reading Abbey was chosen several times between 1171 and 1466. London was avoided sometimes because of the plague but now, on the eve of the Wars of the Roses, the reason was political. The Lancastrian Henry VI badly needed Parliament to approve increased taxes, but Richard, Duke of York, was claiming the throne, and his party was strong in London. Accordingly, Henry transferred the deliberations to Reading, and secured the necessary grants with the aid of a supportive Speaker. Parliament went on to approve the creation of a standing army totalling 20,000 archers, the costs of which were to be met by the shires and chief towns. Thus Reading helped prepare the ground for the Yorkist-Lancastrian struggle that would soon afflict the whole country. The opening of the 1453 Parliament at the Abbey is colourfully portrayed in a large oil painting by Stephen Reid (1873-1940), one of ten Abbey paintings commissioned by Dr J.B. Hurry, now displayed at Reading Museum.

PV (Hurry, J., *Reading Abbey*, 1901)

MARCH 7TH

1628: On this day:

> a controversie risen betwene some of the Souldyers billetted in Towne and divers young men of the Towne, especially Joseph Fillett and John Richardes, apprentices, was heard and examined in the presens of Mr. Druce the Captayne of the Souldyers. It appeared and was manifested that the said men were principals in the quarrell, and would not obey the Constables in their office, they both were enjoyned to find sureties for their good behaviour and for lacke of sureties committed to the Counter [Prison].

A decade later, in 1637, the Corporation heard about more wrongdoing:

> Informacion was geven by William Rider and Thomas Boules that on Sondaye night last William Lawley, a miller, dwelling with Thomas Towns, about 8 or 9 of the clocke, did lead a poore woman named Ann Hersey by the arme into the Ortes and there did abuse her by violently using her body. William Lawley was comitted to Counter and required to finde sureties. The said lady, beinge convented, denyed not the circumstances, but confessed the said William Lawley had use of her bodye, and that she was much overtaken with drinke to her great griefe.

Drink and youth caused as much trouble 400 years ago as they do today.
VC/SG (Guilding, J., *Reading Records: Diary of the Corporation*, 1895)

MARCH 8TH

1794: On this day, the La Tournelle and St Quentin Boarding School in Reading, sometimes known as the Abbey Gateway School, was put up for auction. Jane Austen, her sister Cassandra and their cousin, Jane Cooper, had spent eighteen months at this school eight years previously. Mr Hawkes, the auctioneer, intended to sell household furniture comprising about forty bedsteads and bedding, parlour furniture including a pianoforte and a glass chandelier, and kitchen items such as hams, bacon, a sow, coals and wine. On subsequent days sales took place of books in English and French by 'the most-esteemed authors', books on grammar, geography and chronology, and equipment including a pair of globes, 'magic lanthorns' with historical plates, a barometer and a thermometer, excellent charts and maps, 'amusing and instructive, uniting every improved system of private tuition or public education'.
JP (*Jane Austen Society Report,* 1996)

———— •◆• ————

1937: On this day, the new Odeon Theatre was opened. The architect of the new building was A.P. Starkey of Harrow, whose design offered sleek and simple lines, boldness of character, contrast of colour and effective lighting at night. The Odeon was the last new cinema to be built in Reading for over sixty years.
SG (Phillips, D., *Reading Theatres, Cinemas and Other Entertainments,* 1978)

MARCH 9TH

1739: On this day, John Wesley paid his first recorded visit to Reading en route to Hampshire, where he was due to preach for his friend, Charles Kinchin.

> On Friday morning I set out … and in the evening came to Reading, where I found a young man [the hymn-writer, John Cennick] who had in some measure 'known the power of the world to come.' I spent the evening with him and a few of his serious friends; and it pleased God much to strengthen and comfort them.

Wesley's opinion of Reading rapidly declined; in November he wrote:

> a little company of us met in the evening; at which the zealous mob was so enraged, that they were ready to tear the house down. Therefore I hope God has a work to do in this place. In thy time let it be fulfilled!

The fulfilment was long coming, for it was not until 1777 that Wesley could write:

> In the evening I preached at Reading. How many years were we beating the air at this town? Stretching out our hands to a people stupid as oxen! But it is not so at present. That generation is passed away, and their children are of a more excellent spirit.

JBD (Wesley, J., *Journals*, Everyman, 1906)

MARCH 10TH

1815: On this day, the 'Calculating Phenomenon' George Bidder performed to astonished Reading audiences. Aged only nine, he gave accomplished public demonstrations of his amazing prowess in mental arithmetic. Asked 'What number multiplied by itself will produce 18,207,289?' he answered correctly – in a minute and a half – '4,267'. Despite pressure from his father, a Devon stonemason who wanted to keep him on tour to make money, Bidder was encouraged to continue his schooling. After studying mathematics at Edinburgh, he became an engineer, teaming up with George Stephenson. In 1845 he helped establish the Electric Telegraph Company. A member of the Institution of Civil Engineers for almost fifty years, Bidder became its president in 1860. He died in 1878. The National Portrait Gallery has a picture of him at nine – the age he made his sensational Reading debut.
PV (Cooper, J., *Some Worthies of Reading*, 1923)

———◆———

1863: On this day, Reading celebrated the marriage of Prince Edward and Alexandra. Fun and games included 'jumping in sacks, bobbing for oranges, hurdle races, treacle roll amusement, diving for eels, apple scrambles, climbing the greasy pole, running after a pig, the bucket race, the French omnibus, ball in the ring, winding the string, donkey race and grinning through a horse collar'.
AS (*Reading Mercury*)

MARCH 11TH

1890: On this day, the Reading Scientific and Literary Society met in the Lodge Hotel to hear Dr F.W. Andrewes present a paper on bacteria. The room was packed and those present were fascinated by the slides of the various bacteria that were identified. Dr Andrewes drew attention to the possibility that some of the diseases, which were the scourge of Victorian society, namely tetanus, diphtheria, typhoid and tuberculosis, were almost certainly due to these microbes; and he expressed the hope that research might lead to preventative medicine in time. The speaker also explained the nature of microbes and the progress which scientific research had already made towards treating and eradicating their associated illnesses. Mr Austin, Mr Freeman, Mr Street and Dr Firth all lent microscopes for the use of members, and a magic lantern also enlivened the proceedings. The newspaper report of the event was accompanied by promises that Powell's Balsam of Aniseed would cure any cough, as recommended by members of the church, stage and the bar; sulpholine lotion offered to 'drive away pimples, blotches, redness and disfigurement', and Revd Mr Holmes of Bloomsbury offered a 'cure of all those who suffer from the errors and indiscretions of youth, nervous debility, physical exhaustion and early decay'.

JP (*Reading Observer*)

MARCH 12TH

1910: On this day, the Sisters of Marie Madeleine Postel moved with their students to a new address, from the premises in Castle Hill, Reading, where they had first opened their school in 1902. Over the intervening years more nuns and pupils had arrived from France, and, as initial suspicion of the sisters abated – their large wimples had been an unfamiliar sight in Reading – local girls joined the school. By 1908 Reverend Mother was looking for more spacious premises. She saw Broad Oak in the Whiteknights area and considered it an ideal site – but unfortunately it was not for sale. The sisters made a novena in preparation for the feast day of their patron, St Joseph. Their prayers completed, they were informed that Broad Oak was now on the market! The necessary finance raised, the move was finally made on 12 March 1910 and St Joseph's Convent School was launched; it still flourishes over a century later. Recently renamed St Joseph's College, it is now co-educational. Past pupils include Cardinal Cormac Murphy-O'Connor, Archbishop of Westminster, who as a small boy in the 1930s attended St Joseph's kindergarten, and singers Alma Cogan and Marianne Faithfull.

PMS (Hanley, Sister M., *A Hundred Years A-Growing*, 1994/ *Old Redlands*, Redlands Local History Group, 1990)

MARCH 13TH

1983: On this day, the Reading half-marathon was run for the first time, starting and finishing in Reading University's Whiteknights Park. There were 5,000 runners, and the winner was Mark Curzons, secretary of the university's athletic club, in a time of sixty-seven minutes forty-five seconds. The race has been repeated every year since this date, apart from 2001, when foot and mouth concerns forced a cancellation. The course has varied over the years; it now starts in Green Park, close to the Madejski Stadium, home to Reading Football Club and London Irish Rugby Club. After a circuitous course around the town, the runners finish at the Stadium. The men's course record is sixty-one minutes nineteen seconds, set by Kenyan Patrick Makau in 2008. The female record, sixty-nine minutes thirty-five seconds, was achieved the same year by Liz Yelling, British double Olympian. Reading was one of the first half-marathon town courses to welcome wheelchair racers. The men's record is held by British Paralympian Gold medallist David Weir MBE, with a time of forty-five minutes fifty-nine seconds in 2006, and the women's by Paralympian Shelly Woods, who completed the course in sixty-six minutes thirty-seven seconds in 2004. The half-marathon has continued its popularity, with 16,500 places at the 2013 race.

VC (Reading half-marathon website)

MARCH 14TH

1947: On this day, following months of bitterly cold snow and ice, and reductions in electricity supplies and working hours, the thaw brought with it devastating floods. The Thames rose by 8in, resulting in many properties in Lower Caversham being flooded, and water under railway bridges made travel difficult. Appropriate boats and lorries had to be commandeered as 'ferries'. Voluntary organisations rose to the occasion splendidly, finding temporary accommodation for hundreds. There were reports of fuel shortages – simply because householders could not access their submerged coal stocks! Food and drink were delivered by means of buckets lowered from upper windows. Prompt action by Thames Conservancy saved Caversham Lock. Although it was a week or so before the floods subsided, it was many months, if not years, before life returned to normal for some of those affected. Ironically, the following summer turned out to be one of the hottest on record!
JRS (Currie, I., Davison, M. & Ogley, R., *The Berkshire Weather Book,* Froglets, 1994/Starr, J.R., *Weather and Climate in History,* 2005)

———— • ◆ • ————

2012: On this day, after a third bid, Reading learnt that it was not to become a city. Politicians of all persuasions seemed united in regarding it as a city in all but name.
JBD (*GetReading*)

MARCH 15TH

1968: On this day, the *Reading Chronicle* reprinted an earlier article in the Caversham Park Village publication *Village Voice*, which had been scathing about Reading town. The authors were not strictly within Reading, as, at that time, Caversham Park Village (though not Caversham itself) was outside the town boundaries. Their corporate opinion was expressed by a pseudonymous contributor writing as 'Bumpkin'. 'Reading,' he wrote, 'must be the deadest, dullest, most boring dragsville with the powers and dignity of a County Borough and seat of a university anywhere south of Reykjavik.' From the general he shifted to the particular: 'Forget about Reading. There's one decent department store and a reasonable library service (credit where it's due). For the rest – in the way of culture, shopping or services either look in other directions or let's try to do it for ourselves.' The *Reading Chronicle* splashed the story across its front page with the headline 'Reading is Dragsville'. The people of Caversham Park Village were quite vitriolic in their opinions of Reading, when questioned by a reporter. The reporter returned to Reading with the quotes and, upon presenting the statements to the people of Reading, was met with an apathetic response. In 1977 Dragsville swallowed up Caversham Park Village.

VC (Wykes, A., *Reading: A Biography*, Macmillan, 1970)

MARCH 16TH

1833: On this day, John Carter was hanged at Reading Gaol. He had started multiple fires in his home village of Lambourn on 19 November 1832, in the hope of raising labourers' wages. Although others were involved, Carter alone was charged and convicted with the manufacture of incendiary devices and committing arson. It was a crime he never denied.

VC (Kidd-Hewitt, D., *Berkshire Tales of Mystery and Murder*, Countryside Books, 2004)

1927: On this day, a Reading man appeared in court after his bright idea of taking a fox-terrier to the FA Cup tie against Brentford had unfortunate consequences. Thomas Luker of Upper Vine Buildings dressed his dog in Reading's blue and white colours and took him to Elm Park. Luker saw some fans with a bottle of liquor, asked for a drink and they obliged. However, the dog attacked one of them on the wrist and legs, the injuries needing hospital treatment. The magistrate, the Mayor of Reading, told Luker the animal was not under control and should not be taken to football matches where it might become excited. Luker was ordered to pay 22s 6d (£1.13) damages plus 11s (55p) costs. Meanwhile, Reading won the tie 1-0 and reached the semi-finals.

NS (Local press reports)

MARCH 17TH

1185: On this day, a century after the First Crusade, an unsuccessful crusading revival was attempted at Reading Abbey. The recovery of Jerusalem from Muslim hands was still profoundly important to the Eastern Empire in Constantinople and the Roman papacy. Now, King Henry II (1133-89) received a deputation from the Holy Land under Heraclius, Patriarch of Jerusalem, and Roger de Moulins, Grand-Master of the Knights Hospitaller, who was later killed in battle against Saladin. Heraclius had already visited Italy and France, seeking men and money to fight for the Holy Land. At Reading he reminded Henry of his vow – never fulfilled – to go on crusade after Thomas Becket's murder in 1170. Although professing sympathy, Henry replied that 'for him to accept the kingdom of Jerusalem which they offered him, to go thither and desert England, and expose it to its hostile neighbours would not, he imagined, be acceptable to God since this kingdom was as pleasing to God and as devout as the other'. Henry's son, Richard the Lionheart, would later lead a Third Crusade. But rather than vanquishing the great Saladin he made peace with him: yet another century of crusades failed to regain Palestine for Christianity.

PV (Hurry, J., *Reading Abbey*, 1901)

MARCH 18TH

1994: On this day, Clonmel, Ireland, signed the official twinning agreement with Reading. This link was no doubt backed by Reading's significant numbers of people of Irish origin; it was formed during a period of Labour control of the council (the Irish Labour Party was founded at Clonmel in 1912). Close contacts still continue, with this twin celebrated in the name, Clonmel Walk, in Caversham. 1994 also saw Reading twin with a third-world village, San Francisco Libre in Nicaragua; this place benefits chiefly from educational help from Reading, and is noted in San Francisco Libre Walk near the Hexagon. Our twinning with Düsseldorf goes back to 1946, when Major-General Collins of the Royal Berkshire Regiment appealed for food and clothing to help that shattered city. Reading's new Mayor, Phoebe Cusden, promptly responded, initially through food parcels. Cultural, sporting and school exchanges gradually followed, until in 1975 the twinning became formal. A large commemorative sculpture was unveiled at Dusseldorf Way, facing the Civic Centre, in 1981. Most recently, Reading formally twinned with Speightstown, second town of Barbados, in 2003; our town has the largest diaspora of Bajans outside the Caribbean, and a lively Barbados and Friends Association has flourished since the 1970s.

PV (Daphne Barnes-Phillips, *Hands of Friendship*, Corridor Press, 2003)

MARCH 19TH

1749: On this day, the following notice appeared in the *Reading Mercury*:

William Bethen from London rat killer to his Royal Highness the Duke of Cumberland, now at the White Hart in Duke Street, Reading and who works for most of the nobility and gentry, has a particular way of destroying that sort of vermin which does so much mischief. They are of a different nature from black rats, which they destroy, and who will destroy one another if taken in a trap. NB He cures and keeps the buildings clear for those that employ him by the year, or cures them at present, or sells the stuff with directions of how to use it. It is prepared without poison, and is an infallible cure, which gives satisfaction to all whom he is concerned with. He also clears ships in twenty four hours and sells stuff that will keep for seven years with directions how to use it. He likewise destroys mice and causes them to die out of all buildings. He performs several other curious things too tedious to insert, which are done by no other than himself.

The White Hart inn flourished well into the nineteenth century until it was demolished for road widening.
SG (*Reading Mercury*)

MARCH 20TH

1849: On this day, Trinity Congregational (later United Reformed) Church opened in Reading. The building was packed for the morning ceremony, at which the Revd William Legg from Broad Street Chapel offered prayer. The Revd James Sherman, preaching, considered they now had 'a respectable house suited to the age in which we live'. The *Berkshire Chronicle* in July 1848 reported under the heading 'New Congregational Chapel' that the body of independent dissenters, who had seceded from Broad Street Chapel, and who since had occupied the New Public Hall as a temporary place of worship, had recently purchased a piece of land in Queen's Road, Reading and were about to commence building a chapel, designed in the Early English style by William Ford Poulton, who was himself married in Broad Street in 1850. The new church had seating for 500 worshippers, later enlarged to accommodate 800. Gas-lighting was installed and a school and church hall were added in a matching style. By the 1970s, the congregation had fallen to seventy; unable to attract their own minister, they decided to close the church. It was demolished in 1980 but its name survives in Trinity Hall, student accommodation that was built on the site.

SD (North, L., article in *Reading Chronicle,* 1980)

MARCH 21ST

1890: On this day, *The Times* announced the termination of the partnership between Samuel Soundy and Arthur Eisdell, corn-millers at Reading's Abbey Mills. Soundy & Sons worked the mill until 1957, before its demolition in 1964. Re-development of the site in 2009 brought us Abbey Mill House, which, with its iconic 128m spire, 'The Blade', is Reading's tallest building yet. The mill, once vital to Reading Abbey's existence but possibly pre-dating it, was powered by the Holy or 'Hallowed' Brook – a branch of the Kennet that the monks improved by embankment and clearance. William Grey, a royal crony, acquired Abbey Mill along with other monastic property after the Dissolution of the Monasteries. Under successive owners, it continued to provide the townspeople's flour for another four centuries. By Victorian times, the medieval structure had largely been lost. Soundy's Mill still produced flour for local bakers and shops, and later for biscuit manufacturers McFarlane Lang and Huntley & Palmers. The two undershot waterwheels ceased to turn by 1911, replaced by electric power. Today the mill is no more, yet three of its twelfth-century arches still stand over the Holy Brook, now under English Heritage protection.

PV (*The Times/Reading Standard*, 1957)

MARCH 22ND

2000: On this day, Cormac Murphy-O'Connor was installed as tenth Archbishop of Westminster, leader of the Roman Catholic Church in England and Wales. Born in Reading in 1932, he grew up with five siblings in London Street, where his Irish-born father was a GP. His first school (after St Joseph's kindergarten) was Presentation College in Reading, now closed, where alumni include Mike Oldfield, rock musician, and Lawrie Sanchez, a Reading professional footballer and later football manager. At eighteen, Murphy-O'Connor followed two older brothers into the Church, studying at the English College in Rome. After a decade of pastoral work in Hampshire, he returned to Rome as the college's rector from 1971 to 1977. He once revealed that it was here that he learned to mix a good Martini cocktail. In 1977 he was host to Archbishop Coggan when he visited Pope Paul VI, and at the end of the year he was appointed Bishop of Arundel & Brighton. Made an honorary Doctor of Divinity in 2000 (recognising his work for Christian unity), and Cardinal in the following year, in 2002 he became the first Catholic priest since 1680 to deliver a sermon to an English monarch (Queen Elizabeth II). He retired in 2007 at the mandatory age of seventy-five.

PV (National and local media/private sources)

MARCH 23RD

1907: On this day, the foundation stone of Caversham Library, designed by William Lewton, was laid. This doggerel appeared in the *Reading Standard*:

The sun was shining brightly
The banners streamed around
When a little band of citizens
Stood on crimson covered ground
To lay a grand 'Foundation Stone'
It was their fixed intent
And seriously and solemnly
With heavy steps they went.

For this very doubtful blessing, for
Which the ratepayers will groan,
With a Herculean effort they
Upraised this wondrous stone,
And laid it safely down to rest
In a nicely plastered little nest,
And then they swelled to twice the size
(Unless the sun was in my eyes)

And then one made a little speech,
Which no one could hear,
And then they sang a little song
'Mid trembling doubt and fear,
And then they said 'Twas over, and
Outside we all must pass,
We'd such a lot of policemen, and
We'd such of lot of gas.

SG (Cliffe, D., *Roots and Branches*, Two Rivers, 2007)

MARCH 24TH

1840: On this day, Henry West, aged twenty-four, was killed whilst working on the roof of the new railway station at Reading, plucked from there by a freak whirlwind. Such 'tornadoes', generally associated with intense thunderstorms, are far from unusual in Britain. His wooden memorial 'grave-board', subscribed for by his workmates, may be seen in the churchyard of St Laurence near the path by Forbury Road gate. This 'dead-board' takes the usual form of a length of wood supported by two posts, which keep it from sitting directly on the damp ground. Although these rails do not usually survive, unlike more expensive stone, this example has been kept in good repair, being renovated and repainted when necessary. It is a matter of local speculation whether this 'grave rail' is a traditional shape or appropriately that of a rail from the permanent way. Its inscription includes the following verse:

> Sudden the change, I in a moment fell
> And had not time to bid my friends farewell
> Yet hushed be all complaint. 'tis sweet, 'tis blest
> To change Earth's stormy scenes for Endless rest.
> Dear friends prepare, take warning by my fall.
> So shall you hear with joy your Saviour's call.

PSm/JRS (Epitaph in churchyard)

MARCH 25TH

1908: On this day, the future cinema director, Sir David Lean, was born. He came from a Quaker family and in 1922 was sent to Leighton Park School, the Quaker boarding school in Reading. Lean is said to have been an unwilling pupil; he left to become an even less enthusiastic accountant, but finally found his métier in films, rising from tea-boy at Gaumont Studios to become director of such films as *Brief Encounter, Great Expectations, Lawrence of Arabia* and *Doctor Zhivago*. He died in 1991.
JBD/VC (*Who's Who/Daily Telegraph*)

———•◆•———

1989: On this day, *Catalyst* magazine was launched at Reading Town Hall. Its core was a listings section – live music was happening at the Beehive, the Dove, the Eagle and the Red Lion – but there were also arts reviews, computer advice, political comment and gossip, and a crossword with Reading-based clues. The first issue covered the station rebuild, the San Francisco Libre twinning, the birthday of the Hindu god Siva and news from Friends of the Earth. The magazine was very low-tech; every fortnight a group of volunteers gathered in Park Hall for a convivial paste-up session. The fiftieth and last issue appeared in September 1991 when editor Adam Stout bowed out; efforts to revive the magazine were unsuccessful.
AS (*Catalyst No.1*)

MARCH 26TH

1833: On this day, it was reported: 'This afternoon, 43 individuals, men, women and children, natives of this town and neighbourhood, embarked in a barge at Caversham Bridge for Liverpool, to take their passage to New York. To this has the long period of Tory misrule brought Old England.'
AS (*Reading Mercury*)

———•◆•———

1927: On this day, Reading FC made their only FA Cup semi-final appearance but lost 3–0 to Cardiff City at Wolverhampton Wanderers' Molineux ground. There were more than 7,000 Reading fans in the 40,000-strong crowd. Many of them wore blue and white favours and a buttonhole badge distributed by Huntley & Palmers in the shape of a biscuit. Cardiff City, with eight internationals in their side, were far too good for Reading, who nevertheless had the better of the first twenty minutes. However, Ferguson and Wake gave the Welshmen the lead and Ferguson added another goal after sixty-five minutes to end Reading's hopes. Striker Frank Richardson, fifty years later, described the day as the most disappointing in a long footballing career. Reading scored a revenge victory over Cardiff in the Championship to Premier League play-off semi-finals in 2011, losing in the final to another Welsh side, Swansea.
NS (*Local press reports*)

MARCH 27TH

1952: On this day, a serious accident occurred in Reading involving trolleybus 126. At the junction of Oxford Road with Cranborne Gardens, it overturned as a result of hitting the kerb and mounting the verge at speed. Astonishingly, the driver, conductress and three passengers aboard suffered only minor injuries, mainly from cut glass. It seems that the driver had lost control after looking back into the lower saloon: as a result he lost his job.

JRW (*Berkshire Chronicle*)

———◆———

2004: On this day, Dr Reg Saxton died in Worthing. Saxton, who lived in Kings Road, Reading, during the 1930s, was a pioneer of blood transfusion serving with the International Brigades in the Spanish Civil War. In 1936 he travelled to Spain and was immediately active behind the front line in the battles of Jarama, Belchite, Brunete and Teruel; later he served during the final Republican offensive on the Ebro River, in 1938. Among his patients was Julian Bell, poet and nephew of Virginia Woolf. During the Second World War, Dr Saxton served with the Royal Army Medical Corps in Burma, continuing his work in blood transfusion. After the war he joined the Campaign for Nuclear Disarmament and continued campaigning until his death.

MC (Cooper, M. & Parkes, R., *We Cannot Park on Both Sides: Reading Volunteers in the Spanish Civil War 1936-39*, 2000)

MARCH 28TH

1777: On this day, Mary Latter died at her home in Reading. Mary was not a native of Reading, having been born in Henley-on-Thames in 1725. She indulged her talent for satirical poetry by writing verses descriptive of the persons and characters of several ladies who were inhabitants of the town. Afterwards she disowned the verses in a ludicrous rhyming advertisement in the *Reading Mercury*. In 1759 she published a small volume of miscellaneous works, in which she described herself as living 'not far from the market place, immersed in business and debt, sometimes madly hoping to gain a competency, sometimes justly fearing dungeons and distress'. She was treated with uncommon esteem by John Rich, the manager of the Theatre Royal, Covent Garden, but his death in 1761 put an end to the hopes and expectations she had formed of having her tragedy, *The Siege of Jerusalem,* presented on the stage and the subsequent probable benefits that might arise from its success. Undaunted, she continued writing to support herself until her death. She was buried in St Laurence's churchyard close to the remains of her mother.

VC (Doran, J., *The History and Antiquities of the Town and Borough of Reading in Berkshire*, 1835)

MARCH 29TH

1903: On this day, Arthur George Negus OBE was born in Reading. Arthur went on to become a broadcaster and antiques expert. His family had a long history in the antiques business, and Arthur took over the family firm at the age of seventeen, following his father's death. He first enjoyed television success at the age of sixty-two on the panel of *Going for a Song*, but was best known as the face of *Antiques Roadshow* for its first four years. He died on 5 April 1985 at his home in Cheltenham.
VC (*Oxford Dictionary of National Biography,* OUP, 2004)

1936: On this day, Sir Richard Rodney Bennett was born in Broadstairs, Kent. He is renowned for his film scores and jazz performances as much as for his challenging concert works. During the 1950s he was a pupil at Leighton Park School in Reading. He then became a student at the Royal Academy of Music in London, where he later taught. His compositions include scores for *Murder on the Orient Express, Far From the Madding Crowd* and *Four Weddings and a Funeral.* He lived in New York from 1979. Awarded the CBE in 1977, he was knighted in 1998 and died in December 2012.
VC (Meredith, A., *Richard Rodney Bennett: The Complete Musician*, Omnibus, 2010)

MARCH 30TH

1840: On this day, at 6 a.m., the first train from Reading's barely completed 'station house' left for Paddington station in London, drawn by the *Fire Fly* engine. The *Reading Mercury* reported:

> The novelty of this delightful and expeditious mode of travel, coupled with the extreme beauty of the morning, attracted a vast number of our country friends to the town; indeed we have seldom witnessed a greater influx of visitors than thronged Friar Street and the Forbury on this truly interesting occasion. At the station house, every accommodation was afforded the spectators that could be reasonably expected or desired by them, the extensive platform immediately adjoining the offices having been thrown open to the public, and seats provided, in a most handsome manner, for their convenience – a privilege which was not unduly appreciated by them. In the course of the afternoon, several directors and other gentlemen connected with the line arrived in one of the trains, accompanied by C Russell, Esq., the chairman of the Company, who, we are informed, were entertained by H Simonds at his brewery with a meat-tea. The station is a most commodious and neatly built structure.

Fire Fly took about one hour fifteen minutes to complete the 35¾-mile journey to Paddington.

VC (*Reading Mercury*)

MARCH 31ST

1851: On this day, Reading saw the taking of the census. The head of each family was asked simple questions about himself; Henry Ellis, of Oxford Road, answered thus:

> Henry Ellis, married, aged 38, occupation – Plebeian gardener and Chartist,
> where born – in the City of chimney pots.
> Ann Ellis, aged 39, fruitful wife, safe enough, household and maternal carer
> Mary and Ann, daughters, aged 15 and 13 – parents' housemaids
> Henry, son, aged 11 – much work and little pay
> John, son, aged 9 – helps brother and plays with other
> Charles, son, aged 7 – goes to school whistling as he goes
> Thomas, son, aged 3 – stops at home and plays with brother
> Edward, son, 4 months – nursed tenderly

Asked if deaf, dumb or blind Henry wrote: 'can hear the church bells talk tolerably and wears specs when day grows dim'.

Also on this day occurred England's first and only Religious Census. This showed that in Reading (excluding areas later added to the town) there were twenty-one places of worship with nearly 7,000 adult worshippers in the morning and over 6,000 in the evening, compared with the total population revealed by the main census of 21,436.

SG/JBD (1851 Census of Reading/Tiller, K. (Ed.), *Berkshire Religious Census 1851*, Berkshire Record Society, 2010)

APRIL 1ST

1966: On this day, the murdered body of seventy-one-year-old Alice Beatrice Cox was found at her home in Salisbury Road, Reading. Police were summoned, and the scene was checked and noted: it had all the appearances of a robbery gone wrong. Scotland Yard were called in, and the house dusted for fingerprints. People who legitimately had been in the house were fingerprinted for elimination purposes – and one unidentified set of prints remained. There followed a mass fingerprinting of all males in Reading; over 10,000 prints were taken but none matched. Visiting a house in Cambridge Place, the police took fingerprints in the room of 'Frank', a lodger: the prints matched! Further checks identified Frank as Benjamin Frank Achilles Comas, a native of St Vincent in the Caribbean. His details were circulated, and police spotted him in a café. He gave a false name and address but was taken to be fingerprinted. After first refusing, when faced with detention he consented. His prints matched those at Salisbury Road and Cambridge Place. Found guilty of murder, wounding with intent, housebreaking and larceny, Comas received a life sentence.

VC (Eddleston, J., *Foul Deeds and Suspicious Deaths in Reading*, Wharncliffe, 2009)

APRIL 2ND

1871: On this day, Reading householders were required to participate in the National Census; coincidentally, this was Census Day also in 1911. The census returns, now available, are a prime resource for such studies as the size of families, place of origin (Reading itself or elsewhere), the mix of professionals and artisans, and other fascinating data. Reading's evolution from mere country market-town to by far the largest commercial and industrial centre in Berkshire was clearly evident by 1871. The coming of the railway and such major enterprises as Huntley & Palmers, Suttons Seeds and Simonds Brewery, had generated this growth and its associated social changes. In 1871 Reading townspeople numbered 39,497, doubling to 84,364 by 1911, compared with 156,000 recorded in the 2011 census. The 1871 census also recorded 'blind' or 'deaf' disabilities; as previously, 'trade or occupation' was entered. But in 1911 came greater detail of employment, whereby some even named their employer – invaluable for writing family history! But as 1911 was the Suffragette era, many women – perhaps thousands – boycotted the census to protest against the government's denial of women's right to vote; however, the record is silent on how many of these were Reading inhabitants.
PV (National Archives)

APRIL 3RD

1971: On this day, an ordinary Reading family made television history when the first 'fly-on-the wall' television programme was broadcast. Filming had started in mid-February when the Wilkins family of Whitley allowed the BBC into their home to follow their lives over a period of weeks. This working-class family comprised Terry and Margaret and their four children, not to mention their cat and several cages of budgerigars. From the first, the programme caused controversy and even outrage in Reading as people were bitterly critical of the BBC for showing the town in such a bad light. One Reading MP, Tony Durant, wrote to the Corporation's Director-General complaining that it was bad television and poorly produced. The many criticisms which, perhaps surprisingly, shook the family, included the BBC's handling of taboo subjects: a family affected by divorce, a child born out of wedlock, a mixed-race relationship, and individuals not averse to swearing even in front of the cameras! Despite this reception, the series was a success for the BBC and has subsequently been much emulated. Terry and Margaret Wilkins later divorced and married other partners, and Margaret died in 2008.

JP (*Reading Evening Post*/Phillips, D., *The Story of Reading*, Countryside Books, 1980)

APRIL 4TH

1909: On this day, a Palm Sunday procession brought about a controversy in which Captain Henderson, Chief Constable of the local police, became deeply involved, although the subject was a matter of Church doctrine rather than normal policing issues. On Palm Sunday, the clergy and congregation of St James' Roman Catholic Church had processed through Reading streets displaying the Blessed Sacrament. The procession was orderly and caused no obstruction, but it brought loud protest from members of the Evangelical Lay Churchmen's Union, invoking ancient Acts which prohibited the wearing of robes or public demonstration of 'Roman' worship. The Union demanded that in future Henderson should prohibit such demonstrations; he responded that there had been nothing inflammatory or disturbing about the procession, but he would, of course, implement the Act if so ordered. After he had been so instructed, exchanges of letters followed, involving the Roman Catholic Bishop of Portsmouth, in whose diocese Reading lay. These drew the reply that the last thing Catholics wanted to do was break the law, but since the Home Secretary had given permission for processional worship elsewhere, why should Reading be excepted? Correspondence flew back and forth, with the upshot that Reading Watch Committee revoked their decision to ban similar events in future and recorded their regret for having taken it in the first place.

VC (Wykes, A., *Reading: A Biography*, Macmillan, 1970)

APRIL 5TH

1879: On this day, a Saturday, Reading townspeople could sample for the first time a ride on the new horse tramway – but only along the western half of the line. The Reading Tramways Company had obtained powers to construct the tramway east to west across the borough, boundary to boundary, from the cemetery via Broad Street to the barracks in Oxford Road; but the opening of the eastern section was delayed until 31 May by Reading Gas Company's laying of gas mains. The original trams, twenty-six-seat single-deckers drawn by one horse, were described by the *Reading Observer* as 'commodious and handsome' vehicles, in which 'high and low, rich and poor, deigned to sit shoulder to shoulder'. Adverse criticism was soon to follow: irregular service, over-crowding, cheeky boy conductors. Adding more trams in the 1880s improved the frequency, but the line was never extended, even though the borough expanded. Passengers enjoyed greater capacity and speed when six new and two second-hand two-horse double-deck cars entered service in 1893, after a depot fire destroyed five trams. Subsequently the trams suffered from competition from horse-buses and the tram-track deteriorated. In 1901, after prolonged arbitration, the council exercised an option to buy up the undertaking and to extend and electrify it.
JRW (*Reading Observer*)

APRIL 6TH

1942: On this day, the 'normal' arrangements between Reading's principal bus undertakings were slightly relaxed, when the 1d surcharge on inbound Thames Valley buses was temporarily abolished. The aim of this re-arrangement, which lasted until 1 January 1948, was to make best use of scarce fuel supplies caused by U-boat operations in the Atlantic and to conserve tyre rubber. It also helped passenger mobility and relieved some of the pressure on Reading's transport system. When this small wartime relaxation, on inward journeys only, ended in 1948, the parties returned to the original arrangement, with the 'lost' revenue being transferred in cash to the Corporation! In 1915, when Thames Valley had introduced bus services from Reading into the surrounding countryside, it had been anticipated that the 1d surcharge would discourage travel within the town by passengers who would otherwise use the electric trams. In those days – and, indeed, through to the 1950s – a penny was a lot to spend unnecessarily. For sixty years, it well suited the municipal undertaking to insist on retaining the fare surcharge. The surcharge was finally abandoned in a deal with Thames Valley's successor, Alder Valley, whereby Reading Transport took over the operation of services to Woodley and Twyford from 12 October 1975.

JRW (*Berkshire Chronicle*)

APRIL 7TH

1958: On this day, Easter Monday, over 1,000 'Ban the Bomb' marchers departed from Reading for their protest 'target', Aldermaston Atomic Weapons Research Establishment. The first H-bomb test had recently polarised attitudes to Britain's nuclear policy. Now, protestors joining en route would bring the estimated total demonstrating at AWRE to 12,000. This first Aldermaston March, organised by the pacifist Direct Action Committee, had won the backing of the new Campaign for Nuclear Disarmament only some weeks before. On Good Friday, Canon John Collins, CND chairman, delivered a rousing send-off speech in Trafalgar Square. After two days on the road, accompanied by musicians and peace songs, and buoyed up by conviction, the marchers reached Reading amid snow-flurries and a bitter wind on Sunday. Reading's Socialist MP Ian Mikardo led them into town, but those who supported 'The Bomb' for Britain's defence provoked some angry confrontations. Private homes and, controversially, some local schools provided sleeping accommodation. On Monday morning, again in freezing weather, the marchers plodded out on the Bath Road for the last 8-mile stretch. The *Berkshire Chronicle* (in its page 13 story!) noted: 'Never before can Reading have seen anything quite like this protest march.'
PV (*Berkshire Chronicle*)

APRIL 8TH

1163: On this day, a duel was fought between two knights of the realm on an island in the Thames at Reading. During King Henry II's campaign against the Welsh in 1157, some of the soldiers panicked because, it was said, the royal standard-bearer, Henry de Essex, dropped the standard, signalling that the King was dead. When Robert de Montfort accused Essex of cowardice and treachery, which he denied, the King determined on trial by combat to resolve the quarrel. Before great crowds of spectators, including the King and many nobles, the duel continued for several hours, with blood spurting through the chainmail of both knights. At last, Essex – dazzled by a vision of another knight he had murdered – suffered a 'mortal' wound. He was thereupon judged guilty, and Henry bade the monks of Reading Abbey to carry his body away for burial. But a flicker of life was noticed under the bloodied sheet and he was nursed back to health. As a branded coward and traitor, his estates were forfeit and he later became a monk in the Benedictine order. The island, once called De Montfort Island, is now known as Fry's Island.

VC/NS (Phillips, D., *The Story of Reading*, Countryside Books, 1999/Childs, W., *The Story of the Town of Reading*, 1905)

APRIL 9TH

1941: On this day, Caversham suffered a second incendiary air raid. The first had been a daylight raid on 30 January, when several hundred incendiaries fell over an extensive area, including St Peter's Church, St Anne's Road, Hemdean Road, Rectory Road, Priory Avenue, North Street, Short Street, Westfield Road and Cromwell Road. Shops and houses were hit and a furniture store burnt out. The second raid was less serious. Most incendiaries fell in gardens near Church Street, the Regal Cinema, Caversham Library, Hemdean Road, Oxford Street and Chester Street. Earlier, in the autumn of 1940, Reading had experienced four other bombings, all by lone aircraft. On 1 October a bomber struck the Anglefield Road, Mayfield Drive and Chiltern Road areas of Henley Road. On 3 October, Berkeley Avenue, around St Saviour's Church, received attention, presumably with the intention of demolishing the nearby railway bridge at the head of the coal-yard. On 9 October, for no obvious reason, Emmer Green was bombed, near Reading Golf Club and St Benet's Home in Kidmore End Road. The raid of 26 November was more serious, as houses in Cardiff Road were hit in an attempt to destroy the railway junction. (For Reading's most serious air raid, *see* February 10th.)

JRW (*Berkshire Chronicle*/personal research)

APRIL 10TH

1798: On this day:

> ... a boy of about ten years old, of the name of New, fell into the chalk-pit at Mr. Sherman's brick-kiln, which is above thirty yards deep, and was very materially hurt; his father went down for him, but was so much agitated, that after they were drawn up a considerable height, he let him fall ... his skull was fractured, and he now lies without hope of recovery.

Sherman's kiln was off Southampton Street, possibly where Sherman Road stands today.
AS (*Reading Mercury*)

———— • ◆ • ————

1824: On this day, John Man died in Castle Street, Reading, and was buried in St Mary's Church on 24 April. He was born in 1749 in Whitechapel and baptised on 3 December 1749. After education at Whitgift School, Man arrived in Reading in 1770. In June 1775, he married Sarah Baker at St Mary's and fathered four children. Becoming assistant master at the Hosier Lane academy of William Baker, his father-in-law, he wrote poetry and historical works. His two important books about Reading are *The Stranger in Reading* (1810) and *The History and Antiquities of Reading: Being a History of the Town of Reading* (1816).
VC (Sowan, A. (Ed.), Man, J., *The Stranger in Reading*, Two Rivers, 2005)

APRIL 11TH

1722: On this day, Christopher Smart was born in Shipbourne, Kent. A friend of his late father, the Duchess of Cleveland, paid for his schooling in Durham. Proving to be an able student with a love of literature, Smart entered Pembroke College, Cambridge, where he became a Fellow. When the literary set of the day drew him to London, he became a prolific author, satirist and poet. In 1752 Smart married Anna Maria Carnan, stepdaughter of John Newbery, the renowned Reading publisher (printer of the *Reading Mercury* from 1737). He wrote for Newbery's newspapers and magazines. He produced children's books, composed songs and other pieces for theatres and pleasure garden and translated Horace into prose for the use of students. He also provided material for 'Mrs. Midnight's Oratory', a series of popular entertainments sponsored by Newbery. These were a cross between music-hall and circus, with songs, recitations, dances and performing animals. A bout of religious mania characterised by compulsive praying in public led to his detention in an asylum; but his most acclaimed work, *A Song to David*, appeared on his release in 1763. Bankrupt and ill, Smart died on 20 May 1771; his widow – still running the *Reading Mercury* – and two daughters were fortunately provided for under John Newbery's will.
VC (Cooper, J., *Some Worthies of Reading*, 1923)

APRIL 12TH

1971: On this day, the brief history of Reading's (illegal) Radio Utopia came to an abrupt end. Officials from the Ministry of Post and Communications (alerted by a Theale lady who was receiving phone requests for music to be played!) raided a Tilehurst house and found a radio transmitter hidden in the loft. Although no interference had actually occurred, the transmissions were close to Radio One and the emergency services' wavelengths. On 11 April the broadcasts were traced, using monitoring and tracking equipment. Checking the road, the officials noted an aerial leading from an upstairs window to a nearby tree. The next day they entered the house concerned, with police officers, and found two boys inside; a transmitter hidden in the loft was still warm from use, though disconnected. A third boy, posted as lookout outside, had warned in vain of the officials' approach, and came inside to give himself up. Their defence lawyer claimed that the teenage entrepreneurs, Denis Pibworth, John Ryland and Stephen Dove, had taken pains to ensure that their broadcasts would cause no interference within a 5-mile radius. They had initiated their service in the conviction that the BBC needed an alternative, but zeal for their cause had overcome their judgement. Each was fined £10 with £10 costs.

JP (*Reading Chronicle*)

APRIL 13TH

1813: On this day, the Revd Charles Coates died. Every student of the history of Reading has at some time consulted his *History and Antiquities of Reading*, published in 1802. He first considered the idea in 1791 and sought subscribers. He then delved into intensive research, taking eleven years before the book was finally published in 500 pages with illustrations and a useful map. In 1810 he issued a supplement with corrections and additions. Born in 1746, the son of John Coates, a London watchmaker, and baptised at St Laurence's, Reading, he was educated at Reading School and Gonville and Caius College, Cambridge. After a curacy at Ealing, he held the living at Preston, Dorset, and finally at Osmington, but failed to obtain a Reading parish. Although the health of both his wife and himself hindered his literary activity, before his death he was engaged in a new and enlarged edition of Ashmole's *Berkshire*. But this project was never realised. Of his *Antiquities*, *The British Critic* wrote: 'Mr. Coates has, with unwearied assiduity, gathered all that could prove interesting to the inhabitants of Reading; to whom we have no doubt this work will be extremely grateful'.

SG (*Oxford Dictionary of National Biography*, OUP, 2004/O'Byrne, R., *Representative History of Great Britain & Ireland*, Part 2: Berkshire, 1848)

APRIL 14TH

1860: On this day, the Reading Government School of Art was finally opened after a search of nearly four years to find suitable accommodation. Charles Havell (1828-92), a noted artist and drawing master, was made headmaster of the school, a position he held till 1889 when he was replaced by Henry Dawson Barkas. The main objective of the institution was to teach art to the masses, leading to the subject becoming part of the school curriculum. The rôle of the headmaster, along with his assistant and pupil teachers, would be to teach day and evening students at the school premises, and also to visit private and board schools. Teaching in Science was added in 1870. After Barkas took over, the school's staff was increased. By 1892, with the development of the University Extension Movement, the Reading School of Science and Art (along with other educational institutions) became an original element of the University College. This then evolved into the prestigious Art Department of the University of Reading. In 2010 an exhibition entitled 'Art School' was staged at the Museum of Reading to celebrate 150 years of art tuition in Reading.
SG (Gold, S., 'The Reading School of Art', ms)

APRIL 15TH

1123: On this day, years of site clearance and planning by a work-party of eight Benedictine monks from the celebrated Abbey of Cluny came to fruition. On 18 June 1121 their project, Reading Abbey – the largest church in Christendom – had already reached the point where King Henry I ceremonially laid its foundation stone. Then, using raw materials from far and wide, with the freestone shipped from Caen in France, and local craftsmen and labourers, the monks drove the work forward. The first building phase now culminated in Hugues de Boves, alias Hugh of Amiens, becoming first Abbot of Reading. Hugh, a learned theologian, successfully organised the monastery, recruiting many novices and encouraging royal patronage. He next won the Foundation Charter of 1125, which firmly set Reading on its path to greatness. In September 1130 Hugh was raised to be Archbishop of Rouen and transferred to the King's domains in France. On the death of Henry I, his nephew Stephen claimed the throne; through the next troubled years of Civil War, Hugh gave him, and his successor Henry II, his staunch support. Reading's first abbot died at Rouen in November 1164.

PV (Hurry, J., *The Rise and Fall of Reading Abbey*, 1906)

APRIL 16TH

1802: On this day, the 'New Canal' or 'New Cut' was opened, bypassing the kink in the River Kennet near Reading Abbey and passing under Watlington Street. The *Reading Mercury* reported:

> A barge freighted from London, belonging to the Navigation Company, on board of which was a great number of respectable inhabitants of this town, sailed up it. There was a blue flag and a laurel bough hoisted at the mast-head, and the men were decorated with blue ribbons; she sailed to her moorings amidst a grand discharge of cannon ... Afterwards the Navigation Company dined together in their office, where the day was spent with the utmost festivity and hilarity.

Previously, in 1797, it had been announced that:

> The Committee appointed to carry into execution the plan of a constant and regular Navigation between Reading and London, beg leave to inform the Public, that a Barge will lie at Mr Blandy's Wharf on Thursday next, loading for London. Orders are received at the Counting-House in the Wharf, or at Mr Man's.

The company comprised William Blandy, ironmonger, coal merchant and later Mayor of Reading, in partnership with John Man, best known as author of *The Stranger in Reading*, an entertaining and critical account of the town in 1810. (*See* April 10th.)
AS (*Reading Mercury*)

April 17th

1897: On this day, the funeral of William Silver Darter was attended by a large congregation. He was one of the town's most successful characters, born in London Street in 1803, the son of a carpenter. Darter served the people of Reading for nearly fifty years as councillor, magistrate and Mayor (1850-52). By trade he was a plumber, painter and glazier, with premises in London Street; thus he came into contact with all classes of townspeople, gaining a knowledge of houses both private and public and a strong interest in current events. Darter was an astute businessman and property developer. In 1839 he had a large new house, Swiss Villa, built for him in Kings Road, designed by Henry Briant, architect of the Royal Berkshire Hospital. Later he moved to Sutherlands and finally to Somerleaze, both off Christchurch Road. He is perhaps best remembered today for his articles in the *Reading Observer* in the 1880s, later published in book form as *Reminiscences of Reading by an Octogenarian*. By his wife Maria Jenkins he had at least seven children; his daughter Maria married John Talwin Morris, and his daughter Kate married Edward Morris, both brothers of Joseph Morris, the Reading architect.
SG (Phillips, D. (Ed.), *Reminiscences of Reading*, Countryside Books, 1989/Boorne, Darter Family Tree, ms)

APRIL 18TH

1913: On this day, the Parks and Pleasure Grounds Committee of Reading Council resolved that its best thanks be accorded to Mr Herbert J. Lawrence of Parkhurst, Reading, for two peahens, and to Mr Denzil Cope of Bramshill Park, Winchfield, for a peacock, which they had respectively presented to the Corporation and which had been placed in the grounds at the Mansion House in Prospect Park. A month later they decided that 'the horse which is kept for use in Prospect Park be disposed of as the chairman of the Committee may direct, as it is no longer suitable for the purposes, and that the Borough Surveyor be instructed to hire a horse when one is required for use there'. In July they invited tenders for the right of pasturing sheep in the park. Nearly a year later they resolved to 'make such arrangements as they may deem to be proper with a view to the removal from Prospect Park of the peafowls which are now kept there and which disturb the patients and nurses in Park Hospital'.

AS (Reading Borough Council, Parks and Pleasure Grounds Committee Minutes)

April 19th

1164: On this day, to quote the words of Dr Hurry, the historian of Reading Abbey:

> The great Abbey Church was hallowed, after taking more than
> 40 years to complete. To mark the occasion the King (Henry II),
> and many nobles of the realm travelled to Reading; there came
> too the great Archbishop of Canterbury, Thomas Beckett, and
> ten suffragan bishops. What a spectacle that must have been!
> Think of the magnificent procession of monarch, nobles,
> Archbishop, Abbot and monks in gorgeous apparel, winding
> through aisle and nave past the royal tomb (of Henry I) up to
> the glorious choir. In due order would follow wonder-working
> relics, preserved in golden shrines adorned with sapphires and
> pearls, reputed relics of tutelary saints, absolving from sin and
> preserving from misfortune. And as today you wander through
> the ruins that do survive, you can still imagine, and listen to
> the voice of thanksgiving as the great Archbishop dedicates the
> fabric to the worship of God for ever and ever.

The Abbey later added the skull of Thomas Becket to its relics, which included the hand of St James, St Philip's skull, the jawbone of St Ethelwold, Abbot of Abingdon, pieces of the True Cross and relics of the Virgin.
SG (Hurry, J., *The Rise and Fall of Reading Abbey*, 1906)

APRIL 20TH

1932: On this day, Reading Aerodrome, situated in the south-eastern suburb of Woodley, hosted Sir Alan Cobham's National Aviation Day. His group of pilots was touring the towns of Britain as part of a national campaign to promote flying, and to secure a million signatures on a petition to be presented to Parliament demanding a more progressive air policy. Many people gathered in Woodley to view the magnificent air extravaganza, which started in the morning with a display over the Reading area for the benefit of local dignitaries. In the early afternoon Cobham's Air Circus, composed of airliners and smaller aircraft flown by both men and women, performed a thrilling aerobatic display. Those brave members of the public who were willing to advance £1 were able to experience exciting trips in the planes, the autogyro and the gliders. Spectators also enjoyed demonstrations of parachuting and wing-walking, before the grand finale of an air race around the pylons which was won by a Tiger Moth. Technical progress and innovation was further proved by an aerobatic display directed from ground by telephony! The whole spectacle demonstrated to the public the wonders of technology and the skills of the aviators and aviatrices.

JP (*Berkshire Chronicle*/Temple, J., *Wings over Woodley*, 1987)

APRIL 21ST

1957: On this day, Thames Valley Traction Company commenced an unusual bus service for inland Britain – operation of open-top double-deckers on a tourist 'riverside service' from Reading, meandering through meadowland and picturesque villages, through market towns and over river bridges, to Maidenhead. All double-deckers were open-topped originally but were enclosed by the 1930s. After the Second World War the general exception was using open-topped buses as tourist attractions 'along the prom' at seaside resorts. Tom Pruett, Thames Valley's general manager from 1955, brought the idea with him from Brighton. It was a brave experiment, in the days when most families had little disposable income and probably no car. Despite complete reliance on the vagaries of British weather, the service ran also during the next summers, 1958 and 1959. The weather in 1957 was not particularly good, producing fewer passengers than anticipated, so in 1958 the service began only at Whitsun, and then just at weekends. However, although the route was extended to Windsor, the weather was again poor. It was only a little better in 1959 and it had been deemed prudent to adjust the timetable further. Operation was scheduled to resume in 1960 – and, indeed, publicity had been prepared – but the plug was pulled!
JRW (Lacey, P., *Thames Valley Traction Company 1946-1960*, 2009)

APRIL 22ND

1626: On this day, 'Robert Woodd, a sayler, an apprentice to Captayne Tokeleye of London' was examined by magistrates in connection with a spending spree in Reading's hostelries with money that did not belong to him. His master had sent him to a tailor to collect some money owed to him and instead of returning it to him he had travelled 'to this towne Sondaye last' by way of Brentford, Hounslow and Maidenhead. 'He brought from St. Katherine's with him £23 in money, gold and silver, whereof he spent £10, 11 or 12 in 3 or 4 dayes, and the rest, viz. £13, the Constables had of him.' Woodd had put up 'at the signe of the Bell' for four nights at a cost of 40s, to which he generously added a further 4s in tips to the 'servantes'. Further sums were spent at the Olivant tavern (30s), the George (10s), the Sun (3s) and the Three Tuns (12d). Since the present worth of the currency is about one sixtieth of what it was in the early seventeenth century, the total amount of his master's money squandered by Woodd came to around £600!

JBD (Guilding, J., *Reading Records: Diary of the Corporation*, 1895)

APRIL 23RD

1981: On this day, the 'Cartwheeling Boys' sculpture, located near the Civic Offices, was unveiled by Mayor Marion Absolom and Oberbürgermeister Klaus Bungert to celebrate the long association between Reading and Düsseldorf. This link, founded in 1947 by a previous Mayor, Phoebe Cusden, has given rise to a series of cultural, sporting and other exchanges. In 1971 the Reading Düsseldorf Association organised a Friendship Fortnight, when Düsseldorf children came once again to Reading to take part in sporting and dance activities. Following this particularly successful event, Düsseldorf City Council presented Reading Borough Council with a sum of money to be spent on a special project to commemorate the link. After much thought, it was decided that a piece of sculpture representing children would be appropriate. A legend exists in Düsseldorf of a boy said to have saved the life of Prince 'Jan Wellem' (Count Palatine Johann Wilhelm) in the seventeenth century; when a wheel of the Prince's carriage worked loose on the way to his wedding in 1678, the boy was able to hold the wheel in place by cartwheeling. This is the legend represented in the sculpture, designed by Brian Slack and made of aluminium, set against a brick wall background. It was cast at Brunel University.

SG (*Hands of Friendship*, Reading, 2003)

April 24th

1929: On this day, came the long-awaited opening of the Cadena Cafe at 101 Broad Street, Reading. The new building stood on the site of former car showrooms. It had a beautiful bronze shop-front, and a contemporary report described it as 'a cafe which must rank amongst the finest in the Royal County and certainly one of the most beautifully equipped in Reading'. The opening ceremony was performed by Mr J.W. Williams, who was chairman of the Cadena board of directors. He revealed that he had been born in Reading and was 'one of the first boys to enter the new Reading School'. The Cadena Cafe Company had its headquarters in Bristol but had long wanted to open a branch in Reading. The new amenity could accommodate up to 300 persons and was fitted with an oak dance floor on the second floor. The architect was William J. Stenner FRIBA of Bristol. Many older Reading people will remember the aromas of coffee being brewed at the Cadena wafting across Broad Street; however, this one-time Reading landmark seems to have fallen victim to the redevelopment of the town centre in the 1970s. Will the new-fangled coffeehouse chains come to inspire as much affection?

SG (*Reading Standard*)

APRIL 25TH

1594: On this day, an inventory of the goods of William Laud, father of the future Archbishop of Canterbury, was drawn up. He had been a master shearman, a skilled cloth finisher, and a member of the Clothiers' and Clothworkers' Gild. The dates of his death and burial are unknown but the churchwardens' accounts show he was buried in St Laurence's Church. His wife, Lucy, the administrator of his estate, gave 2s to the poor at his funeral and spent 5s on food and drink for his neighbours. He had been ill for a time; the physician's fee was the large sum of 10s. He left a modest estate, valued at £52 17s 2d, but when his debts to several tradesmen, two cloth workers (possibly his employees) and £28 to Richard Lawde were paid, there was a deficit of £13 11s 6d. His was a comfortable home, several living rooms, chambers (bedrooms) for family and resident employees, a courtyard with a well, a stable, and two gardens with poultry, peas and beans. Several workshops were equipped for finishing the broadcloth for which Reading was renowned, and in the gardens were racks for stretching cloth. He owned a book for use at church services but not a Bible.

JoD (Berkshire Record Office)

APRIL 26TH

1670: On this day, Joseph Coale died; he was one of three Reading Quakers who perished during the persecution of Nonconformists which followed the Restoration of the Stuart monarchy in 1660. Joseph Coale, a Mortimer man, had been one of the first to become a Quaker in Reading, in 1655 when he was about nineteen years old and an apprentice weaver. After he had finished his training the next year, he felt a call to spread the Quaker gospel and for the next five years preached through Cornwall, Devon and Dorset, suffering imprisonment at least five times. Finally, in 1664, he was arrested at a Reading Quaker Meeting. This was part of a sustained persecution led by Sir William Armorer, Justice of the Peace, which saw most of Reading's Quaker men and women imprisoned. Quaker worship was continued only by the children, who were often beaten and abused. As Quakers observe the biblical injunction to 'swear not at all', they were readily trapped by the authorities for refusing to swear the Oath of Allegiance. They thus became effectively 'non-people' whose property and lives were forfeit. Joseph Coale spent the next six years in Reading Gaol, where he continued to write and publish until his death.

CJS (Sowle, T., *Some Account of the Life, Service, and Suffering of ... Joseph Coale*, 1706)

April 27th

1801: On this day, the *Reading Mercury* and the *Oxford Gazette* advertised an auction sale of the contents of the Austen family home in Steventon, Hampshire:

To be sold by auction: Chariot, and harness, 200 volumes of books … cows and calves … The furniture comprises four post and fields bedsteads … fine feather beds and bedding, mattresses, pier and dressing glasses, floor and bedside carpets, handsome mahogany sideboard, modern set of circular dining tables … Pembroke and card ditto, bureaus, chests of drawers and chairs, a piano forte in a handsome case, a large collection of music by the most celebrated composers … an 18-inch terrestrial globe and microscope, mahogany library table … tea china, a table set of Wedgewood ware, eight-day clock, side of bacon, kitchen, dairy and brewing essentials, an end of hops, set of theatrical scenes &c &c.

The Revd George Austen and his wife Cassandra, who were both in their sixties, had decided to leave their Hampshire home after more than thirty years and move to Bath with their two daughters, Cassandra and Jane. The family were selling their effects because of the difficulty of transporting them to Bath. Catalogues for the sale were available from, inter alia, The Angel, Reading. (*See also* March 8th.)
JP (*Jane Austen Society, Collected Reports, 1986-1995*).

APRIL 28TH

1991: On this day, a team from Reading, the Cambridge Arms 'A', was the first winner of the prestigious Morland Original Bitter Quiz League. This was the culmination of a contest for pubs and clubs across Berkshire and Oxfordshire, selling Morland's beer, to compete in area leagues. The Cambridge won the Reading League, narrowly beating the second-placed County Arms 46-45 in the last match. The play-offs that followed included a home and away leg against the winner and runner-up of the Wokingham League. The Cambridge team beat the Plough and Harrow, Warfield, to reach the competition finals. The finals took place at the Dog House near Abingdon. Having seen off Mr Warricks Arms in the semi-finals, the Cambridge was pitted against the Black Horse in the Grand Final. The quiz began disastrously for the Cambridge, but with two former soldiers in the team it was backs-to-the-wall, and, with the help of the Quiz-Master who disallowed a basically correct answer from the other side, the Cambridge won a 48-45 victory, lifting the trophy presented by Morland Head Brewer, Bill Mellor. The Cambridge appeared in the next three years' finals, winning again in 1993, but thereafter lost form. Despite its sporting prowess the Cambridge Arms closed in 1998, followed by the demise of Morland's Abingdon brewery in 2000.

JBD (Author's diaries)

APRIL 29TH

1854: On this day, aged eighty-six, died Henry Paget, 1st Marquess of Anglesey, who had been a distinguished general during the Napoleonic Wars. As such he gave his name to a recruiting campaign in Reading in 1807 by the 7th (Queen's Own) Hussars, formerly known as the 7th Light Dragoons. Paget had commanded this regiment since 1801, saw distinguished service with them at Coruña, and later fought as a Lieutenant-General at Waterloo, where he lost a leg. The recruiting campaign in Reading held out the prospect of being 'comfortably and most handsomely clothed and mounted on the finest Blood Horses England can produce' along with 'the pleasure of dining every day upon all the luxuries of the Season, with a set of the jolliest Fellows in the World'. Those tempted were invited to apply 'to Captain Duckinfield or Serjeant Hough, at the Sign of the Sun, Reading. God Save the King!' No mention of going off to fight Boney in the Peninsular War but we know that Henry Duckinfield was drowned in 1809 when the troop transport *Despatch* sank off the Lizard in Cornwall, and it seems all too likely that some of the fine fellows he recruited at the Sun went down with him.

JBD (Hamblin, I. & Dearing, J., 'This Sun of Reading', ms)

APRIL 30TH

2012: On this day, 18.8mm (0.75in) of rain fell at Reading; only two days earlier 17.6mm (0.7in) had fallen, making these the wettest April days since 3 April 2000. This was the culmination of an unusually wet month that saw 119.9mm (4.8in) of rainfall. At some 250 per cent of the long-term average, this was the wettest April at the University since 2000 (when 132.6mm was recorded). One hundred and fifty-three Flood Alerts were issued nationwide by the Environment Agency, forty-three in the South East. This wet month (in which there were only four days with no rainfall) coincided with the announcement of the start of a hosepipe ban, following drier-than-average conditions over the preceding eighteen months! Indeed, in December 2011 the *Reading Chronicle* had announced: 'The River Pang is running dry'; it highlighted the 'Protect the Pang' scheme which emphasised that this was everybody's problem, and urged all to conserve water at a time when resources were running low. Following a very stormy early June, which wrought havoc with the Queen's Diamond Jubilee Celebrations, the hosepipe ban was lifted later that month by Thames Water.

JRS (Brugge. R., University of Reading Weather Data)

MAY 1ST

1823: On this day, William Henry Timms published his *Twelve Views of Reading*. Son of William Timms, proprietor of the Lower Ship Hotel, he was born in Reading in 1791 but lived for a time in London and later settled in Margate. His *Views*, advertised in the *Reading Mercury* of 26 May 1823, depicted London Road; Horne Street with St Giles; Duke Street seen from the bridge; King Street; Market Place; St Mary's Church; Castle Street seen from the turnpike; a view from Red Lane; Coley House; Holme Park; Caversham Park and Caversham Bridge. The price was £1 11s 6d per set, or two guineas for a half-bound edition. Publication of further views, promised for the autumn, failed to materialise, perhaps because sales of the first set were sluggish. Five years later the two-guinea sets were still unsold despite being reduced to 10s 6d. Today, a coloured bound set can sell for over £2,000! Curiously, while Timms' surviving works show him chiefly as a landscape painter and engraver, the 1851 Census and his death certificate of 1858 term him 'portrait painter'. His prints were made into postcards, also commonly appearing in books to illustrate Reading in the 1820s.

SG (*Reading Mercury*/Amos, K., Family Tree, 2008)

MAY 2ND

1906: On this day, legendary cricketer W.G. Grace (known as the Doctor) brought the London County Bowling Club to Reading Bowls Club, Kendrick Road, to play in celebration of the previous winter's laying of a new green in Cumberland turf. Grace's team included Tom Robertson, president of the English Bowling Association and gold badge winner, and internationals including Joe Hay, R. Pearson, J. Gillespie and Stephen Fortescue. The day being very wet, even the presence of celebrities failed to attract many spectators and the teams played in mackintoshes and carried umbrellas. A closely contested game resulted in a 54–52 win for Reading. In fact, the outcome depended on the Doctor's last bowl, a firing shot which just failed to win the match.
NS (Archives of Reading Bowls Club)

———— •◆• ————

1997: On this day, Reading awoke to a change in the political landscape with two Labour MPs for the first time: Martin Salter in Reading West and Jane Griffiths in Reading East, having majorities of 2,997 and 3,795 respectively. Salter went on to win two more elections before retiring, while the local constituency association de-selected Griffiths – leading to a Conservative gain in 2005.
JBD (Waller, R. & Criddle, B., *Almanack of British Politics*, Routledge, 1998)

MAY 3RD

1833: On this day, Hilton's and Wombwell's travelling carnivals came to blows on the Oxford Road near Reading:

> Even the freaks took part. The fat man made for the living skeleton with a door-hook; the skeleton battered the fat man with a peg-mallet. Windows and doors of caravans were smashed ... There came a terrible diversion ... elephants, mad with fright, smashed the sides of the wagon to splinters and made their way out, rushing hither and thither, and turning over everything in their path. No lives were lost, but the turmoil will never be forgotten ...

AS (Sanger, G., *Seventy Years a Showman*, Dent, 1927)

1930: On this day died a twenty-one-year-old Reading hero – Bernard Lawrence Hieatt, flyer and motorcyclist. His statue in East Reading Cemetery shows him in 1930s 'leathers' and describes his death as occurring '... at the moment of his greatest triumph', creating two world motorcycle and sidecar records at Brooklands. Bernard was killed instantly when his sidecar struck a verge, in driving rain. Recording 'death by misadventure', the coroner called him 'one of the finest riders on the track – an all-round man'. *Berkshire Life* likened his exploits to something from *Boys' Own* magazine. At his funeral in St Bartholomew's, the gates were locked to control the crowds, while aeroplanes circled overhead.

JRS (Memorial inscription/*Berkshire Life*, 2010)

MAY 4TH

1810: On this day, John Berkeley Monck married Mary Stephens. John, the second and favourite son of John and Emilia Monck, was educated for the bar. When delicate health forced him to give up London life he moved to the country, settling at Coley Park on Reading's outskirts and marrying Mary, daughter of a Reading alderman. He was Member of Parliament for the town from 1820 to 1830, working for both the Reform Bill and the Beer Bill, and was very active in municipal affairs. When he died on 13 December 1834, up to 400 people followed the funeral cortège from Coley Park to St Mary's Church. Mary Russell Mitford, one of his close acquaintances, described him thus:

> He is a Great Grecian, and a Political Economist ... living in a lodging close to the House, with an old woman, who cooks him alternatively a beefsteak, a mutton chop, or a veal cutlet; he does not indulge in a lamb chop till after Easter. He votes sometimes with one party and sometimes with another, as he likes their measures; respected by all, notwithstanding his independence; and idolized here in the country for his liberality, his cheerfulness, his good-humour and his unfailing kindness.

VC (Cooper, J., *Some Worthies of Reading*, 1923)

MAY 5TH

1914: On this day, a new gymnasium was presented to the University College by Dr and Mrs Hurry. The lack of this essential part of university life had been felt by both the authorities and the students, but shortage of funds had prevented any progress. Dr and Mrs Hurry had come forward with the necessary finance and the new building, designed by Charles Steward Smith, fitted in well with the other university buildings, most of which had been designed by the firm of Smith and Son. Over its entrance door a coat of arms was carved, together with a relief panel reproducing the Discobolus (the iconic 'discus thrower' of ancient Greece), executed by J. Daymond and Son. At the opening ceremony, a gymnastics display was presented by a team of twelve students. Mr Wansdell, president of the Men Students' Union, thanked the donors, saying that 'by using the gymnasium the athletes would be better able to improve their physique, and the new facility would also provide a training ground for the eights and teams'. Responding, Dr Hurry concluded with the hope that the gymnasium might produce some future Olympic competitors. The building still stands and, having recently been modernised, continues to be used as a gymnasium.
SG (*Berkshire Chronicle*)

MAY 6TH

1843: On this day, it was reported that the first interment had taken place on the previous Monday afternoon, in Reading's new general cemetery situated just beyond what was then the town's eastern boundary. The deceased was a young woman of a respectable dissenting family and this Nonconformist burial was well attended by 'a considerable number of spectators'. The minister of the Broad Street Independent Chapel officiated. Because the Dissenters preferred the unconsecrated section of the cemetery, which was nearer to the archway entrance, this event could happen a month before the Bishop of Oxford came in June 1843 to consecrate the Anglican portion with its chapel, which was further from the entrance. This private company cemetery was an early development important both as a public health measure because of over-crowded parish burial grounds and also as it allowed Nonconformist ministers to conduct the funeral rites when there was no vacant burial space adjacent to their places of worship. The new cemetery was also equipped with chapels for the use of both Anglican and dissenting ministers but, regrettably, these have been demolished, although the entrance lodge, designed by William Brown, remains as a distinctive feature of the area.

PSm (*Reading Mercury/Berkshire Chronicle*)

MAY 7TH

1970: On this day, the Reading Centre of the National Trust was formed. A group of local enthusiasts wanted to create in Reading an association of National Trust members who could meet others with similar interests. There would be talks, visits, day trips, holidays, a social programme and recruiting and fund-raising events, as well as the opportunity to help the National Trust. The launch was a phenomenal success with Sir John Winnifrith, the National Trust's Director General, as the guest speaker. Sir John Betjeman had agreed to become president and nearly 400 attended the inaugural meeting in the Great Hall of the University; they all joined the new group. Within a few years the membership peaked at over 1,000, and the group soon became a leading local society with a large programme of cultural events. In 1970 there were only thirty-six such groups in England but now there are over 200. All surplus funds are passed to the National Trust, and during this time the Reading Centre has raised a quarter of a million pounds. In 1979, when Basildon Park was opened to the public, the National Trust needed to recruit 150 volunteer stewards; half of these were found through the Reading Centre.
SG (Personal records)

MAY 8TH

1852: On this day, the *Reading Chronicle* reported a curious incident: 'On Saturday an inquisitive cow entered the Wheel Inn in Friar Street and contemplated a seat at the bar, but was politely informed she was lacking those distinguishing qualities by which judicial honours are secured, and on the door being closed coolly and complacently walked away.' Originally called the Catherine Wheel, the Wheel Inn stood opposite St Laurence's Church. In 1633 the Corporation ruled that an annual sum of 4*d* should be paid to its cofferer for the 'standing of the signe-post at the Katherine Wheele'. At around this time the inn featured in a court case when one Augustine Chapman, a horse-dealer, was accused of staying at the 'Katrene Wheele' with a woman named Cicelye Addams 'as man and wief' and was 'committed to be carted'. The Wheel finally closed its doors in 1882; one of the last landlords was Dymore Boseley, who also carried on a brickmaking business. The inn then became the premises of Gregory, Love & Co., grocers. In 1943, the buildings on this site were damaged by Reading's one major air raid of the Second World War.

JBD (*Reading Chronicle*/Guilding, J., *Reading Records: Diary of the Corporation*, 1895)

MAY 9TH

1913: On this day, a squad of young men climbed aboard the boat-train at Charing Cross, clutching football kit and tickets for the long journey to Italy: it was Reading Football Club's first overseas tour. After crossing Paris in 'omnibuses' they boarded the night train for Genoa, on a tour that would end with a grand dinner in Turin. The club, founded in 1871, was nicknamed The Biscuitmen (by association with Reading's major employer, Huntley & Palmers). After 1895 the team became partly professional and enjoyed good results in the Southern League. In 1913, after contact with football enthusiasts in Italy, Reading FC undertook a short end-of-season trip to play five friendly matches with Italian sides. The tour was a pronounced success. Starting with a win over Genoa, they went on to beat AC Milan 5–0. Although they lost the next game 2–1, they then beat Pro Vercelli, the Italian champions, 6–0. The triumphant climax to the tour came on 18 May when they defeated the full Italian national team by 2–0. They had earned their final banquet. The comment of Italy's leading paper *Il Corriere della Sera* was generous: 'Without doubt, Reading FC are the finest foreign team seen in Italy'.

PV (*Berkshire Chronicle*)

MAY 10TH

1915: On this day, Monica Enid Dickens was born. She died in Reading on 25 December 1992. Great-granddaughter of Charles Dickens and herself a celebrated authoress, she became one of the bestselling women novelists of her time. Having been expelled from St Paul's Girls' School, she attended drama school before being presented to Court in 1935. With no career training, she took a job as cook-general in a variety of houses and soon, by chance, met a publisher who encouraged her to write about her experiences 'below stairs'. Dickens took just six weeks to complete her first book, *One Pair of Hands*, which has never been out of print since first published in 1939. In the 1940s she wrote about her wartime nursing experiences. With every book came literary recognition and praise. In 1951, on her marriage to Roy Stratton, a Commander in the US Navy, she moved with him to Washington and later to Massachusetts. A close friend of Chad Varah, founder of the Samaritans in the UK, Dickens set up the US Samaritans. After her husband's death she returned for her final years to her small cottage in Reading. Dickens had a love of animals and a generous nature; 'she helped many people through hard times'.

VC (*The Independent*)

May 11th

1893: On this day, there was great commotion over a fire at Reading's Tramway Company stables in Oxford Road, supposedly caused by a spark from the blacksmith's anvil falling on loose hay. Flames spread rapidly to the stables and other buildings. Fortunately the horses were turned loose before the fire got a hold, but the car sheds and five trams were destroyed. At nearby Brock Barracks a soldier noticed the pall of smoke, whereupon fifty soldiers and the crew of the 3rd Royal Berkshire Regiment's horse-drawn steam-pump were dispatched to the fire. On arrival, Major Edwards assessed developments, then ordered demolition of an unburned section of stables as a firebreak to save nearby housing. Meanwhile, the town centre police station had been alerted. The Volunteer Fire Brigade was mobilised, closely followed by the Maiden Erleigh brigade and a further ten-man volunteer fire brigade, with the Head Constable in command. The latter, in civvies, began a stand-up row with Major Edwards, claiming that only he should be fighting fires in the borough, the troops should not be there and the unburned stabling should not have been torn down. Thereafter ensued a war of correspondence between military and civil authorities, the end result of which was the establishment of the full-time Reading Borough Fire Brigade. **JRW** (Local press reports)

MAY 12TH

1868: On this day, the long-awaited restoration of St Laurence's Church, Reading, was completed and a service of dedication held. The work, begun a year earlier, included removal of the galleries and pews, relocation of monumental tablets to the interior of the tower, installing a new altar-rail and restoration of the pulpit. The most noticeable alteration was external: the demolition by order of the Board of Health of the attractive Blagrave Piazza attached to the south wall, which had been erected in 1619 and is a distinctive feature of early prints. The architect Joseph Morris inserted five beautiful traceried windows into the newly bare south wall, for which he was congratulated. The *Reading Mercury*, however, commented:

> There was one marked defect in the arrangements at which considerable annoyance was manifested; we allude to the condition of the seats, the staining of which (we understand) was not completed many hours before the service commenced. The result was that many ladies had their handsome dresses injured, by the quantity of oil absorbed from the seats. It would have been by far the wisest course, if time did not permit the staining of the seats, simply to have left them in an unvarnished state, by which the annoyance now so generally complained of would have been avoided.

SG (*Reading Mercury*)

May 13th

1867: On this day, the *Reading Mercury* reported:

Henry Chesterman succeeded in landing a fine trout at Caversham-bridge. The fish weighed 7lbs., and measured 2ft. long by 5¾ inches. After the trout had been hooked, the man found it difficult to land it, and upwards of twenty minutes elapsed, during which the fish took a run of about 200 yards before it was hauled into the boat, with assistance. This is the first trout that has been caught in the neighbourhood this season.

VC (*Reading Mercury*)

———— • ◆ • ————

1896: On this day the facsimile of the Bayeux Tapestry (*see* June 28th) was:

removed at Her Majesty's desire to Windsor Castle, where it was privately inspected by the Queen … Arthur Hill had the honour of attending and personally explaining the details of the historic pictures to the Queen who was pleased to express much interest in the subject and asked many questions about the work. The fact that Her Majesty has shown such interest in this unique work of the olden time will greatly add to its value, and the people of Reading will henceforth appreciate, more highly than they already do, the forethought and generosity which secured this treasure for the town.

SG (*Reading Mercury*)

MAY 14TH

1868: On this day, as reported by the *Reading Mercury*:

The Forbury Gardens are in their summer luminance and floral beauty which the present delightful weather has so generally produced. On Thursday they were honoured by a visit from his Grace the Duke of Marlborough who spent an hour inspecting the Abbey Ruins and grounds. He expressed very great pleasure at all he saw and spoke highly of the place as a resource for the inhabitants of what he termed 'a spirited town'. Approval from the possessor of Blenheim is no slight compliment.

SG (*Reading Mercury*)

————— • ◆ • —————

1921: On this day, Dora Carrington, painter and member of the Bloomsbury Group, wrote to the writer Lytton Strachey: 'And so in the café in the vile city of Reading I said I'd marry him [Ralph Partridge]'. Michael Holroyd, in his biography of Strachey, says 'she [Carrington] seemed a mess of odd moods: impulsive, self-conscious, restless. Eager to please – losing herself in ceaseless activity. "You are like a tin of mixed biscuits", Iris Tree told her. "Your parents were Huntley and Palmer".'
AS (Holroyd, M., *Lytton Strachey*, Heinemann, 1968)

MAY 15TH

1856: On this day, Charles Russell, former Chairman of the Great Western Railway, committed suicide by shooting himself. Born in Reading in 1786, he served in the Bengal Army before becoming Conservative Member of Parliament for Reading from 1830-7 and 1841-7. During his first term in office he was an influential supporter of the Great Western Railways Act of 1835. He was elected Chairman of the GWR in 1839 and, with Brunel, Saunders and Gooch, he formed the great quartet that built the Great Western broad gauge into a major national system. Vigorous in his establishing and nurturing of the GWR, he was described by one writer as 'one of the greatest early Victorian railway chairmen'. Russell had keenly championed the rights of the company's employees, who, when he retired in August 1855, showed their gratitude by collecting funds for a portrait of him to be painted by Sir Francis Grant RA. The picture was placed in a position of honour in the boardroom at Paddington. Suffering from dementia and old age, Russell took his own life only nine months after retiring. Curiously, an earlier Reading MP, George Spence (1826-27), had committed suicide in 1850 by cutting his throat.

VC (MacDermot, E., *History of the Great Western Railway, Volume I, 1833-1863*, 1927)

MAY 16TH

1931: On this day, the flying ace, Amy Johnson, came to Woodley Aerodrome for the opening of Reading Aero Club's new headquarters. The celebrations included a ladies' race in which Miss Johnson participated: a triangular course was flown from and back to Woodley via Wokingham Church and Twyford station. Johnson won the first heat, averaging 88.5mph, but came only third in the final.
NS (Temple, J., *Wings over Woodley*, Aston, 1987)

———•◆•———

1939: On this day, the trial began of Sidney Pricket, charged with murdering his wife of seven years, Edith, at Reading the previous January. The couple lived in Rodway Road in Tilehurst, where their constant arguments were the bane of their neighbours' lives. Edith had confided to a neighbour that she thought Sidney was going insane. On 16 January Pricket telephoned the police and informed them that he had killed his wife. Police duly arrived at the house and found Edith's body in the bedroom, strangled. In court, it took the jury thirty minutes of deliberation to find Pricket 'guilty but insane', whereupon he was committed to Broadmoor Criminal Lunatic Asylum.
VC (Long, R., *Final Commitment: An Anthology of Murder in Old Berkshire*, Berkshire Books, 1994)

MAY 17TH

1897: On this day, Oscar O'Flaherty Wills Wilde, the well-known playwright, poet, storyteller and wit, spent his last night in Reading Gaol. Wilde had been transferred to Reading from Pentonville on 13 November 1895 and for the last eighteen months of his sentence for gross indecency was known as C3.3. This was not the happiest episode in the life of the self-declared genius, but it led him later to write perhaps his most lasting contribution to poetry, *The Ballad of Reading Gaol*, inspired by the execution at the gaol in 1896 of Trooper Charles Woodbridge. Wilde also exercised his social conscience by protesting at the brutal policies of the governor, Lt Col Isaacson, who was transferred to another prison; and he helped the warders with their entries in newspaper competitions, winning a silver tea-set for one and a grand piano for another! Also inside, he wrote a long self-pitying letter to his onetime lover, Lord Alfred Douglas, which was published as *De Profundis* and has often been regarded as one of his least palatable works. On his release the following day, Wilde proceeded via Twyford station to Pentonville for a final night in custody. He then crossed to France, where he died in 1900.
JBD (Southerton, P., *Reading Gaol by Reading Town*, Berkshire Books, 1993)

MAY 18TH

1931: On this day, a film romance in real life was played out at Reading railway station, where two of the world's most famous film stars were reunited. Mary Pickford met her husband Douglas Fairbanks after four and a half months apart, amid rumours of marital difficulties. When Pickford landed at Southampton Docks in the morning, 'an elaborately fitted-out car' awaited her on the quayside – a present from Fairbanks. She telephoned her husband at Westward Ho! and learned he had lost in the first round of the Amateur Golf Championship. He was returning to London later – and the train would stop at Reading. She raced up from Southampton in the car, at times touching 70mph, and after an affectionate meeting on the platform at Reading, the couple motored up to London together. **NS** (*Berkshire Chronicle*)

———— •◆• ————

1973: On this day, the *Reading Chronicle* reported on the biennial rally of the Christian Colportage Association held on 12 May at Greyfriars Church, Reading. This evangelical body still exists under the name 'Outreach UK', but no longer has 'colporteurs' selling tracts door-to-door. The word, from the French, referred to a box or tray hung from the vendor's neck. **AS** (*Reading Chronicle*)

MAY 19TH

1359: On this day, Reading was the scene of great rejoicing, tournaments, dancing and a pageant, as a significant dynastic marriage was solemnised at the Abbey Church. Prince John of Gaunt (fourth son of King Edward III, reigned 1327-1377) wed his cousin Blanche, daughter of Henry Plantagenet and heiress to the vast Lancaster estates. The King, his four sons and nineteen knights took part in the jousting, which lasted a fortnight. Reading's chronicler John Man suggested that 'King's Mead' (now Kings Meadow, still a grassy open space) might have been the location of these festivities. Blanche died young in 1369, her death being mourned by Chaucer in his first major poem, *The Book of the Duchess*. One of the sons of their marriage later became Henry IV (1399-1413), while the latter's son, Henry V (1413-22), pursued the Plantagenet family's claim to the throne of France. A large, richly coloured painting of the marriage ceremony of John and Blanche was produced by Horace B. Wright in 1914. It is one of ten which Dr Jamieson Hurry, the historian of Reading Abbey, commissioned from various artists and gifted to Reading Art Gallery; they are now on public display there and in the Town Hall.

PV (Hurry, J., *Reading Abbey*, 1901)

MAY 20TH

1939: On this day, Reading said goodbye to its electric trams. At 10.30 p.m., a gathering of civic dignitaries departed Mill Lane depot for Tilehurst in two new trolleybuses, then returned to the Pond House to ride Tram No.13 on its final journey. Several hundred witnessed its departure, escorted by around fifty youthful cyclists. The Mayor and the Transport Committee Chairman took turns at driving. Progress, although often impeded, was described as 'triumphal'. Oxford Road was lined with onlookers, some bursting into choruses of *Auld Lang Syne*. In Broad Street the Mayor had difficulty manoeuvring through the throng. With gong clanging, the tram entered King Street, six policemen leaping aboard the already full car to deter souvenir hunters. In Duke Street, 'The Harmony Kids' band from The Ship set the crowd singing *Lambeth Walk* and *He's a Jolly Good Fellow*. One young lady, in a long evening dress (which she clutched knee-high), was the heroine of the crowd, for she had stepped alongside the tram for half a mile – in high-heeled silver shoes! Reading's last tram reached the end of the line just before midnight. The town had lost a trusty friend of thirty-six years' standing.

JRW (Jordan, H., *Tramways of Reading*, 1957)

MAY 21ST

1939: On this day, a Sunday, twenty-five shiny new trolleybuses replaced Reading's trams on the 'main line', which included an extension along Wokingham Road to the Three Tuns and another beyond the Pond House to serve Tilehurst, terminating at the Bear Inn. All is recorded as having gone exceedingly well on the first day's operation, apart from a power failure in the afternoon on the Tilehurst section, because more vehicles than had been envisaged were drawing power on Norcot Road hill. Subsequently, sub-station capacity was increased. It was fortunate that Reading implemented the conversion to trolleybuses at this time. With the country plunged only four months later into a war which would last six years, a large fleet of brand-new trolleybuses using home-produced electricity brought many blessings to the town in those years of adversity. Reading's population swelled by about 70 per cent and by 1945 the transport undertaking was carrying more than twice as many passengers as it had in 1938, with the addition of only six extra trolleybuses. While motorbuses (running on petrol and diesel fuel) were subject to progressively more acute fuel rationing, resulting in earlier daily curtailment of services, the trolleybuses remained largely unaffected.

JRW (Hall, D., *Reading Trolleybuses*, Trolleybooks, 1991)

MAY 22ND

1893: On this day, Alexander Buller Turner was born in Reading, the son of Captain Charles Turner of Berkeley Avenue and the Royal Berkshire Regiment, and grandson of Admiral Sir Alexander Buller. Educated at Wellington College, he subsequently joined the 1st Battalion of the Royal Berks Regiment, with whom, as Second Lieutenant Turner, he saw service in France in the First World War. For the following action he was awarded the Victoria Cross. On 28 September 1915 at Fosse 8, near Vermelles, when regimental bombers could make no headway, Second Lieutenant Turner volunteered to lead a new bombing attack. Making his way down the communication trench almost alone, he threw bombs incessantly with such dash and determination that he forced the Germans back by about 150 yards. His action enabled the reserves to advance with few losses. He continued to cover the troops as they withdrew, thus averting the loss of many men. Severely wounded, Turner died three days later. He is buried in the Military Cemetery at Chocques. During the Second World War, at the 2nd Battle of El Alamein, Alexander's younger brother Victor, born in Reading in 1900, also won the VC.

SG (Batchelor, P. & Matson, C., *VCs of the First World War – The Western Front 1915*, Alan Sutton, 1999)

MAY 23RD

1910: On this day, Henry Bilson Blandy laid the foundation stone of St Luke's church hall, Erleigh Road, Reading. The architect (and churchwarden) was Spencer Slingsby Stallwood; the contract price was £1,368. Just seven months later, on 16 November, the Mayor declared the hall open. At this date St Luke's was part of the parish of St Giles. The building of the new church hall was timely for, four years later, in 1914, under the leadership of Commandant Lady Abram, it became a Voluntary Aid Detachment (VAD) Hospital for the wounded of the Great European War. A plaque in the hall records that nearly one thousand wounded soldiers were treated here. At the Berkshire Record Office, a *Book of Quotations* can be viewed which was assembled by parishioners in 1908 to support the Building Fund. A later publication, *Our Own Cookery Book* (1927), was sold at 1*s* (5p) to raise money for the Hall Extension Fund, which enabled the addition of a kitchen. A century later, the Parish Hall of St Luke with St Bartholomew (now so named) has been refurbished, thanks mainly to donations and grants from local bodies. It offers a main hall and a committee room, plus a splendid kitchen, as a facility for local organisations.

JRS (*St Giles' Parish Magazines*)

MAY 24TH

1912: On this day, Reading residents celebrated Empire Day – as they had done annually for a decade. Canada had originated the Day in the 1890s, as Victoria Day, marking the birthday of the Queen-Empress Victoria (1819-1901). After her son Edward VII succeeded her, the event spread as the focus for patriotism and pride in the achievements and future of the British Empire. It would remain significant for the next century in Australia, India, Canada and many lesser outposts of Empire. As the Commonwealth evolved, in 1958 the name was changed to Commonwealth Day, and it is now celebrated in March. In 1912, with Victoria's grandson, George V, on the throne, Reading, like most other places, treated the Day as primarily a young people's affair. The *Berkshire Chronicle* reported: 'The spirit of true Imperialism has pervaded all the elementary schools of the town, and thousands of children at the most impressionable period of their lives have been taught the lessons of the glories and the responsibilities of Empire.' Special history and geography lessons started the Day, followed by an exciting programme involving patriotic songs, saluting the Union Jack, marching in procession, and hearty cheers for King and Queen and Empire. Oxford Road Infants School even staged a pageant, featuring a pre-teen Britannia with attendants.

PV (*Berkshire Chronicle*)

MAY 25TH

1880: On this day, J.J. Colman, MP for Norwich, laid the foundation stone for Wycliffe Baptist Church, to be built at Cemetery Junction, Reading. Ebenezer West, headmaster of Amersham Hall School in Caversham, had invited Colman to perform the ceremony, and Revd William Anderson of King's Road Baptist Church handed him the silver trowel for the purpose. Among the guests were Revd F. Trestrail, president of the Baptist Union, and Reading's MP, George Palmer. The church was designed by local architect, William Ravenscroft, in the Byzantine style of Northern Italy. The builders were Collier and Catley; the cost of building was set at £3,700. Frank Attwells, a local musical firm, supplied the organ at reduced cost. Memorial stones of the new Sunday schools were laid in 1888. Initially the schools had more than 300 youngsters attending, their teachers numbering twenty-one. When, in 1978, a new community centre was being built, a glass jar was discovered in the foundations, containing artefacts from 1880. That same jar was employed again, filled with artefacts from 1978 and placed between the walls of the new extension and the church, with the idea that it may come to light again during any future rebuilding.

SD (*Reading Chronicle*)

MAY 26TH

1795: On this day, Sir Thomas Noon Talfourd MP was born in Reading. Son of a Broad Street brewer, he took his middle name Noon from his grandfather, the Revd Thomas Noon, who had been minister at Broad Street Congregational Chapel. As a boy, Talfourd had a brief spell at the Commercial and Classical School in Chain Street, followed by eighteen months as a pupil of Reading School. After marrying in 1822 he supplemented the family income by working as a legal reporter on the Oxford Circuit. Talfourd served several terms as MP for Reading until 1849, when he was appointed a judge of the Court of Common Pleas. The *Law Magazine* described him as 'a sound rather than first-rate lawyer'. During his parliamentary career he was involved in the abolition of the pillory as a punishment, but perhaps his most significant achievement was to father the Copyright Act of 1842. Talfourd was a literary man as well as a legal one, publishing plays, poems and critical works, and he was on friendly terms with literary men of the day, including Dickens, Coleridge, Charles Lamb and Wordsworth. He died suddenly of apoplexy while addressing the jury at Stafford Assizes in 1854. Talfourd Road, off Wokingham Road, is his permanent memorial in Reading.

VC (Wykes, A., *Reading: A Biography*, Macmillan, 1970)

MAY 27TH

1839: On this day, the Royal Berkshire Hospital was opened. Accompanying celebrations included a procession from St Laurence's Church to London Road, with marching bands, over 2,000 children, members of various societies, building and hospital staff and the Corporation all participating. Although the Reading Dispensary had been founded in 1802, there was no proper hospital to serve the fast-growing population. In 1836 a suitable site was found, the land being given by Lord Sidmouth. An architectural competition, attracting fifty-five entries, was won by Reading architect Henry Briant. The foundation stone was laid on 13 May 1836, just months before the death of King William IV. Thus it is William's coat of arms which graces the tympanum above the main entrance, symbolising the royal patronage which his successors have continued. Briant's design included the main central block of eleven bays and six giant Ionic columns with pediment above. Subsequent additions, all maintaining the dignified classical Bath stone appearance of the 1836 building, were designed by Thomas Rumble (1840s), Joseph Morris (1860s), Morris and Stallwood (1870s-90s), and Charles Smith and Son (early 1900s). The excellent twenty-first-century rebuild of many departments and wards has recently been completed.

SG (Railton, M. & Barr, M., *The Royal Berkshire Hospital, 1839-1989*, RBH, 1989)

MAY 28TH

1827: On this day, the *Reading Mercury* reported on the Bulmershe Revel and its prizes: 'A gold-laced hat to be played for at cudgels by old gamesters, and a good hat for young gamesters … also a hat to be wrestled for, and a cheese to be bowled for.' The paper later described a Whitley Wood event, where a maying-house was erected and cricket played for ribbons. Again, in 1832, we read: 'the first Maying of this year will be held at Spencer's Wood, near this town, where a comfortable bower is to be erected and a band of music to be in attendance.' Backsword and wrestling were the chief sports, attracting bloodthirsty aficionados. Some years earlier, in 1812, 'Octogenarian' witnessed Whitsuntide sports on 'Bunny Sheath' (dialect version of 'Bulmershe Heath'!) and deplored some nasty work with cudgels: 'I soon had enough of it, for I saw a fellow's head cut and blood flow. But the people shouted a chorus of "A head! A head!" with clapping of hands.' Revels and mayings were popular, with townspeople needing a day in the country with inexpensive entertainment as relief from Reading's cramped and busy streets. By the twentieth century these bucolic pursuits had largely died out.

PV (*Reading Mercury*/Darter, W., *Reminiscences of Reading*, 1888)

MAY 29TH

1838: On this day, the magistrates of Reading Borough thought it prudent to apply that night for military aid from Windsor to ensure that 'no attempt was made to disturb the public peace', because the workmen labouring at the western end of Sonning Cutting had taken strike action (the contractor having not paid them for the last two weeks). However, the men who walked to Reading were reported as 'behaving with great forbearance', even though a further promised payment was not forthcoming. They were reduced to appealing for charity and local people responded well, in one case a large number of them being treated to 'a substantial supper'. The Sonning Cutting was a difficult task and Brunel's general policy was not to pay a contractor until work was completed. By the following Friday morning the men, having gathered 'in groups around the town', were assembled in the Forbury where they were addressed by the Mayor and Mr J.J. Blandy, who told them that the secretary of the Great Western Company had authorised an offer of pay on condition of their returning to work. 'After a little consultation' this was accepted and work on the vital cutting recommenced.

PSm (*Reading Mercury*)

MAY 30TH

1906: On this day, Park Hospital was opened, as Reading's 'special' hospital for isolation cases such as diphtheria and scarlet fever; it was set near Prospect Park on the outskirts of the town. Reading had long needed an isolation hospital and the project finally came to fruition, largely through the efforts of Dr Alfred Ashby. In his speech at the opening ceremony, Mr Smith (of Charles Smith and Son, architects) explained the differences between an isolation hospital and an ordinary hospital. His terms of reference had been to spend as little as possible on external appearance and nothing at all on ornament! The buildings, which included separate pavilions for scarlet fever and diphtheria patients, residences for matron and staff, a kitchen annexe and a laundry, were all detached units.
SG (*Reading Standard*)

———— • ◆ • ————

1929: On this day, in Reading, Michael Foot, the future Labour Leader, won his first election, standing as a Liberal. As a sixteen-year-old pupil at Leighton Park School, Foot took part in a mock election, polling fifty-six votes against thirty-eight for the Conservative and eleven for the Labour candidate. In the General Election on the same day, Reading followed the national trend, electing Dr Somerville Hastings for Labour.
JBD (Morgan, K., *Michael Foot*, HarperCollins, 2007)

May 31st

1882: On this day, the second phase of Reading's Municipal Buildings was opened. The first phase, designed by Waterhouse, had been completed six years earlier, and thoughts soon turned to an extension to house the Organ, Museum, Art Gallery and Library, and also provide premises for Reading School of Science and Art. All this was now possible, following Reading School's relocation to Erleigh Road. Thomas Lainson, an architect well known for his Romanesque and Gothic designs in Brighton, was appointed adjudicator for a design competition, but was eventually awarded the contract himself, while Messrs Chappell of London were appointed as the main building contractor. Much thought went into the exterior decoration: the plan provided for a decorative frieze of Corshill stone to extend along the whole Blagrave Street frontage, with an effigy of Henry III in a niche below his coat of arms, and panels depicting scenes from Reading's history. Unfortunately, expenses overran and most of this work was left undone. The space intended for Henry III was later filled with a statue of Queen Victoria; together with the single historical panel which was completed, this may be viewed by today's passers-by. The collections for the Museum and Art Gallery were started with donations from the Blandy, Palmer and Goldsmid families.

SG (*Berkshire Chronicle*)

June 1st

1911: On this day, Caversham Electric Theatre was opened by Admiral Sir Francis Powell KCMG. The newspapers hailed it as a building that would be reckoned one of the most valuable assets of the entertainment-loving part of Caversham's population. The opening drew a representative audience, including the Mayor of Reading, Alderman W.J. Martin, and other notable persons. The *Reading Standard* reported: 'The theatre, situated next to the Free Library in Caversham, has an ornate façade, and the interior is well planned, the floor being laid on a considerable gradient, so that every person in the auditorium has a clear view of the screen, and the exits being numerous.' The theatre was designed by F.E.B. Ravenscroft and built by R. Bell and Sons. It was owned by a small limited company and remained an independent cinema until the late 1940s when Harold Baim Cinemas of London took it over and renamed it the 'Glendale'. It closed as a cinema in 1977, and the following year members of the New Testament Church of God bought the building for use as their church. It retains some of the original cinema features, including the balcony.

VC (*Reading Standard*)

JUNE 2ND

1931: On this day, sixteen-year-old Reading School pupil, Horace (Tom) Dollery, opened the batting against the MCC and carried his bat for an unbeaten 104, in a total of 115 all out. Next highest score was 3 by No.10 batsman, G.D. Heath. Remarkably, when the score reached 50, Dollery had amassed every run. His innings repeated his century against the MCC in 1930 – a team which included South African Test bowler Sid Pegler. On each occasion none of Dollery's team-mates managed double figures. Subsequently he played four Tests for England; in 1951 he became the first professional cricketer to captain a county side (Warwickshire) to the Championship.
NS (Local press reports)

---◆---

1941: On this day actor Stacy Keach was born in Georgia, USA, son of an actress and a theatre director. It was thus no surprise that both Stacy and his brother, James, pursued acting careers. Stacy played stage and screen rôles in *Frost/Nixon, Hamlet, Barnum*, and *Jesus of Nazareth.* On television he took the title rôle in *Mickey Spillane's Mike Hammer.* In 1984 he served nine months in Reading Prison after pleading guilty to the charge of entering the UK carrying cocaine.
VC (*New York Times*)

JUNE 3RD

1908: On this day, Reading's West End Library was ceremonially opened in Oxford Road next to Battle Hospital. The day's programme included tea, speeches and Dr Hurry's handover of the deeds to Mayor Edward Jackson. The two men had laid the foundation stone only the previous October. As Treasurer of the Voluntary Committee, Hurry had long striven for this amenity for West Reading's inhabitants, who numbered some 13,000. While the Committee raised £1,360 for the site and the library's maintenance, the major contribution was £4,000 from the Scots-born philanthropist, Andrew Carnegie (with whom Hurry was principal negotiator). The council was (quite properly) concerned that a new library would overload municipal finances. The building was designed by local architect Frederick William Albury. During its first decade, it loaned around 21,000 books annually; it also, unlike Caversham Library, had a juvenile department from the start. This success was achieved without the services of a professional librarian; financial strictures meant that only Reading Central's Chief Librarian was qualified at this time. Requisitioned for 'war service' in 1916, as annexe for Battle Hospital, it resumed normal activities in 1923 and was later renamed Battle Library. **SD/PV** (Cliffe, D., *Roots and Branches*, Two Rivers, 2007)

JUNE 4TH

2003: On this day, Lord Carrington, Chancellor of the University of Reading, ceremonially cut the turf for a new national resource at St Andrews Hall, Redlands Road: the Museum of English Rural Life (MERL). MERL now constitutes a unique archive, storage and conservation centre for England's rural heritage. Dating from 1951, the museum gained recognition over succeeding decades with donations of artefacts, documents and publications, underpinned by funding from individuals, university grants and a recent £5.2 million Heritage Lottery cheque. From its first home, the Waterhouse-designed Whiteknights House, the collection moved to temporary buildings on the university campus. MERL then relocated to another Waterhouse building, St Andrews Hall, most recently a student residence. The removal entailed completely refurbishing the hall and constructing a purpose-built wing to display wagons, machinery and tools. As a protected building with Grade II listing, which had lasted the years less well than expected, the house proved highly challenging. After the turf-cutting, two years of building and rebuilding culminated in the museum opening its Reading Room in May 2005, to allow researchers access to the library and archives; two months later MERL welcomed the first visitors to its public galleries.

PV (MERL records)

June 5th

1949: On this day, a Sunday, the first of two trolleybus route extensions to the south of Reading (to serve the developing Whitley housing estate) was inaugurated. The original trolleybus route from Caversham Bridge to Whitley Street had been suspended soon after the end of the Second World War, and much road reconstruction was needed in the town centre and Southampton Street, with the removal of cobbles and old tram rails. At the same time, hundreds of steel traction poles were planted down Basingstoke Road and Whitley Wood Lane as far as the Engineers Arms, and down Buckland Road and Northumberland Avenue, terminating just beyond Hartland Road roundabout. Next, overhead wires were erected, and two electrical sub-stations built and equipped, one at Christchurch Gardens, the other near the Savoy cinema. In those austere times there were delays bringing these costly projects to fruition. Even so, this day saw the first trolleybuses running on their original route from Caversham Bridge and finally into Northumberland Avenue. It is recorded that scores of Whitley inhabitants turned out to welcome the new service. The Whitley Wood route opened in August; but another thirteen years would pass before the inhabitants of the southern end of Northumberland Avenue would enjoy easy access to the trolleybuses.

JRW (Hall, D., *Reading Trolleybuses*, Trolleybooks, 1991)

JUNE 6TH

1876: On this day, Reading's new Town Hall, designed in the Gothic style by Alfred Waterhouse, was officially opened. Plans had been mooted soon after the adjoining old St Laurence vicarage was pulled down in 1870. William Woodman, borough surveyor, produced plans costed at £3,000 to £4,000 but, following a dispute with a contractor, this scheme was set aside. A year or so later the borough commissioned Waterhouse, who had long been associated with Reading. Waterhouse's first, far more ambitious, plan costing £40,000 was rejected, but his second design costing approximately £10,000 proved acceptable. The foundation stone was laid on 8 October 1874. The remit was difficult as the council wanted to retain the recently restored Assembly Room of the 1786 Town Hall, now called the Victoria Room. Waterhouse had to incorporate this structure with the new offices and clock tower on an awkward double-aspect site, but overcame these difficulties to achieve the impressive results we see today. He also designed the armchairs and other furniture; they were manufactured and upholstered by Blowers and Son of Minster Street. Although most of the furniture has been sold off, several pieces may still be found within the building.

SG (*Berkshire Chronicle*)

JUNE 7TH

1675: On this day, Ann Fiennes, niece of Lord Saye and Sele, died in Reading of smallpox and was buried at St Giles. Her sister, Celia, the intrepid traveller, later visited 'Redding … which is a pretty large place, severall Churches, in one lyes buried one of my sisters … her monument of white marble.' **JBD** (Morris, C. (Ed.), *The Journeys of Celia Fiennes*, Cresset, 1947)

———— • ◆ • ————

1819: On this day, Pall Mall was scene of the auction of the magnificent private library and other valuable possessions of George Spencer-Churchill, Marquess of Blandford (1766-1840). Blandford had acquired Whiteknights Park in 1798 and subsequently spent inordinate sums landscaping its grounds with beautiful gardens and a lake with ornamental bridges. For the library, he recklessly bid for such rarities as a 1471 Boccaccio and the Bedford Missal, once owned by John, Duke of Bedford. Paintings by Rubens, Holbein, Titian, Tintoretto and Gainsborough were bought to grace the walls. By 1812 Blandford had so far fallen into debt that Whiteknights had to be mortgaged. When his father died in 1817, he became the 5th Duke of Marlborough; creditors continued to hound him, so the celebrated Whiteknights library had to be sold, followed piecemeal by the paintings, statues and other furnishings. **PV** (Hunter, J., *A History of Berkshire*, Phillimore, 1995)

JUNE 8TH

1898: On this day, the Athenaeum Club's new premises at 28 Friar Street, Reading, were opened by the Mayor, W. Bligh Monck, whose father, J.B. Monck, had opened the club's previous habitat in 1842. The building was designed by local architects Millar Galt and William James Nasmyth, using S. & E. Collier's terracotta and bricks. Construction and furnishing cost about £8,000, most of which was met by J.C. Fidler, a local property developer and seed merchant. The club's main rooms were reached by an ornate stone staircase and included a three-tabled billiard room and dining room; reading, smoking and cards were also well provided for. The club placed emphasis on good food and the steward's server was 22ft long with a lift to an overhead kitchen. The long-case clock from the old building was upset by its move, losing half an hour and then stopping altogether! In 1972, the Athenaeum Club merged with the Berkshire Club, moving four years later into premises in Blagrave Street, whereupon the Friar Street building was sold off. The Blagrave Street premises now house a pub called the Oakford Social Club.

SD (North, L., *Reading Chronicle*, 1979)

JUNE 9TH

1910: On this day, Reading was subject to a devastating series of hailstorms. Unconfirmed rain intensity of 10cm was unleashed in one hour! Hail up to 2cm in diameter fell in Caversham, causing damage to roofs, nursery plants and Post Office instruments. Roads were flooded – Oxford Road became impassable. Lightning strikes damaged property and caused several pupils of Miss Smee, a teacher, to faint from terror; she herself suffered burns and temporary paralysis.
JRS (Currie, I., Davidson, M. & Ogley, R., *Berkshire Weather Book*, Froglets, 1994)

———◆———

1945: On this day, Felix Bowness, future star of the 1980s sit-com *Hi-de-Hi!*, had a busy time. He was one of four lads from Reading Aero Boxing Club, taking part in an open-air tournament at Guildford. He was the only one to fight after rain wiped out the other bouts. Bantamweight Bowness beat his opponent in six fierce rounds, then raced back to Reading to participate in a talent competition at the Palace Theatre, which he won with his impersonations. Bowness (1922-2009), who hailed from Harwell and later lived in Woodley, Reading, played a different sporting rôle in *Hi-de-Hi!* – that of the jockey, Fred Quilly.
NS (*Reading Standard*)

JUNE 10TH

1841: On this day, Charles Dickens turned down an invitation to stand for election as one of Reading's MPs. Dickens stated his reasons: 'The sum you mention … is greater than I could afford for such a purpose; as the mere sitting in the House and attending to my duties … would oblige me to make many pecuniary sacrifices, consequent upon the very nature of my pursuits.'
JBD (Forster, J., *Life of Charles Dickens*, 1872-4)

———•◆•———

1896: On this day, Amelia Dyer, the Baby Farmer, was hanged at Newgate. She had been convicted at Reading of murdering Edith Marmon, an illegitimate baby placed in her care by a Cheltenham barmaid. Evelina Marmon had read Dyer's newspaper advertisement, offering to board children at a cost of £10. Since the previous summer, forty babies' bodies had been found in the Thames at London, with further discoveries in Reading's waterways. The first, accidentally pulled up by a bargee, was wrapped in a brown paper parcel, marked: 'Mrs Dyer, Kensington Road, Reading'. The police soon assembled a cast-iron case and arrested Dyer. Her plea of 'guilty but insane' was to no avail and she was sentenced to death.
NS (Gaute, J. & Odell, R., *The Murderers' Who's Who*, Harrap, 1979)

JUNE 11TH

1971: On this day, John Hudson from Earley, Reading, achieved a remarkable hole-in-one on successive holes during the second round of the Martini Golf Tournament at Royal Norwich. The former Sonning assistant, professional at Hendon, had aces at the 195-yard 11th and the 311-yard 12th. He was four over par when he came to the 11th and his four iron shot dropped 10ft short before rolling into the hole. There was a delay of twenty minutes on the tee before he took his driver downwind, using the same ball; it landed five yards short, bounced on the green and disappeared into the cup. He held his nerve for a second par 72 and ended the tournament in joint ninth place on 287.
NS (Local press reports)

———— • ◆ • ————

2012: On this day, and its predecessor, a month's rain fell in Reading during the wettest spring since 1910. On the 12th a man was pulled from the swollen waters of the Kennet and Avon Canal by a water rescue team. Warnings had been issued of the dangers of fast-flowing rivers – the man's companion turned up safe at home having climbed out by himself!
JRS (Brugge, R., Reading University Meteorological Dept/ *Reading Chronicle*)

JUNE 12TH

1833: On this day, a second auction of Crown Lands took place in Reading, following an earlier sale in November 1832. About 130 acres were offered, stretching from what is now called King's Road at 'Jackson's Corner' to the cemetery. This area included Orts Road and the Orts Farm Estate, land on either side of Forbury Road, land between the Kennet and the Thames, Eldon Road and the left-hand side of London Road and Watlington Street. Many of the Crown Lands were originally owned by monasteries; at Reading they passed to the Crown at the dissolution of the Abbey. Except for a few isolated houses, the land at Reading had remained open countryside. Many speculators, including architects, builders and property developers, acquired sites. This was a real turning-point in the growth of Reading. Further adjacent sites were released in 1833 and 1834, creating Queen's Road, Sidmouth Street and South Street. A sale advertisement reads: 'a great choice of eligible sites, for the erection of private dwelling houses and villas, being most favourably situate on a remarkably dry and salubrious soil, commanding most delightful views over Caversham Park and the intermediate rich country'.
SG (Sale Catalogue/*Reading Mercury*)

JUNE 13TH

1971: On this day, an ecumenical service, second event in the two-month Festival of Reading, was held. The Festival had begun the previous day, commemorating the first mention of Reading in the *Anglo-Saxon Chronicle* (AD 871) and the 850th anniversary of Reading Abbey. Activities included a procession of floats, a beer festival, dancing at The Top Rank Suite and a steam train ride; those of more cultural tastes could enjoy an exhibition of Reading's history and architecture, an art exhibition and an open-air production of *Macbeth*. Musical interests were catered for by the Royal Liverpool Philharmonic, the Reading Concert Orchestra and the first-ever Reading Pop Festival (*see* June 25th). Sports enthusiasts had badminton and tennis competitions, an amateur regatta and a charity cricket match. For the less athletic, there were bus tours which, for 20p, took passengers on a scenic 30-mile tour of Reading suburbs, with commentary. Unfortunately, very heavy rain plagued the first week's events and the streets of Southcote were flooded, giving rise to conspiracy theories that Thames Conservancy had allowed this flooding so as to prevent inundation of the Kings Meadow festival site. The appropriately titled festival song *Two Many Rivers* had its world premiere on 14 June.
JP (*Reading Chronicle/Evening Post*)

JUNE 14TH

1887: On this day, Dr J.F. Mackarness, Bishop of Oxford, laid the foundation stone of St Saviour's Church, Berkeley Avenue, Reading. The new church replaced the 'tin tabernacle' previously used for services. Initially, St Saviour's was a chapel-of-ease to St Mary's but it later passed to the care of St Giles'. Designed by Frederick William Albury and built at a cost of £5,891, St Saviour's was unfinished at the time of its consecration; a planned campanile was never built. In 1900 Albury designed the Sunday school, where Christmas breakfasts were a popular event. The church formerly possessed a carved wooden lectern depicting a pelican pecking its breast to draw blood to feed its young, which is now in St Giles'. In the 1980s, the church faced redundancy but in 1987 the Elim Pentecostal church acquired it, adding a tasteful extension in 1992. More recently, the congregation has sought its rebuilding. Three hundred and fifty local residents opposed this plan, but after unsuccessful attempts at listing by Reading Borough Council and the Victorian Society, its future remains uncertain. The former church hall is used by Churches Together in Reading as their drop-in centre for the homeless.

SD (*Reading Chronicle*)

JUNE 15TH

1926: On this day, the *Reading Chronicle* reported on activity at the Trades Union Club in Minster Street, as Reading played its part in the General Strike. Prominent trade unionists were arrested for allegedly intimidating a strike-breaker and even clipping the ear of a young 'blackleg'. The Chief Constable congratulated those strikers who had 'played the game'. Biscuit Factory workers (as food producers) were initially held back; the strike ended just as they were about to join the action. Reading's Conservative council, taking a hard line with striking tramway workers, gave a £2 gratuity each to five blacklegs.
KJ (*Reading Chronicle*/Records of Reading TU Club)

1970: On this day, Justin Fletcher was born in Reading, the son of songwriter Guy Fletcher. After studying at the Guildford School of Acting, he decided on a career in children's television. Having sketched out various comic characters, he put together a show reel called *Justin Time*, featuring two notable characters: Anna Conda, the myopic warden of a reptile house, and Arthur Sleep, a regional newsreader who has the utmost difficulty staying awake. Both Anna and Arthur later reappeared in his show, *Gigglebiz*. Fletcher was awarded an MBE in 2008 for services to 'children's broadcasting and the voluntary sector'.
VC (*Guardian*)

JUNE 16TH

1668: On this day, Samuel Pepys, Admiralty Secretary under Charles II and James II, visited Reading during his travels through England on Navy business. This journey, begun on 5 June, took him with his wife and others through Oxford, Bath, Bristol and Marlborough. Thence, via Newbury, 'in the evening betimes come to Reading, and I to walk about the town, which is a very great one, I think bigger than Salisbury. A river runs through it, in seven branches, which unite … and runs into the Thames. One odd sign, of the Broad Face.' (This hostelry, located in the High Street, was demolished in 1926.) Next day, Pepys' account continues: 'Rose, and paying the reckoning, 12s.6d; servants and poor, 2s.6d; musick – the worst we have had … So set out with one coach in company …' Returning to London by horseback, as they had come, Pepys arrived by nightfall. From modest origins, Pepys became a 'man about town' at ease in aristocratic circles, enjoying London society, the playhouses, the ladies and the gossip of the day. His 'warts and all' diary, written from 1660 to 1669, is a unique record of contemporary society and Pepys' own Admiralty work.
PV (*Diary of Samuel Pepys*, Everyman, 1906)

JUNE 17TH

1968: On this day, Speedway first came to Reading, with the opening match at the Reading Greyhound Stadium, Tilehurst. Reading Racers' opponents were Nelson Admirals, and a crowd of just under 5,000 fans paid 5s (25p) each to view the event. However, the evening ended in farce. In the last heat, the Admirals gained a 5–1 win for a 39–all draw, but referee Day ruled that their reserve, Gary Peterson, was ineligible and the heat was re-run. Nelson Admiral's Terry Shearer was then excluded for causing a pile-up and unaccountably he was replaced by Peterson, who won the heat. Reading Racers took second and third places for a 41–37 success overall. It was 'third time lucky' for Racers, who had lost their first two British League Division 2 matches away to Plymouth Devils and Berwick Bandits. On an evening far from incident-free, Reading's Dene Davies demolished the safety fence, leading to delays, and there were complaints that the loudspeakers were inaudible. Despite this difficult start, Racers went from strength to strength and, over the years, provided many exciting evenings for their fans.

NS (Local press reports)

JUNE 18TH

1909: On this day, the Memorial Cross to King Henry I was unveiled at the Forbury Gardens, Reading. This day coincided with Henry's foundation of Reading Abbey in 1121. When he died at Rouen in 1135, his embalmed body was brought back and buried before the High Altar in the Abbey Church. The rite took place on 4 January 1136 in the presence of King Stephen. On the twentieth-century occasion, the guest of honour performing the ceremony was Augustine Birrell, Chief Secretary for Ireland, who was met at the station by Rufus Isaacs MP for Reading, the Mayor, the Town Clerk and Dr Jamieson Hurry, donor of the Cross. Tickets for the event had been distributed with great care, for fear of disruption by Suffragettes, as Birrell opposed votes for women. The Cross was designed by William Ravenscroft and carved by Maile and Sons of London in grey Cornish granite. Standing over 20ft high, it bears the Beauclerc arms, the arms of the Abbey and a suitable dedication. Exactly four years later, Dr Hurry gave the plaque that commemorates the thirteenth-century motet 'Sumer is icumen in', which was composed at Reading Abbey. The plaque is now mounted in the Chapter House.
SG (*Reading Standard*)

JUNE 19TH

1908: On this day, Joseph Eggleton died 'through being knocked off his bicycle in Silver Street, Reading'. His gravestone records in doggerel verse that:

Injuries great not long he bore,
Physicians tried in vain,
Till God did please to take him,
And ease him of his pain.

JBD (Gravestone in Reading Cemetery)

———◆———

1915: On this day, the *Reading Standard* reported that a collection box at the Sun Inn for the 'Comforts for Wounded Soldiers Appeal' had raised 8*s* 11*d* (45p). Licensed victuallers' collections for the Royal Berkshire Hospital and the War Hospitals Supplies Depot were reported later in the 1914-18 war. In May 1917, a sum of 5*s* 9*d* (29p) from Mr Davey of the Sun is recorded, double that contributed by the Lyndhurst Arms (also run by Davey) – but somewhat outshone by the 8*s* and one halfpenny (40p) given by Mr Absolom of The Horn. It was also during this war that Reading experienced government measures to restrict access to liquor. Charles Roberts of the Sun received instructions to limit the drinking of hospital patients and not to serve women before the hour of 12 noon!
JBD (Hamblin, I. & Dearing, J., 'This Sun of Reading', ms)

JUNE 20TH

1785: On this day, the Reading Paving Act was passed. Like other medieval towns, Reading had utterly lacked proper paving and draining. Even its main streets were described in 1550 as laid with flints and cobbles. By the eighteenth century, leading citizens decided that improvements were overdue; the borough needed a Paving Act. Although many townspeople were opposed, fearing increased taxes, the Mayor and one of Reading's MPs endorsed the project. In 1785, Parliament passed the Act authorising the appointment of Commissioners for 'paving, watching and lighting the town'. The first slab was laid in August, with church bells rung, fireworks and a grand dinner at The Ship. Ten years on, paving was still incomplete, and complaints continued. A writer of 1800 denounced the 'shameful state' of streets; another in 1823 declared there was 'no town in England where there was less attention paid to this point'. In 1826, new legislation, nicknamed the 'All-Perfection Act', brought in Commissioners with greater powers. The year 1841 saw asphalt paving introduced, and in 1845 King Street and most of the Market Place lost their cobblestones and were finally macadamised.

PV (Childs, W., *Town of Reading in the Early Nineteenth Century*, 1910/Phillips, D., *History of Reading*, Countryside Books, 1999)

JUNE 21ST

1897: On this day, the sixtieth anniversary celebrations of Queen Victoria's reign began ignominiously, as rain and wind swept the South East. Later the sun burst through to crown 'The Queen's Day'. At St Laurence's Church, the Bishop of Reading extolled the progress brought by the reign: triumphs in the arts, sciences, engineering, welfare, resources and invention. No wonder Reading celebrated – even the weather rose to the occasion.
JRS (Currie, I., Davidson, M. & Ogley, R., *Berkshire Weather Book*, Froglets, 1994)

———◆———

2006: On this day, in Reading Abbey's Chapter House, local publisher Two Rivers Press launched its illustrated edition of *Sumer is Icumen in*, the amazingly advanced round composed on the site in around 1250. All present were encouraged to join in the moving experience of performing a 750-year-old piece in its place of origin, led by members of Reading Bach Choir. On the wall of the Chapter House is a plaque bearing a facsimile of the manuscript, which was found tucked into the Abbey Cartulary and is now in the British Library. At its unveiling in 1913, one speaker described it as 'one of the landmarks in the whole history of music – as important as the appearance of Wagner's *Tristan and Isolde*'.
AS (*Sumer is Icumen in*, Two Rivers, 2006)

JUNE 22ND

1954: On this day, the *London Gazette* announced that the George Medal was awarded to a Reading nurse, Freda Holland, for outstanding courage in single-handedly rescuing fifteen new-born babies from their burning nursery in Dellwood Maternity Hospital in the early hours of 18 April. Nurse Holland, alerted by the other nurse on duty, repeatedly entered the inferno and carried out all fifteen babies, beating down the flames with her nurse's cap and struggling through suffocating smoke. She suffered burns to her face and arms and was taken to hospital, along with the babies. Despite her valour, all but two of the babies died within three days; Nurse Holland was not informed until she herself was no longer in a critical condition. At that time it was not unusual for babies to sleep in a nursery, to allow the mothers to rest. The fire, which had probably been smouldering for twenty to thirty minutes, was caused by a faulty boiler, installed according to regulations. In April 2004 a memorial service was held to commemorate the fiftieth anniversary of the fire. Freda Holland died in January 2010, just short of her ninety-seventh birthday. One of the two survivors attended her funeral.

JP (*Evening Post*)

JUNE 23RD

1931: On this day, Mrs Maxine Freeman-Thomas, known as Blossom, and F.G. Miles flew for the first time together into Reading Aerodrome at Woodley. He had been her flying instructor in Shoreham and she later divorced her husband to marry him. Miles set up in business at Woodley with the Phillips & Powis Company, which was already well-known in aviation circles. During the next two decades, the Miles Aircraft Company designed many popular planes, with Blossom working as an aviation engineer alongside her husband. At first the company catered for the privileged few with enough money to buy a small plane (the Hawk in 1933 had a price tag of £395). During the six years of the Second World War they designed, developed and repaired aircraft for military use. In that period, they undertook sixty-seven design studies, constructed over 4,000 planes and repaired more than 2,000 Spitfires and other planes in Woodley. Thanks to the pioneering Blossom, female staff were recruited for technical rôles in the factories and eight blind men also trained for the work. She instigated lunchtime exercise classes, a 'Miles Magazine', an amateur dramatics group and music and sports clubs for the workforce.

JP (Fostekew, J., *Blossom*, Cirrus, 1998)

JUNE 24TH

2012: On this day, the Revd Nigel Hardcastle, vicar of St Luke with St Bartholomew since 1999, celebrated forty years of full-time ministry (and his retirement) in a service at St Luke's attended by the Deputy Mayor, the Bishop of Reading, the Archdeacon of Berkshire and many friends and family. Speeches clearly showed appreciation for Nigel's years of service to the church and community. Nigel was born and bred in Reading, where he gained a degree in physics at the University. While there he felt the call to serve God in the ordained ministry. In 1969, he entered Queen's College, Birmingham, theological college; it was on this training course that Nigel met his future wife, June. Following his ordination in Birmingham Cathedral in 1972, he served several Birmingham parishes and was a driving force in the British Council of Churches' computerisation programme. In 1989, he returned to Reading, initially taking the helm at St Barnabas, Emmer Green. Recently Nigel received a 'Pride of Reading' Award as a Community Champion for his work with churches in East Reading and for encouraging understanding between various faith groups via the Faith Forum.

JRS (*GetReading/Grapevine*: St Luke with St Bartholomew Parish Magazine)

JUNE 25TH

1949: On this day, at the Royal Counties Agricultural Society and Hackney Horse Society's Reading Show, a brass band played a varied selection, comprising *Martial Moments*, *Zampa*, *Wedded Whimsies*, *Tesoro Mio*, *High Button Shoes*, *Mickey Goes A-Whistling* and *Amparito Roca*.
AS (Printed programme)

———————•◆•———————

1971: On this day began the first of Reading's now annual Pop Festivals. Initially part of the Festival of Reading (*see* June 13th), it is the sole component to have survived. The Festival began in controversy: battle lines were drawn up by local residents and businessmen who barricaded their properties with barbed wire, whilst letting fly insults about the allegedly lawless and 'great unwashed' youngsters about to bring mayhem to the town. Approximately 20,000 fans descended upon Reading, to hear pop and rock music covering all styles for the princely sum of £2 for a weekend ticket, along with the almost obligatory heavy rain. £17,000 was spent on policing the event, including production of a Six Point Safety Code for residents. This offered helpful advice such as bringing the milk in off the step and locking car doors. The promoter, Harold Pendleton, hoped to see the Festival repeated and was sure that the weather could not be as bad again.
JP (*Evening Post/Berkshire Chronicle*)

JUNE 26TH

1926: On this day, the Prince of Wales, later King Edward VIII and Duke of Windsor, made a visit to Reading which included a call at Simonds' Brewery. A photograph shows the Prince raising his bowler hat as he approaches a reception party that includes a sturdy shire horse. Founded by William Blackall Simonds in Broad Street in 1785, and moving to Bridge Street in 1789, the firm grew to become the town's principal brewery, benefitting from contracts to supply the Army and (following the 1830 Beer Act) meet the boom in public houses. By 1938, annual production was 279,000 barrels, up from 58,000 in 1871, and in the 1950s Simonds controlled 1,400 pubs and four breweries. However, in 1960 it was decided to merge its interests with those of Courage Barclay to form one of the 'Big Six' national brewers. The Bridge Street operation closed in 1980, being replaced by a new brewery at Worton Grange near the M4; to the chagrin of 'real ale' fans, this produced keg beer only. Within The Oracle development built on the brewery site, an information board, funded by the Simonds family and Reading Civic Society, commemorates Simonds' influence on the town.

JBD (Corley, T. & Simonds, R., *H&G Simonds Ltd*, 2009)

JUNE 27TH

1857: On this day, the *Reading Mercury* reported a fatal fight
that had occurred in Kings Meadow on 25 June. George
Shackel of Earley Court Farm entered Reading police station
to report that he and his manservant, Joseph Lawrence, had
been set upon by two labourers. Superintendent Henry Peck,
following protocol, took details of the informant and of the
event, but, being a stickler for the rules, said the police could
not get involved unless someone was seriously hurt, or a
policeman present as a witness. Shackel became indignant at
Peck's attitude and complained to the first magistrate he could
find. Meanwhile, the unfortunate Lawrence had been killed by
his two attackers! William Appleton, who had already served
time for the death of a woman at Newbury and for stealing
coppers at Mortimer, was found to have dealt the fatal blow. At
the hearing before Reading Borough Magistrates on 26 June,
George Shackel described the assault and the subsequent
dialogue between himself and Superintendent Peck. Appleton
and his accomplice Holmes were found guilty as charged of the
unlawful killing of Lawrence. Appleton was sentenced to three
weeks' imprisonment and Holmes to a mere three days.
VC (*Reading Mercury*)

June 28th

1895: On this day, William the Conqueror made his long-awaited appearance before the general public in Reading – courtesy of the copy of the Bayeux Tapestry executed by the ladies of Leek Embroidery Society in 1885/6. In the evening, Revd J.M. Guilding, the Reading antiquarian and archaeological expert who had previously advised Alderman Arthur Hill that the tapestry was for sale, gave an explanatory talk to the public. He and Alderman Hill wanted to see how far Reading townspeople were interested in acquiring the tapestry, amidst fears it might be sold to America. On the previous afternoon, the great and the good of Reading society had come, at the invitation of Alderman Hill, to partake of light refreshments, after which they proceeded to view the tapestry (more correctly, the embroidery). Guilding had addressed the assembled group, which included G.W. Palmer MP, Mr Blackall Simonds, Mr H.B. Blandy and Mr Dryland Haslam, highlighting the 623 men (unlike the original, all are fully clothed, to preserve Victorian sensibilities!) and approximately 800 animals, buildings and trees. Such was the enthusiasm, that when Alderman Hill offered to buy the Bayeux embroidery for the town, the Corporation gratefully accepted his offer.

JP (*Reading Mercury/Reading Chronicle*)

JUNE 29TH

1968: On this day, the adaptation of Reading's trolleybus system to the new Inner Distribution Road reached an important stage: the trolleybus overhead was slewed over the new westbound bridge, connecting the two halves of Oxford Road across the cutting between Caversham Road and Castle Street. Work then started on the eastbound half. The previous August the trolleybuses had been routed via a temporary carriageway between Alfred Street and Thorn Street, to enable building of the new bridge. Traffic had thus become one-way westbound on the temporary carriageway and eastbound via Bedford Road and Chatham Street. Buses, however, continued operating both ways, with their drivers controlling time-delay traffic lights. The first half of the new bridge was built while excavation work, sheet-piling and retaining-wall construction continued on the IDR. However, by the time all the work was completed, Reading's trolleybuses had stopped operating. This section of the IDR opened in 1969, and a plaque on Oxford Road Bridge commemorates its completion between Caversham Road and Southampton Street in February 1971. Financial constraints prevented further work for another twenty years, when existing roads on a larger loop were used rather than the original contentious route through Forbury Gardens.

JRW (Reading Transport Society/British Trolleybus Society Journals)

JUNE 30TH

1934: On this day, a twenty-year-old Reading athlete, Phyllis Bartholomew, achieved a remarkable treble at the Women's AAA Championships at Herne Hill. Bartholomew collected a third successive national long jump title with a leap of 18ft 2¾in (5.56m). That summer she went on to achieve even greater glory by taking the long jump Gold medal in the British Empire Games at the White City.
NS (Local press reports)

———◆———

2007: On this day, Reading Town Regatta was held. Reading has a long history of rowing regattas, coming and going in several guises over the past 150 years, as the tide of support waxed and waned. Reading Regatta, later renamed Reading Amateur Regatta, was the first to be held in 1842 and is going strong to this day. Reading and Caversham Regatta followed in 1870, taking place near Caversham Bridge. Reading Working Men's Regatta began in 1877, on the Dreadnought Reach below the lock, and this evolved into the Reading Town Regatta. Fire devastated the boathouse in 1996, but a replacement was built on the site of the old. Thames Valley Park Regatta is the newest event, starting in 1990, for junior and school teams.
VC (Clark, G., *Down By The River*, Two Rivers Press, 2009)

JULY 1ST

1916: On this day commenced the Battle of the Somme, in which British and French forces attempted to break through the extensive German army's fortifications of the Western Front in the First World War. October rains put an end to the carnage, with only a few miles of ground captured; over 1 million soldiers had been killed. Of the three Royal Berkshire Regiment Battalions in action, only the 6th was involved on 1 July. For them the day ended with six officers killed and five wounded; of other ranks, seventy-one were killed, 254 wounded and eleven missing.
PMS (Fox, C., *On the Somme: The Kitchener Battalions of the Royal Berkshire Regiment*, University of Reading, 1916)

———— • ◆ • ————

1968: On this day Reading awoke to a red, pink, beige and rust-coloured Martian-like landscape! 'Technicolour rain from Spain and the Sahara' was the headline describing Caversham's dust-covered cars and washing! The harmless deposits proved to be Saharan sand raised by winds, carried to Britain on a strong southerly airflow, then washed out by storms, particularly over southern England. Small dust deposits are not infrequent but the amount which fell in 1968 was very unusual; only in 1755 and 1903 did Reading have similar occurrences.
JRS (*Reading Gazette/Weather Magazine*)

JULY 2ND

1870: On this day the *Berkshire Chronicle* devoted ten closely typed columns to a detailed and enthusiastic account of the exciting event of the previous day – a royal visit to Reading! The Prince and Princess of Wales had come, amidst much pomp, to lay the foundation stone for Reading School's first building at its new site in Erleigh Road. Queen Victoria's eldest son, Albert Edward – the future King Edward VII – was a dashing young man of thirty, and his young wife, Princess Alexandra of Denmark, a renowned beauty. The loyal people of Reading, wildly excited at the prospect of the visit, had put much effort and expense into setting up suitable decorations for the royal route: 'Flags and banners, and Prince of Wales feathers, were suspended with much taste at every corner, every bend of the route. When all was complete the streets presented a sight such as has never been witnessed in Reading before and may never be again.' The lengthy procession of horse-drawn carriages bearing the 'royals' and their entourage wove its way to Erleigh Road, and later, back to the station, accompanied throughout by hearty cheers. One hundred and forty years later, the names of nearby Denmark Road and Alexandra Road still serve as reminders of that glorious day.

PMS (*Berkshire Chronicle*)

JULY 3RD

1876: On this day the transfer of the licence of the Sun in Castle Street took place before Messrs W.S. Darter and G. Palmer, sitting on the Reading Borough Bench. Robert Parker, who had held it since 1860, gave the licence to Charles Roberts, then aged thirty-three. Roberts was also a farmer, leasing Pilgrim's Farm at Burghfield for £30 per annum, and a keen man of the turf with a racehorse that competed in the Cesarewitch and the Derby. For local journeys by trap, he kept a pony, which was permitted as a special treat on market days to come into the Market Room. This contained a round table made from a large beer barrel; the pony would climb onto this and make a 360 degrees turn for the amusement of the customers, its reward being a pint of stout! Charles Roberts' forty-year tenure came to an end when he sustained a fall while hunting, suffering a fractured pelvis with complications leading to pneumonia. While in hospital he learned of his wife's death, which may have taken from him the will to live. Albeit, he died on 23 December 1916, succeeded briefly by his second son, William.

JBD (Hamblin, I. & Dearing, J., 'This Sun of Reading', ms)

JULY 4TH

1949: On this day, a Monday, work commenced installing a 'bone-shaped' roundabout at the oblique crossroads at Cemetery Junction, in East Reading, where Kings Road and Wokingham Road intersect London Road; this also removed the police box and controlled traffic lights installed in August 1932. The 1901 St John's coffee stall which had stood at the end of Kings Road had already relocated to Rupert Street. The next task was the removal of tram rails. Following this came adjustment of road kerbs and changes to the trolleybus overhead line, before the one-way scheme was implemented with kerbs forming the 'bone', which was subsequently grassed and planted. The new arrangement came into full use on 4 September. It lasted many years, until the present arrangement with traffic lights was introduced. Originally, this crossroad marked the eastern borough boundary, where, in 1843, a private company established a cemetery; in 1879 it became the eastern terminus of the horse tramway. The borough expanded in 1887 and took in the cemetery, which became 'municipalised'. The term 'Cemetery Junction' came with the introduction of electric trams in 1903, because it was here that the tram routes divided. It is now internationally known as the title of the 2010 Ricky Gervais film.

JRW (*Reading Evening Post*/personal research)

JULY 5TH

1253: On this day, King Henry III granted the Charter that created Reading's first Merchant Guild. Ever since the founding of Reading Abbey in 1121, its abbot had held supreme administrative powers over Reading, including control of its commerce. Increasingly unacceptable to merchants and master craftsmen, this had led to bitter quarrels and even violence. By 1253 it was recorded that 'burghers lay in wait day and night for the Abbot's bailiffs … and assaulted them in the execution of their office'. With ill-will at such extremes, the Merchants Guild then put together the sum of £100 – over £50,000 at today's value – to pay for a Royal Charter permitting them to buy and sell in Reading and throughout England, free from all tolls. Continuing quarrels led in 1254 to a 'Final and Endly Concord', whereby the abbot agreed that the Guild could operate markets and legally hold property, including their own Guildhall. The abbot retained the right annually to appoint their warden, who was effectively the town's Mayor. The abbots of Reading continued in conflict with the Guild, trying to reclaim absolute rights over local trade and government, for another two centuries, until their power came to an end with Henry VIII's Dissolution of the Monasteries.

PV (Hunter, J., *A History of Berkshire*, Phillimore, 1995/ Hurry, J., *Reading Abbey*, 1901)

JULY 6TH

1893: On this day a holly tree was planted at the Forbury Gardens in Reading to celebrate the marriage of Prince George, Duke of York (later King George V), to Her Serene Highness Princess Mary of Teck. The Mayor and Corporation, local magistrates, Mrs Palmer (wife of Reading MP George Palmer), the headmaster of Reading School, and many borough officials followed the mace-bearer in procession from the Town Hall to Forbury Gardens. Speeches of loyalty and good wishes were delivered and the Mayor formally planted the tree, after which the council and borough officials threw in earth. Some thirty years earlier, a previous Mayor, Mr J. Okey Taylor, had planted an oak tree in the Gardens as a memorial on the occasion of the marriage of the Prince of Wales (later Edward VII) to Princess Alexandra of Denmark. However, on the 1893 occasion it was a holly tree or, to be more exact, an *Ilex Aurea Variegata*; this had been the choice of experts who had been consulted as to the best tree to hand down to posterity. The tree still stands in the Forbury Gardens today, together with its commemorative plaque.

SG (*Berkshire Chronicle*)

JULY 7TH

1896: On this day, Trooper Thomas Charles Wooldridge was hanged at Reading Gaol. Thomas was a soldier in the Royal Horse Guards at Windsor, and it was there that he met his future wife, Laura Glendell, a Post Office employee. As a soldier, Thomas needed permission to marry, but he neglected to apply. The couple wed secretly and set up home in Windsor; however, the joys of love soon faded as Thomas had an explosive temper, especially after drinking. He was posted to Regents Park but, as they had married without permission, Laura could not accompany him. She started to see another soldier. Unaware of this, Thomas thought that they would be reunited and arranged to meet Laura, but she didn't turn up. Thomas then discovered that she was seeing someone else. Returning to Windsor, he gained access to the house, outside which he slashed Laura's throat three times with a razor. Thomas calmly gave himself up to the first police officer on the scene, with the words, 'Take me – I have killed my wife!' After conviction, he was sent to Reading Gaol to await execution. One day, during exercise, Oscar Wilde noticed him; thus was Trooper Wooldridge immortalised in Wilde's poem, *The Ballad of Reading Gaol*.

VC (Eddleston, J., *Foul Deeds and Suspicious Deaths in Reading*, Wharncliffe, 2009)

JULY 8TH

1723: On this day the *Reading Mercury* began publication, one of the earliest provincial newspapers, pre-dating *The Times* by over sixty years. Its founder, William Carnan, died in 1737 and his widow married John Newbery, former apprentice printer and later renowned children's books publisher. Newbery's stepdaughter Anna Maria married the poet Christopher Smart. In 1785 the *Mercury* passed to their daughter Mary Ann and her husband Thomas Cowslade, who built up circulation in and around Berkshire. Under the next owner, Francis Peter Cowslade, it backed the Whigs' great Reform Bill. When this Bill passed, the *Mercury*'s support was acknowledged with a silver cup inscribed 'Noble Engine of Freedom, may thy energy never be cramped by the minions of despotism and corruption!' William Wallace Cowslade (1818-1915), Francis Peter's nephew, joined the business at seventeen. He began by collecting the newsagents' takings twice a year, from Southampton to Oxford, accompanied by a groom and carrying pistols to protect the moneybags. Becoming sole proprietor, after fifty years William transferred the *Mercury* to his sons Frederick and Henry but, in 1914, following 129 years of Cowslade ownership, the newspaper was sold. When Frederick died in 1925, the family became extinct, not only in Berkshire but worldwide.

PV (*Berkshire Archaeological Journal*: A Vanished Berkshire Family, 1933)

July 9th

1908: On this day, Ian Mikardo was born in Portsmouth, the son of Jewish refugees from the Russian Empire. Educated in Portsmouth, he attended a rabbinical seminary as well as primary and secondary schools. Injustice and inequality in his boyhood led Mikardo to attend political lectures in London in the 1920s, and then to join the Labour Party and Poale Zion, the Zionist Workers' Movement. As a Zionist, Mikardo had given his first public speech at the age of thirteen. He settled in Stepney after leaving school, married in 1931 and had two daughters. He became a freelance management consultant, and during the Second World War he worked at increasing efficiency in aircraft and armaments manufacturing, based at Woodley Aerodrome in Reading. Settling in Reading at the end of the war, he was selected as Labour Party candidate for Reading at the 1945 general election. He overturned a large Conservative majority to become Reading's MP. Known as Mik, he was the Labour member for Reading until 1959. After he lost his Reading seat, he became MP for Poplar at the 1964 general election. Mikardo remained a back-bencher throughout his forty years in the House of Commons. Retiring from Parliament in 1987, he died on 6 May 1993.

VC (*New York Times*)

JULY 10TH

1911: On this day, two memorial plaques were unveiled in the Chapter House of Reading Abbey by Sir William Osler, a medical friend of the donor, Dr Jamieson Hurry. The plaques, each carved from a single slab of Forest of Dean bluestone, commemorate the first and last abbots of Reading. On one, Abbot Hugh de Boves, supported by his tonsured brethren, is shown receiving his insignia of office from King Henry Beauclerc (Henry I), whose men-at-arms are standing by. The border of the plaque is decorated with the coat of arms of Reading Abbey and a carving of a bull (a 'rebus' for the abbot's name: 'boves' is Latin for 'bulls'). The other plaque shows Abbot Hugh Faringdon (whose coat of arms also appears) standing at the foot of the gallows, a rope around his neck, addressing the burghers of Reading. Nearby, in front of burghers and soldiers, stand two other monks, John Rugge and John Eynon, waiting to be hanged, drawn and quartered. (Their abbot was more fortunate: he died on the gallows, thus escaping the ghastly sequel – to the disappointment of onlookers.) The sculptor was William Silver Frith (1850-1924), and the architect of the setting for the memorials was William Ravenscroft. (*See* November 16th.)

SG (*Berkshire Chronicle*/Hylton, S., *Reading Places, Reading People*, Berkshire Books, 1992)

JULY 11TH

2012: On this day, the Olympic torch was paraded through Reading. Having arrived the previous evening, it continued its journey around the country, in the lead-in to the London 2012 Olympic Games, by heading through the town towards Newbury. Locals who shared in carrying the flame included ninety-two-year-old George Weedon, who had competed as a gymnast at the 1948 London Olympics. Reading had its Olympians in 2012 too. With its Thames-side location, rowing is a major sport in Reading, hence a high number of Olympic rowers from the town. Reading residents Helen Glover and Heather Stanning won Gold in the women's pairs. University of Reading graduate Richard Egington gained a Bronze medal in the men's eight, while sweethearts Natasha Page and Sam Townsend, who were due to get married after the Games, each came fifth in their respective events, women's eights and men's double sculls. Anna Watkins and Kate Grainger won Gold in the women's double sculls, and Zac Purchase won Silver in the men's lightweight pairs. Away from rowing, diver Chris Mears came fifth in the 3-metre synchronised diving and ninth in the 3-metre springboard event. Reading hockey players were also selected for Team GB, with three in the men's team and six in the women's, gaining fourth place and Bronze respectively.
VC (*GetReading*)

JULY 12TH

1311: On this day, Greyfriars Church came into being. The friars, followers of St Francis of Assisi, had first come to Reading in 1233 and nearly fifty years later began building their church on what was then called Newe Street, on a site measuring 344ft by 335ft (105 x 102m); their chief object was 'to rear a church suitable for the crowds who flocked to hear their zealous preaching'. Restored for worship in 1862 after a 300-year gap (in which it was put to secular and sometimes ignoble uses) Greyfriars Church is said to be the oldest Franciscan church still used for worship.
JBD (Spriggs, G., *History of the Church of Greyfriars*, 1965)

———— • ✦ • ————

1819: On this day, Redingensians found a novelty offered for their health and pleasure: 'Cold, Warm, Vapour and Shower Baths'. The *Reading Mercury* advertisement proclaimed: 'The Ladies and Gentlemen of Reading and its vicinity are respectfully informed that these Baths, replete with every necessary convenience, will open for their reception on Monday 12th inst. Particulars on application at the Baths, Bath Court, London Street.' From the book *Reading Seventy Years Ago* we learn that a 'Dr Hooper' created the Baths – whether a qualified man or quack is uncertain.
PV (*Reading Mercury*/Ditchfield, P., *Reading Seventy Years Ago*, 1887)

JULY 13TH

1841: On this day, leading local surgeons and doctors founded the Reading Pathological Society (RPS) – to promote 'discussion of medical and surgical subjects, of cases and of other matters connected with the profession'. One of the oldest such bodies in the UK, it pre-dates the Pathological Societies of London (1846) and Manchester (1885). The resources it developed include a valuable library, a medical museum and a portrait gallery of members and others. These treasured facilities are still at the Royal Berkshire Hospital (opened in 1839), where the RPS held its meetings from the start. Reading had had a Medico-Chirurgical Society from as early as 1824, and they had originated the library which the RPS built up. This earlier, less prestigious body continued as a separate institution until absorbed by the RPS in 1899. One of the main functions of the RPS remains the regular presentation of papers by members and eminent guests, always reflecting the best practice of the day and characterised by conscientious, painstaking research. An early record emphasised that 'Great interest was taken in morbid anatomy, no evening being allowed to pass without the exhibition of several specimens'.

PV (Hurry, J., *History of The Reading Pathological Society*, 1909)

JULY 14TH

1868: On this day, Christchurch National Schools (Infants, Boys and Girls) were opened in Reading. These were not the first schools in the Whitley area (the Spring Gardens Wesleyan School preceded them), but they were the first to be purpose-built. The buildings were funded mainly by local subscriptions and collections, with additional funds from the government, the Diocesan Board, and the National Schools Society. Only a five-minute walk from the newly built Christ Church, the schools were in Milman Road and had room for 381 children. In 1871, the *Reading Chronicle* reported that there were 190 children in attendance and thirty-seven in the Night School held there. Punishments were severe, and were meted out for what we might deem small offences, such as having dirty hands or being careless when doing sums. By 1909 the schools had expanded to accommodate 564 pupils with an average attendance of 514. The three schools continued until 1927 when Christchurch Junior Mixed and Infants (Primary) came into being. The school was run by women for two decades; the only men having access were the vicar, a part-time games master, an attendance officer and the caretaker. Christchurch Primary School continues to this day, a happy and well respected school. **VC** (Barnes-Phillips, D., *The Top of Whitley*, Corridor Press, 2002)

JULY 15TH

1868: On this day, two prize fighters, Tim Collins and Bill Gillam, were amongst the crowd attending the Reading Races held at Kings Meadow. It was a very hot day, over 90°F (32°C). After the last race, these two started arguing and it was decided to sort out their problem by fighting. A ring was quickly formed, a referee appointed and a purse of £10 collected. After fifteen rounds of severe slogging, both fighters collapsed to the ground, feeling the effects of the heat. Gillam was the first to get up, but, as Collins was rising, Gillam was ruled to have kicked his opponent and the referee awarded the prize money to Collins, after thirty minutes of fighting. Dissatisfaction was expressed at this result and both fighters agreed to fight a re-match for another £10 purse. The fight was going very much like the first, until in the ninth round Collins managed to throw Gillam, who crashed heavily and injured his shoulder. As he was unable to defend himself, his seconds threw in the towel, thus avoiding further punishment.

SG (Hill, M., *Old Prize Fights in and around Berkshire*, 2010)

JULY 16TH

1556: On this day, Julius Palmer, former Master of Reading School and Reading's only Protestant martyr, was burned at the stake in Newbury. Palmer had fled from Reading but, returning to collect some belongings, took a room at the Cardinal's Hat in Minster Street. There he was arrested, having been betrayed by one of his assistant masters.

JBD (Oakes, J. & Parsons, M., *Reading School*, DSM, 2005)

———◆———

1801: On this day, James Dormer, of High Wycombe, was executed at Reading Gaol for the murder of John Robinson, a pedlar from Hurley, shot dead on the Maidenhead to Henley road. Dormer, a deserter from the Royal Marines, and a certain Richard Alder were duly arrested and tried. Reporting on the crime and execution, the *Mercury* recounted how Dormer, having fallen into bad company, was persuaded to support his family by a life of robbery. The two originally intended to rob a coach. This failing, they set upon Robinson, who was travelling home in his cart. The pedlar resisted but swiftly paid with his life. Although both men acknowledged the crime, each denied being the killer and Alder was acquitted. At the gallows, Dormer made a lengthy speech to those gathered, and at 1.30 p.m. he was hanged.

VC (*Reading Mercury*)

JULY 17TH

1933: On this day, a new Reading Labour Exchange was opened in South Street, the previous premises having been in London Street. The number of unemployed at the beginning of 1933 was 5,000, but was down to 3,000 by the time of the opening. All the men employed in its building were engaged through the Exchange. The architect, Charles Michael Childs Associate of Royal Institute of British Architects of HM Office of Works, designed the Exchange in a free interpretation of Georgian architecture. Every effort was made on the opening day to have jobs available, and thus they were able to announce that Huntley & Palmers wanted a hundred girls, Huntley, Boorne and Stevens required twelve workers and Reading Borough Council needed twenty strong labourers. The Labour Exchange remained at South Street until about 1974, when the building became a medical centre. After the Borough Council acquired it in 1989 for social and community groups, it was launched as 21 South Street Arts Centre. The Labour Exchange, now called the Job Centre, relocated to St Mary's Butts, and is now situated in Friar Street. To celebrate its fifth birthday in 1994, the Arts Centre commissioned a piece of sculpture from Eric Stanford entitled *Guardian for the Gate of Sparta*, which is displayed in the garden.

SG (*Berkshire Chronicle/Evening Post*)

JULY 18TH

1832: On this day, a huge outdoor dinner was held in Reading to celebrate the passing of the Reform Act of 1832. This Act was intended to make the House of Commons more representative of the population. The struggle for the legislation was as long and hard-fought in Reading as elsewhere in the country. To celebrate the greater freedom and justice which the new law would confer, it was decided to hold a public dinner for all the townspeople. At dawn on 18 July a cannon boomed from the Forbury; drums beat and church bells rang. Throughout the town houses were decorated with laurel, and thousands of strangers flocked in from the surrounding countryside. At 3 p.m. the company sat down at 116 tables, each 50ft long, and laden with food and decorations. The tables stretched down London Street, Duke Street, King Street, Minster Street, Broad Street, Friar Street, and the Market Place. Some dined on barges which had been dragged into the streets on waggons or rollers. Besides those seated at the tables, nearly 4,000 others joined in the feast. At 5 p.m. the whole company moved to the Forbury, and the evening passed in sports and amusements.

VC (Childs, W., *The Story of the Town of Reading*, 1905)

JULY 19TH

1836: On this day, the Revd James Sherman tendered his resignation as minister of Castle Street Chapel to the Trustees. Born in Finsbury in 1796, Sherman was apprenticed to an ivory-tuner, making chess pieces and billiard balls, but was later ordained into the Countess of Huntingdon's Connexion in 1818. After terms in Bath and Bristol, he came to Reading in 1820 on a probationary basis, commencing his permanent ministry in April 1821. During his time in Reading, Sherman was notable for his vision of taking the gospel to the surrounding villages, setting up satellite chapels or 'outstations' in Caversham Hill, Binfield Heath, Theale, Wargrave and Woodley. The first two are still active to this day. His call to succeed Rowland Hill at the Surrey Chapel, Southwark, was followed by the successful negotiation by the chapel in Reading for a place in the Church of England. The chapel then became known as St Mary's Episcopal Chapel. Members who dissented built their own chapel on the opposite side of the road, a building now trading as Club Evissa. In later life Sherman wrote the introduction to the first English edition of *Uncle Tom's Cabin*. He finally entered 'into the joy of his Lord' on 15 February 1862.

JBD (Dearing, J., *The Church That Would Not Die*, Baron Birch, 1993)

JULY 20TH

1775: On this day, William Marsh DD was born. He came to his first curacy, St Laurence's, Reading, at Christmas 1800, and eloquently preached his first sermon in Reading. 'That evangelical young Marsh,' as the Vicar of Basingstoke called him, had been a friend and disciple of William Cadogan, the Vicar of St Giles, who described him as 'his son in the faith'. This was in the days of pluralities in the Church, and Marsh, in addition to his curacy, accepted the two small livings of Nettlebed and the parish adjoining, the gift of Mr Stonor, their liberal-minded Roman Catholic patron. The Catholic squire and the ultra-Protestant vicar became firm friends and Marsh stayed with Stonor on his frequent visits to the parish. He held the St Laurence curacy for eleven years, and whenever it was known that he was to preach, the church would be crammed full, for his was 'a ministry of spiritual power, happily combined with a gentle winsomeness and unselfish devotion'. 'Most heavenly-minded of men' is the description of him given by Charles Simeon of Cambridge. Dr Marsh left Reading in 1811 but returned in 1836 to preach at the opening service in St Mary's, Castle Street, after it was licensed for Anglican worship.

VC (Cooper, J., *Some Worthies of Reading*, 1923)

July 21st

1967: On this day, an article appeared in the *Reading Chronicle*, in which some lines of verse headed a feature on a young local poet, John Harflett. He was about to publish a book of poems called *The Fire in My Blood*, and the stanza from a poem called 'Reading Town' read as follows:

A strangled gasp of shops and streets,
Where dead men hurry home at night, lost
In their own grey worlds of silence …
In this cold cancer of a town,
No man calls another 'friend' …

Alan Wykes has commented:

Far from expressing any resentment at this, nobody seems to have raised an eyebrow. Whether because poetry doesn't count, isn't to be taken seriously … or because the accusation was too ludicrous to be considered and therefore beneath the dignity of a letter to the editor is impossible to assess. It may have been that Mr Harflett was considered to have hit the nail on the head, or, anyway, to have slyly revealed a bit of the truth that everyone suspected to be lurking under the surface.

Whatever the reason, the young poet escaped the pillory!
VC (Wykes, A., *Reading: A Biography*, Macmillan, 1970)

JULY 22ND

1903: On this day, there was much merriment in the town as gigantic crowds witnessed the inauguration of the municipal electric tramway system. Contemporary photographs show huge crowds in Mill Lane, Duke Street, King Street and Broad Street, as a procession of ten trams full of invited guests (one third of the original fleet) set off for Pond House before journeying along the 'main line' to Wokingham Road. The first tram was decorated and driven by the Mayor. On the procession's return to Broad Street, the complete service was opened to the public; all cars carried substantial loads throughout the day. The trams went on to serve Reading well for thirty-six years, nearly always making a profit which was ploughed back into the transport undertaking. Not every route was profitable, mainly because apart from the 'main line' the routes were constructed, not with the advice of professionals as to their viability, but rather at the whim of certain worthies sitting on a committee of the whole council. Thus a route to Bath Road, which barely crested Castle Hill and served an area where most owned their own carriage, lasted only to 1930, and one serving Erleigh Road fared little better, being withdrawn in 1932.

JRW (Jordan, E., *Tramways of Reading*, Light Railway Transport League,1957)

JULY 23RD

1883: On this day, George Lovejoy of London Street was buried. Lovejoy, a bookseller who created a noted circulating subscription library, also owned a post office and a stationer's in Reading. The *Reading Mercury* reported:

His death was unexpected, and occurred suddenly on Thursday morning [19 July]. Until within the past few days, notwithstanding his advanced age, he had appeared in his usual activity, health and spirits. His energy was remarkable, and to this, his sound judgment and great tact, his success in business was attributable. His advice was sought by all, and his opinion on business matters and the transfer of landed property was highly valued. To philanthropic objects he was ever ready to give his aid and to those who had seen 'better days' and who had become reduced in circumstances, he was a kind and generous benefactor. Although not filling any public capacity, save the post of borough auditor, he was well and widely known. His sterling worth, good common sense, and honesty of purpose will cause him to be greatly missed and his memory to be long cherished by the people of Reading. The funeral will, we understand, take place at the Cemetery on Monday next.

Reading Museum holds a fine portrait of Lovejoy by Charles Richards Havell.
VC (*Reading Mercury*)

July 24th

1962: On this day, work commenced on what proved to be the last extension of Reading's trolleybus system, a quarter-mile stretch down Northumberland Avenue from the existing terminus (just south of the Roman Catholic church of Christ the King) to the junction with Whitley Wood Road. This was in anticipation of the imminent building of more council housing. At the time it was intended that there would be a further extension, along Whitley Wood Road, to link up with Whitley Wood terminus at the Engineer's Arms, but this never happened. The Northumberland Avenue extension was very straightforward, carried out by the transport undertaking's own overhead line department. Traction poles, already in stock, were 'planted', and by mid-October 1962 all the overhead line and supporting wires were aloft ready for attaching to the insulated fittings, for tensioning and connecting to the rest of the system. However, it took until Christmas to complete the task and, on Boxing Day, Reading was treated to a heavy dose of snow. On Sunday 13 January 1963, finishing touches were carried out in the severe semi-Arctic conditions which had now developed, and passenger service over the extension began the next day. Many years after trolleybuses disappeared from Reading, traction poles on this extension survive, supporting street lighting.

JRW (Hall, D., *Reading Trolleybuses*, Trolleybooks, 1991)

JULY 25TH

1890: On this day, the Revd Hubert Brooke, minister of St Mary's, Castle Street, Reading, signed what became known as the Keswick Letter. A number of those participating in the annual Keswick Convention with an interest in missionary affairs wrote an open letter to the Church Missionary Society (CMS) calling for a thousand missionaries 'within the next few years', to meet the needs of Gospel work in China, India and among the 'recently discovered' African tribes. CMS largely responded to the call with the enthusiastic support of Archbishop Benson. In Reading, Brooke's vision inspired some twenty-four missionaries to go out over the next decade. The first of these, leaving Reading in 1891, were Thomas Simmonds for China and James Redman who was to work in what is now Tanzania. Redman went out as Castle Street's 'own missionary' but he died of a fever shortly after arriving at his post the following year. Others called to the mission field included three sisters, Louisa, Mary and Sibella Bazett, who all went to East Africa. Mary married another of the twenty-four, the Revd Harry Leakey, who had been a French master at Reading School; they became the parents of Louis Leakey, the renowned anthropologist.

JBD (Dearing, J., *The Church That Would Not Die*, Baron Birch, 1993)

July 26th

1602: On this day, young Richard Edwards was buried at St Mary's, Reading. The notice said: 'The child was killed by a blocke that fell on him, which blocke was found by the Coroner's Jury to be guilty of his death.'

AS (St Mary's Parish Register)

———— • ◆ • ————

1799: On this day, there was tremendous excitement at Bull-Marsh (or Bulmershe) Heath, east of Reading. King George III was reviewing a parade of the Berkshire Volunteer Corps, including the Woodley Cavalry. These were perilous times. Napoleon's armies had occupied Italy and forced an armistice with Austria; would England be invaded next? When Henry Addington of Bulmershe Court, Speaker of the Commons, raised the Woodley Volunteer Cavalry in 1798, support was prompt; local gentry with their own mounts comprised the officers, with infantry drawn from labourers. In 1805 the King watched an even greater show at Bulmershe when he returned to inspect the Berkshire Yeomanry and Infantry Corps, 1,000 strong. A ninety-two-page manual was prepared (1804) by an Army sergeant-major for the 'amateurs', preparing them for such reviews and indeed for eventual war service. Twenty thousand spectators, double Reading's population, thrilled to the noise and colour of the marching and riding manoeuvres and military music.

PV (Hunter, J., *A History of Berkshire*, Phillimore, 1995)

July 27th

1887: On this day, the Duke of Cambridge unveiled Reading's statue of Queen Victoria, carved by local sculptor George Simonds – a commission Simonds won while engaged on the Forbury Lion (*see* December 18th). When the council allocated £1,000 for Victoria's Golden Jubilee celebrations, Simonds sent immediately to Carrara for suitable marble. Transportation and other problems delayed its arrival until January, leaving six months for a sculpture that would normally require a year. Simonds worked fifteen hours a day, and the statue reached its pedestal the day before the unveiling. According to myth, Queen Victoria disliked Reading as she had been jeered during a visit, so wanted her statue to face away from the town – but in fact she never visited Reading, and the orientation was selected by the Corporation. Because of the haste, the statue lacks some of its intended fine brocading. The differences show clearly in another Victoria that Simonds sculpted for Weymouth.
SG (North, L., *Reading Chronicle*, 1979)

———◆———

1932: On this day, the County War Memorial was unveiled in Reading. It was designed by Leslie Gunston and sculpted by John Harvard Thomas. The original project, costed at £8,000, was scaled down when subscriptions reached only £1,000.
SG (Slade, C., *The Town of Reading and its Abbey*, MRM, 2001)

JULY 28TH

1906: On this day one of the first balloon races of the Aero Club (now called the Royal Aero Club) started from Reading Gasworks. In a 'hare and hounds' chase, the Hon. C.S. Rolls (1877-1910) was 'hare', piloting his balloon 'Midget', with a five-minute start over five other balloons commanded by other well-heeled 'aeronauts' and their daring lady passengers. A gentle south-westerly bore them away over the astonished heads of Reading earthlings, to land safely in Essex. Rolls made his ballooning debut at twenty-one, and at twenty-four was a founder of the Aero Club. He was no stranger to Berkshire; before Eton, he had attended a Mortimer prep school. In 1903 he piloted the maiden flight of 'Vivienne II' from Prospect Park, Reading – and survived its crash-landing. A motoring enthusiast since Cambridge, and a founder member of the RAC, Rolls commenced car importing while still ballooning for sport. In 1906 he joined with Henry Royce to establish the world-renowned Rolls-Royce engineering firm. Rolls' passions moved on to aeroplanes; he won a gold trophy for the first non-stop return flight across the Channel, but died a month later when his bi-plane crashed at Bournemouth.

PV (Helps, D., *The Reading Gas Company*, 1912)

JULY 29TH

1816: On this day, Madame Tussaud brought her famous waxworks to Reading and the *Reading Mercury* published the following announcement:

MADAME TUSSAUD By permission of the Worshipful Mayor of Reading, lately arrived from Salisbury and last from Newbury, Madame Tussaud, artist to the late Royal Highness Madame Elizabeth, sister of Louis XVIII, most respectfully informs the Nobility, Gentry and the public of Reading and its vicinity, that her unrivalled COLLECTION OF FIGURES as large as life consisting of eighty-three public figures, which has lately been exhibited in Paris, London, Dublin, Edinburgh &c will be open for inspection at a commodious house, opposite the Town Hall, when she hopes to receive that encouragement she has universally met with in all the first cities and towns in the Empire.

A week later the paper reported:

We are happy to hear that Madame Tussaud's collection of figures continues to draw crowds of visitors, who, upon its first arrival entertained prejudices against this type of exhibition, have been prevailed upon to call at the exhibition room, and allow that the excellence of the figures have removed that aversion which inspection of inferior collections had naturally inspired.

SG (*Reading Mercury*)

JULY 30TH

1920: On this day the Reading Borough Police Force Roll of Honour for the First World War was unveiled. Twenty constables were called up as reservists when war broke out and thirty-two more enlisted voluntarily. Pensioners and Special Constables replaced some of them, but by 1918 the Force's strength was thirty below the establishment of 113. Of the fifty-two men who served, three were killed in action: Albert James Lawrence (11856) of Reading (born Woodnesborough, Kent), Grenadier Guards, killed 10 December 1916 in the Somme; Russell Freeman (2543) of Briants Avenue, Caversham (born Framlingham, Suffolk), Life Guards, died of wounds 14 July 1916 in France; and Arthur Percy Dorey (24015) of Century Road, Staines (born Stoke, Surrey), Grenadier Guards, killed 25 September 1916 in the Somme. Claude Victor Bowra (2682) of East Dulwich (born Coombe, Dorset) died during home service, and is also commemorated. Of the forty-seven constables who returned to police duty, three had won the Military Medal and one the Distinguished Conduct Medal. The Roll of Honour recording their names was unveiled by the Mayor, Dr (later Sir) G.S. Abram in the entrance hall of the police station in Valpy Street. This was moved to the new building when Reading's central police station was erected in Castle Street.

VC (Wykes, A., *Reading: A Biography*, Macmillan, 1970)

JULY 31ST

1820: On this day the philanthropist and writer William White was born in London Street, Reading. He was the sixth son of John White, and ninth of his thirteen children. More serious than his brother Walter, the traveller and writer, William was equally energetic in mind and body. As a boy at Castle Street Academy, he was much interested in the elementary science and history taught by Isaac Holden (later a captain of industry and a baronet). Forty years after Holden left Reading, he renewed his friendship with William White; they remained friends until Holden's death. Aged nineteen, William became an abstainer. He was no sour-faced reformer, but a lover of fun and humorous in his speech. His most notable publication was *A History and Description of the Town of Reading* (1841), illustrated by another brother, John White. William White settled in Birmingham, where he died in 1900.

VC (Cooper, J., *Some Worthies of Reading*, 1923)

———— • ◆ • ————

1826: On this day, Notice of Information was given to Messrs Cocks & Son, of the Reading Sauce warehouse, for 'suffering a wild animal, commonly called a turtle, to be at large without a muzzle', being contrary to the statute 7 Geo. IV folio 41 [the Reading Paving Act].

AS (*Reading Mercury*)

AUGUST 1ST

2001: On this day, Brian Brindley died at his seventieth birthday party – a seven-course dinner at the London Athenaeum – suffering a heart attack 'between the dressed crab and the boeuf en croûte'. Born in London, Brindley was educated at Stowe, where he developed 'a love of country houses and a strong dislike of Low Church worship'. After Oxford, national service and a brief flirtation with the Law, he settled, to the surprise of his friends, for a career in the Church. For twenty-two years, he was vicar of Holy Trinity in Reading's Oxford Road, during which 'he managed to turn Holy Trinity from an undistinguished 1820s Gothic box into the boldest and gaudiest of Anglo-Catholic shrines'. A flamboyant and eccentric character who liked to dress like an eighteenth-century monsignor, complete with red high-heeled shoes, he hit the headlines in 1989 when the *News of the World* published an exposé on his liking for young men. As a result Brindley lost his job, his house and his seat on the General Synod of the Church of England. He retired to Brighton, where he decorated his house in the manner of the Brighton Pavilion. In 1992, in response to the Anglican Church's decision to ordain women priests, he converted to Roman Catholicism.
VC (*Daily Telegraph*)

AUGUST 2ND

1554: On this day, Reading received royal visitors of unusual significance. Henry VIII's turbulent reign had given way to that of his sickly son Edward VI, who ruled as a minor for six years, succeeded in 1553 by his elder half-sister, Henry's daughter Mary Tudor. Edward had keenly supported Protestantism but Mary was a devout Roman Catholic. Anxious for an heir, within a year Mary married – in Winchester Cathedral – the king of Spain's son, Philip, also a Catholic – and insisted, in a move unpopular among her subjects, on bestowing on him the title 'King of England'. Eight days later, travelling towards London, the newly-wed sovereigns reached Reading. With inhabitants and burgesses attending 'in their best apparellys', Mayor Robert Bowyer welcomed Mary and Philip on bended knee 'at the upper end of Sivear strete [Silver Street]'. He then 'rode before the king and queen through the towne into the King's place [Reading Abbey] … he presented them with iiii greate fatt oxen'. Mary responded by ordering that Roman Catholic altars and images be restored in Reading, and by granting pensions to former monks of Reading Abbey. After a night in Reading, the happy pair proceeded to Windsor.
PV (Doran, J., *The History and Antiquities of the Town and Borough of Reading in Berkshire*, 1835)

August 3rd

1829: On this day, the *Berkshire Chronicle* reported an early 'motoring' event – with a steam engine fuelled by coke! Reading had previously admired Cornish engineer Goldsworthy Gurney's 'steam-coach' passing westwards on a London-Bath excursion; now returning, it survived collision with the mail-coach and a 'Luddite' attack at Melksham. The vehicle, 'destined to make so great a change in travelling in this country', resembled 'a four-wheeled dogcart', having a steersman and mate outside and four passengers within. Behind trailed 'a sort of barouchette, with six more passengers'. Capable of 12mph, it coped easily with hills.

PV (*Berkshire Chronicle*)

———— • ◆ • ————

1940: On this day, when, following Dunkirk, German invasion threatened, Reading's road and railway name-plates were removed by government order. The council even renamed transport termini, believing residents would recognise the new names, but strangers (German parachutists?) would not. Tilehurst became Bear Inn, Lower Caversham became Donkin Hill and Emmer Green became Chalgrove Way. Lower Whitley became Wood Lane Junction and London Road became Liverpool Road. The word 'Reading' disappeared from bus-stops and bus-sides – but Thames Valley buses still ran into town proclaiming 'READING'! Reversion to pre-war names, with some new ones, came only in 1947.

JRW (Reading Corporation Transport documents)

AUGUST 4TH

1988: On this day, a new bronze sculpture was unveiled in Reading's Abbey Garden. Named *Robed Figure* and created by world-famous English sculptor Dame Elisabeth Frink, it represents a draped figure of indeterminate sex, striding forward. The statue had been purchased from the artist, for an undisclosed sum, by one of the directors of the development company, Metestates. Opinion was somewhat divided: one critic saw the figure as 'sad and sexless, but of importance'; another felt it appropriate to its site close to the Abbey ruins, since at first glance it is possible to interpret it as a monk. Dame Elisabeth, the Mayor and the directors of the company were in attendance at the unveiling. The sculpture is in fact part of a three-piece set of statuary called *The Martyrs at Dorchester*, created by Frink for Dorchester (county town of Dorset) where the original is displayed. The group commemorates two sixteenth-century martyrs and their intending executioner. Like most artists, Frink made more than one model; the Reading figure is a replica of the original 'executioner'. Now moved from its original site to the sunken garden attached to Abbey House, it remains controversial – you either like it or you hate it.

SG (*Evening Post*)

AUGUST 5TH

1768: On this day William Talbot became Vicar of St Giles-in-Reading, having exchanged his City of London parish with the previous incumbent. A follower of Lady Huntingdon, he exercised a powerful evangelical ministry over the next six years. He appeared in an unusual light in 1771 when he was asked to visit Jonathan Britain, who had been detained in Reading's Compter prison on charges of forgery. Talbot became convinced that society would be better off without Mr Britain and that only when he was confronted by the gallows would he be brought to repentance. He himself turned detective and brought to light evidence that eventually convicted Britain, as well as exposing as fantasy the latter's claims to have discovered a French-inspired plot to set fire to the naval dockyard at Portsmouth. Unrepentant and claiming that Talbot had abused his confidence, Britain was executed in May 1772. Not all approved of Talbot's actions. Verses appeared in the *Berkshire Chronicle*:

> A priest of late got Britain hanged.
> Ye sufferers! Cease to mock:
> Who knows? When first he has harangued,
> Perhaps he'll hang his flock.

William Talbot died on 2 March 1774 from a fever he caught from a sick parishioner.
JBD (Talbot, W., *The Rev. Mr. Talbot's Narrative of the Whole of his Proceedings Relative to Jonathan Britain*, 1771)

AUGUST 6TH

1896: On this day, Reading Borough Bench was prosecuting parents for failing to have their children vaccinated against tuberculosis. Fear of contracting the disease appears to have been the main reason for not vaccinating, as cases of children developing symptoms of the disease post-vaccination were cited in several instances.

VC (*Reading Observer*)

———— • ◆ • ————

1933: On this day, Mr Jack Freeman, proprietor of the Wynford Arms on the King's Road, arranged an outing for his regulars to Hastings.

A special corridor train was engaged exclusively for the day; there were no stoppings and only members were allowed to travel. As many as 342 took advantage of the trip – a record we should think for any public house in Reading. Thanks to the Southern Railway Company, the Guard's van was transformed into a bar and the excursionists could thus obtain what refreshment they required with the minimum of trouble. In addition to the above outing there are two others for men and one for women only. Members pay 6d a week and are already putting by for the next occasion.

At the present time the Wynford is perhaps best known as Reading's premier gay pub.

AS (*The Hop Leaf Gazette*, House journal of H.G. Simonds Ltd)

August 7th

1862: On this day, a wet Thursday, Christ Church was consecrated by the Right Revd Samuel Wilberforce, Bishop of Oxford. The church was incomplete through lack of funds, internal paving had been made of the cheapest materials and the tower lacked a top and a spire. Some £4,000 was still required to complete the work. A new church was required in the parish of St Giles, since the old St Giles' Church could no longer cope with the growing population as families were drawn into the area by the availability of work at nearby Simonds' Brewery and Great Western Railway. The land upon which the Christ Church stands was donated by William Milman (remembered today in the name of nearby Milman Road). The Ecclesiastical Commissioners gave £3,000 and a mysterious, unnamed clergyman, unconnected with the parish, donated £4,000. The Revd D.A. Beaufort was later disclosed as the secret donor. The church, designed by eminent Victorian architect Henry Woodyer (responsible also for several other ecclesiastical buildings in Berkshire including St Paul's, Wokingham, and the convent at Clewer, Windsor), was finally completed in 1874. On its elevated site – a ridge on the south side of Reading – and with its tall, elegant spire, Christ Church is a striking landmark, visible for miles.

SD (North, L., *Reading Chronicle*, 1983)

AUGUST 8TH

1990: On this day, the Kennet and Avon Canal was reopened by the Queen, as a through route from Reading to Bristol. The day crowned decades of voluntary restoration effort, and the canal now provides a valuable amenity resource for 'messing about in boats', for lovers of fauna and flora, and for seekers of congenial food and drink at the water's edge. The 87-mile waterway (linking three separately built sections: Bristol–Bath, Bath–Newbury and Newbury–Reading) opened to barges and boats in 1810. The oldest section, from Newbury to Kennet Mouth where it joins the Thames, had already been in operation since 1723. The river, canalised in stretches where its depth makes a separate canal unnecessary, enters Reading at County Lock. Here once stood the large Simonds' Brewery, which gave this twisting, narrow stretch its traditional name, 'Brewery Gut'. (This is *not* named after a physical affliction of beer-drinkers, as some have thought!) The Gut, replete with waterside restaurants and pubs, is now a major feature of The Oracle shopping centre. From this point, the river-canal flows under the eighteenth-century High Bridge into a stretch that has been navigable since the thirteenth century or earlier; here, busy wharves once gave Reading importance as a major river port. Now they are gone, but the Kennet remains for all to enjoy.

PV *(Various sources)*

AUGUST 9TH

1611: On this day, John Blagrave died and was buried in the same grave as his mother in St Laurence's Church, where an elaborate monument was erected in his honour. A notable mathematician, he was born in Reading, the son of John Blagrave of Bulmershe Manor, Woodley, and his wife Anne, who was a daughter of Sir Anthony Hungerford of Down Ampney, Gloucestershire. Young John received his early education in Reading, afterwards entering St John's College, Oxford, where he did not, however, take a degree, instead retiring to his patrimony at Southcote Lodge in Reading, where he devoted himself to his favourite study, mathematics; he later published four mathematical works. Blagrave was distinguished for his charity, bequeathing legacies to the town of Reading, one of which provided annually the sum of 20 nobles (gold coins) to be competed for by three maid servants of good character who had served for five years under one master, to be selected from the three parishes of the town. The whimsical conditions of this bequest required that the maids should appear on Good Friday in the Town Hall before the Mayor and aldermen, where lots were cast for the prize. He married a widow, who was named in his will, but they had no children.

VC (*Dictionary of National Biography, 1885-1900*)

AUGUST 10TH

1513: On this day, the churchwardens of St Laurence's 'payed for a hope [hoop] for the joyaunt and for ale to the Moreys dawncers on the dedicacion day threepence'. This is the earliest reference to morris dancing in Reading.
JBD (Kerry, C., *A History of the Municipal Church of St Lawrence, Reading*, 1883)

———•◆•———

1864: On this day, the bodies of Emma Legge and her children, Flora, Louis and Napoleon, were found in the Thames. Nine days previously, Emma and the children, with husband James, had arrived in Reading from Tunbridge Wells. On the morning of 10 August Emma rose early, dressed herself and the children, hired a perambulator, and headed towards the river. Some time later, William Jacobs, working in a garden on the opposite bank, spotted an empty pram and then noticed a body floating in the water. Jumping into a boat, he found four bodies – the three children cold, the woman still warm. At the inquest, a sorry tale emerged of a woman with a 'husband' who drank heavily and frequently disappeared for days on end. The jury returned a verdict of 'found drowned', as there were no marks of violence on any of the bodies, and Emma had fed her baby shortly before their deaths.
VC (Van der Kiste, J., *Berkshire Murders*, The History Press, 2010)

AUGUST 11TH

1849: On this day, *Reading Mercury* quoted from *The Daily News*: 'Reading has a dishonest reputation. With the single exception of Mr Talfourd, not a member has sat for this town for years except by the well-understood purchase of voters.' This was no lie. With an electorate numbering only hundreds (prior to the 1832 Reform Act) and no secret ballot, parliamentary candidates influenced the vote by both fair means and foul. While polling could last up to eight days, voters could withhold their vote until the final day, in order to sell it at the highest price. Meanwhile, supporters of opposing candidates could be rendered incapable by drink, or forcibly prevented from attending. Other entertaining features were elaborate processions, barrels of free beer, threats and fighting – even on the Town Hall steps. Bribery could include cash, offers of a job on the railway or even tenure of a public house. Candidates were routinely slandered. In 1812, shouts of 'No Popery' derided the respected Mr Monck – who had never been a Catholic; in 1826 Mr Spence was ridiculed as 'a tooth-drawer's son'. The lawyer Talfourd, Reading's unusually honest MP, made charitable donations rather than throwing cash to the populace.

PV (Childs, W., *Town of Reading in the Early Nineteenth Century*, 1910)

AUGUST 12TH

1965: On this day, an accident occurred involving a fire engine on an emergency call. A man, his young daughter, his wife and a baby in a pram narrowly escaped injury when the fire tender mounted the pavement in Caversham Road and crashed into a trolleybus standard. The tender, driven by fireman Ronald Tyler from The Meadway, Tilehurst, had just left the Caversham Road fire station. Following another fire engine, it was negotiating traffic at the junction with Vachel Street, when it struck the pavement. Walking along the pavement was Mr Joseph Kelly, who owned a nearby furniture store. With him was his five-year-old daughter, Kim. 'I just stopped and shut my eyes,' he said afterwards. He flattened himself and his little girl against the wall and the fire engine missed them by inches. As the engine hit the trolleybus standard, a fire-hose nozzle flew off the engine and went straight through Mr Kelly's shop window, narrowly missing his wife, Cora, who happened to be standing beside it. A baby in a pram outside the sweet shop next door narrowly escaped being hit by flying glass from the engine's windscreen. Fireman Tyler was taken to the Battle Hospital after the crash, but was not seriously hurt.
VC (*Reading Mercury*)

AUGUST 13TH

1912: On this day died Octavia Hill, great Victorian campaigner for the housing and welfare of Victorian London's most deprived classes. Although her career centred on London, Octavia maintained Reading connections through her brother, Arthur Hill (Mayor 1883-7). She was godmother to Arthur's daughter Constance, and in 1884 attended her niece Harriet Kate's wedding at All Saints', Reading. It was reported in 1898 that she brought some 200 poor people from Southwark for the day, to be 'hospitably entertained in a large tent' at Erleigh Court, Arthur's home; similar treats were given in other years. In November 1911, Octavia and her sisters, Emily and Florence, were honoured guests at the inauguration of Reading's new Arthur Hill Memorial Baths. Octavia's funeral in 1912 was attended by two of Arthur Hill's daughters, while his son, Revd Frederick Hill, was one of the officiating clergy. Apart from her social work, Octavia was an early fighter for London's Green Belt, creator of a prototype Army Cadet Force, and a principal founder of the National Trust. Among the first supporters of the Trust were her niece Gertrude and her husband Dr Hurry of Castle Street, Reading, while the architect Conrad Willcocks (designer of the Baths) left his house in Caversham to the Trust.

PV (*Reading Mercury/Berkshire Chronicle*)

August 14th

1921: On this day, Harrington Clare Lees was consecrated bishop in St Paul's Cathedral, going out to Australia the following year to become Archbishop of Melbourne. By all accounts he was a distinguished and efficient prelate. At the start of his career he had been a young curate in Reading, under Hubert Brooke at St Mary's, Castle Street, serving from 1892-4. Lees also served with distinction as vicar of Christ Church, Beckenham, from 1907-21 and was a prolific author of devotional works such as *The Divine Master in Home Life*. However, ill-health prevented him from fulfilling his ambition of undertaking overseas work for the Church Missionary Society and in the end caught up with him again, for he died aged fifty-eight on 10 January 1929. During the previous year he revisited Reading and opened a fête for his old church, which had to be held in All Saints' church hall on account of wet weather. He was recalled as 'a rather portly, bow-legged gentleman, dressed in a three-quarter length coat and black silk top-hat ... looking as if he had stepped straight out of the pages of Trollope'.

JBD (Dearing, J., *The Church That Would Not Die*, Baron Birch, 1993)

AUGUST 15TH

1826: On this day:

This town was amused, about half past four in the afternoon, by the unexpected passing through it of a wheeled carriage, drawn by two kites, conveying two gentlemen, who had made their passage from Marlborough. The vehicle had five wheels, one of which, as in a Bath chair, gives the desired direction to the carriage; to which was attached, by a line capable of being (by means of a windlass behind) let out or drawn in at pleasure, a kite, formed of muslin covered with tissue paper painted in imitation of a balloon, measuring 20 feet in height. Through the straighter of this is passed another line, to which is fixed a smaller (or pilot) kite, which has the effect of assisting to support the larger one. The power acquired by the use of these kites is such as, in several instances, to have drawn the vehicle at the rate of 20 miles within the hour. A little difficulty occurred in passing by St Giles's church, in the steeple of which the lines became entangled …

A similar problem arose with a tree at Shepherd's Hill.
AS (*Reading Mercury*)

AUGUST 16TH

1843: On this day, horse racing was revived in Reading, public response to the first meeting at Kings Meadow being beyond the wildest dreams of the organisers. Contemporary estimates varied but a crowd of between 7,000 and 10,000 attended despite a morning of heavy rain. The course was ideally situated, only five minutes' walk from the railway station. On the opening day, the gentry and their families drove to the course in carriages, with the ladies, as at present-day Royal Ascot, dressed in their finery, adding much colour to the scene. All four-wheeled carriages were charged 5s while two-wheeled vehicles were admitted for 2s 6d. Race-goers were entertained by side-shows which included 'shooting at a target, throwing at snuff-boxes and fortune-telling by gypsies'. There were five races on the cards, all over a mile and a half, one of them a walkover. The three-year-old filly, Slane, ridden by Toby Wakefield who was sporting the white jacket and green cap of owner Isaac Day, had the honour of being the first winner at the new course. To round off a successful day, a dinner for sixty racecourse dignitaries was held at the Lower Ship Inn, Duke Street.

NS (Sutcliffe, N., *Reading: A Horse-Racing Town*, Two Rivers, 2010)

AUGUST 17TH

2007: On this day, the international Mills Archive opened its facilities to 'Friends' in all countries, also publishing the first issue of the journal *Mill Memories,* featuring news related to the history and technology of watermills, windmills and mills of other types. The Mills Archive Trust was set up in April 2002 to conserve documents, images and artefacts of molinological importance from around the world. Already, within two years, it had created a website and online catalogue of over 3,000 items. The archive vastly expanded through acquiring four large collections (including that of the Society for the Protection of Ancient Buildings) and a flow of lesser donations, establishing it as the world's largest resource in its field. In 2005 it moved into Watlington House, Reading, which is now the hub of the organisation, offering storage, library and research facilities. By 2007, with committed supporters becoming almost 100 strong, the Trustees deemed it time to formalise the membership category. 'Friends' now have enhanced access to ever-expanding web pages, discount at the archive's internet bookshop and other benefits. The Trust is independent of any commercial or government body, but has received a National Lottery Grant and enjoys occasional income from bequests and book sales. Archiving, cataloguing and research are undertaken by a small team of volunteer staff.

PV *(Mills Archive Trust records)*

AUGUST 18TH

1953: On this day, Reading-born Peter May was helping England regain the Ashes at the Oval, but at Cintra, Reading, there were equally stirring events. Berkshire bowler George Langdale, a tutor at Sandhurst, took all 10 Dorset second-innings wickets for 25 runs in 19 overs to spin his side to victory. Berkshire had made an enterprising declaration but the fast bowlers were unable to make inroads until the Langdale joined the attack. Berkshire's eventual eight-wicket victory was another step towards winning the Minor Counties Championship in Coronation Year.

NS (Local press reports)

———— ◆ ————

2011: On this day, a 'floodbath' of torrential rain amounting to some 60mm (2½in) fell in the Reading area – a record fall for an August day since records began in Reading in the early 1900s. There were reports of abandoned vehicles on the M4 and on the A33 near the Madejski Stadium. Platform 4 at Reading station was inundated, as well as underpasses at Cow Bridge, Vastern Road and Caversham Road. Areas of Broad Street Mall were cordoned off because of a leaking roof. But the resilience of shop owners shone through and they swiftly cleared the mess and soon reopened.

JRS (University of Reading Climatological Site data; *Reading Chronicle*)

AUGUST 19TH

1897: On this day, in his eightieth year, died George Palmer, formerly proprietor of Huntley & Palmers biscuit manufactory in Reading. The idea of keeping biscuits fresh by packing them in specially made tins – and selling them to travellers waiting at London Street's Crown Inn while fresh horses were supplied – was the innovation of Joseph Huntley (founder of the business) and led to the company's initial success. George Palmer, however, is credited with making the project a major Victorian achievement, by employing industrial manufacturing techniques and using the railways for distribution. At its zenith early in the twentieth century, the company employed over 6,000 workers and the biscuits were exported worldwide. In addition to his business career, Palmer served as Mayor of Reading and represented the town as a Liberal Member of Parliament from 1878 to 1885. On one and the same day in November 1891, George Palmer was made an Honorary Freeman of Reading, a statue of George Palmer was unveiled in Broad Street, and Palmer Park (a gift of the Palmer family) was opened. In 1930, by which time the statue was becoming an obstacle to traffic flow, it was moved – appropriately – to Palmer Park. There, top hat and umbrella in hand, Palmer still stands today.

VC/SG (Hylton, S., *Reading Places, Reading People*, Berkshire Books, 1992)

AUGUST 20TH

1832: On this day, Holy Trinity Church in Reading's Oxford Road was consecrated, six years after it had opened. A contemporary account records: 'The attendance was numerous and respectable.' The church was built at the sole cost of Revd George Hulme, its first incumbent, to the design of E.W. Garbett. It was the last church built in Reading with burial vaults (catacombs) before they were outlawed. In 1845, the church's fabric required extensive repair. Revd William Phelps engaged local architect John Billing to carry out this work. He rebuilt the façade, replacing the tower with a bell gable and three lancet windows, and also raised the pitch of the roof. Phelps had a residence built for himself behind the church known as Trinity Parsonage, and designed two houses flanking it to the east (named Hulme Villas) and also a Sunday school. Shortly after this time, the church was photographed by pioneer photographer W.H. Fox Talbot, whose studio was in nearby Baker Street; Holy Trinity was probably the first church to be photographed. In 2011, about half the congregation, including the priest, elected to join the Ordinariate within the Roman Catholic Church because the Church of England General Synod seemed inclined to vote in favour of consecrating women bishops.

SD (*The History of Holy Trinity Church, Reading*, 1910)

AUGUST 21ST

1787: On this day, the Mayor and Corporation of Reading, attended by many of the town's principal inhabitants, processed from the Town Hall to Duke Street where the Mayor laid the first stone of the new High Bridge. This, constructed entirely of stone, would at great expense replace the old, unsafe, wooden bridge over the River Kennet. The *Reading Mercury* had carried an advertisement for contractors to build the bridge, announcing: 'The plans can be seen at the Council Chamber or with the architect Mr. Brettingham of London.' Work moved apace, it being recorded in November that the bridge was so near completion as to be passable by horsemen and carriages. The first person to cross the bridge on horseback, Mr Knight of Whitley, gave the workmen half a guinea to drink his health. A plaque on the Bridge itself reads: 'THIS BRIDGE WAS REBUILT BY THE CORPORATION ANNO DOMINI 1788.' The architect, Robert Furze Brettingham, was further engaged in 1791 to design a new County Gaol for Reading, but the justices were not satisfied with the result. Finding many faults, they resolved 'that Mr. Brettingham be never employed again by the County'. The present gaol was built in 1844 by Scott and Moffatt.

SG (*Reading Mercury*/Gold, S., *Dictionary of Architects at Reading*, 1999)

AUGUST 22ND

1874: On this day, at Reading Cricket Club, for the benefit of Trueman, the Club's professional bowler, a match was played between teams of one-armed and one-legged players. The efforts of the one-legged players in chasing the ball when fielding often resulted in a fall, and when a fielder could not get up again, much 'amusement' was afforded to the spectators. One one-legged man fell, broke his wooden leg and had to be carried from the field. The one-armed cricketers emerged victorious by 103 runs to 62.
NS (*Berkshire Chronicle*)

1905: On this day died Alfred Waterhouse RA, one of England's most distinguished nineteenth-century architects. Coming to Reading in 1867, he acquired land on the Whiteknights estate and built himself a house, Foxhill. Reading is blessed with numerous surviving buildings by Waterhouse, including the Town Hall, Reading School and chapel, Leighton Park School, St Bartholomew's Church and vicarage, Caversham Free Church (Baptist), Christ Church parsonage, the Rising Sun Institute, 'Somerleaze' and 'East Thorpe'. Nationally, Waterhouse is best known for Manchester Town Hall and the Natural History Museum. He was also an accomplished watercolour painter and exhibited often at the Royal Academy; while, with his wife, he produced 'arts and craft' work.
SG (Gold, S., *Dictionary of Architects at Reading*, 1999)

AUGUST 23RD

1796: On this day, a society was founded at the home of Mr John Prew at the Rising Sun in Castle Street, Reading (now known as 'the Sun'). 'Instituted on the 1st of August' in that year and 'established on the 23rd of the same Month', this body was a friendly society with some very laudable rules and regulations, which were published in a pamphlet reprinted by Snare and Man, Printers, Reading, in 1813. The members 'agreed to associate ourselves in unity and good-will to each other, and to the utmost of our power, promote good order, and support these our following Rules and Orders, for the good and benefit of every member belonging to us'. Membership was denied to members of 'any other Benefit Society, nor soldier, sailor, bargeman, brewer's servant, nor bricklayer's labourer, shall be admitted'. There was an entry fee of 'sixpence for the articles, and sixpence to the clerk' and every member subsequently had to pay at each meeting 'one shilling and threepence to the stock, and threepence to be spent'. The Society met at the inn on the last Tuesday of every month, from 7 to 10 p.m. in summer months and an hour earlier in winter.

JBD (Hamblin, I. & Dearing, J., 'This Sun of Reading', ms)

AUGUST 24TH

1829: On this day, William Pratt Swallow died. A worshipper at St Laurence's Church, Reading, he is buried there with his wife and several children. His obituary notice in the *Reading Mercury* recorded that: 'He was a man of strong mind who possessed a great religious feeling, untainted by bigotry and intolerance. Liberal in all his pursuits, he was ever ready to stand forward in defence of the rights and privileges of his fellow townsmen'. He resided at 'Swallows', Russell Street (now No. 2 Bath Road) – a large, detached, red-brick house built in the 1780s. He developed much of the property in the vicinity, particularly Prospect Street, Russell Street itself and Sydney Terrace on Oxford Road. Swallow was also a talented botanist and horticulturalist, and his knowledge in these matters was in demand from both noblemen and florists. It is plausible to suggest that the Marquis of Blandford, who was himself a botanist, may have sought his advice after purchasing the Whiteknights Estate in 1798 and that Swallow may, therefore, have contributed to the estate's international fame.
SD (Gold, S., *Dictionary of Architects at Reading*, 1999/ North, L., *Reading Chronicle*, 1983)

AUGUST 25TH

2004: On this day, English Heritage awarded Grade II listed status to Reading's historic Kings Meadow Ladies' Swimming Baths. Built beside the Thames in 1902, they were opened by Mayoress Mrs Holland Bull in May the following year as 'The Ladies Riverside Bath', the ceremony being attended by many local VIPs. The Kings Meadow had been given to the people of Reading in the 1890s by the famous philanthropist and biscuit manufacturer George Palmer, of Huntley & Palmers. The baths were 'ladies only' at first, with men being allowed access only for the annual Inter-School Gala. (The men had their own pool on the other side of the road, but this has long since disappeared.) Until 1952 the Baths were river fed. They continued in use until 1974, when they were closed for the installation of new filtration units – but were never again opened. By 2002, when the Kings Meadow Campaigners produced a plan for restoration, the building was in a sad state of decay. The gaining of listed status helped to stave off several development threats. The present structure, fundamentally the original building with minor late twentieth-century alterations, is the subject of a passionate campaign towards restoration to its former glory, for the enjoyment of the people of Reading. **VC** (Kings Meadow Baths website)

August 26th

1896: On this day, the new bandstand in Forbury Gardens was opened and used for the first time. In his speech the Mayor remarked that it had been something of a dream that a bandstand should eventually appear: today that dream had become reality. The committee had sought £350 for a handsome iron structure but, as so large a sum was not forthcoming, it was decided that, rather than let the idea fall into abeyance, a wooden bandstand would be constructed from the funds received so far. It was considered that a flat ceiling made of wood would act better as a sounding board than a domed one conventionally constructed of iron. The stand is octagonal, measuring 24ft across and 14ft high; the floor is raised 4ft above the ground with a large storage space below. The roof is of red tiles with an ornamental iron finial, the whole supported by elegant turned columns, brackets and iron diagonals from column to column. The architect of the whole project was George W. Webb. The Mayor having declared the bandstand open, the band of the Scots Greys played the National Anthem. Later in the day they were joined by the band of the Bedfordshire Regiment.

SG (*Berkshire Chronicle*)

AUGUST 27TH

1849: On this day, there occurred in Reading the death of fifty-seven-year-old Italian priest Father Dominic Barberi. Born in 1792 near Viterbo in the Papal States north of Rome, Barberi had been sent to England in 1841 as a member of the Passionist Order to propagate the Roman Catholic faith. He is perhaps best remembered for receiving John Henry Newman, the former leader of the Oxford-based Tractarian Movement, into the Catholic Church in 1845. He suffered a heart attack four years later on a railway journey from London to Worcester but, after leaving the train at Pangbourne, found that there was 'no room at the inn', as the two hotels in the village apparently suspected him of having contracted cholera in the 'big city'. So he was taken back to Reading where he died at the more compassionate Railway Tavern, Caversham Road (later the 'Duke of Edinburgh'; now demolished and replaced by flats). Father Dominic seems to have had a presentiment of his coming death and murmured 'Thy will be done' on reaching Reading. Beatified in 1963, Barberi shares the dedication of the Roman Catholic church in Earley with Our Lady of Peace.
JBD (Gwynn, D., *Father Dominic Barberi*, Burns and Oates, 1947)

AUGUST 28TH

1935: On this day, Reading's first evening newspaper, the *Evening Gazette*, was launched. Headline news was Mussolini's intention to send 20,000 troops to East Africa, while a new electric railway line to London was mooted. On the sporting scene, Steve Donoghue on 100-8 shot Museum won the Ebor Handicap at York. The *Gazette* folded soon after the outbreak of the Second World War.
NS (*Evening Gazette*)

———— ◆ ————

1943: On this day, top jockey Tommy Carey rushed from Ascot, where he had ridden five winners, to complete a Derby double at Cintra – the venue for the Reading Borough Special Constabulary's Horticultural Show and Fête. Earlier in the summer Carey had won the wartime English Derby at Newmarket on Miss Dorothy Paget's Straight Deal. This time round it was success in the Pony Derby on Mr G. Roe's George's Folly. In front of a crowd of 8,000, Carey saw off the challenge of Teddy Gardner and third-placed Michael Beary. Champion jockey Gordon Richards was unplaced on Capt L.A. Simonds' Mild Beer. There was plenty of amusement for the onlookers when the legendary Steve Donoghue finished 40 seconds behind the winner in a qualifying race. The profits from the event went to the Royal Berkshire Hospital.
NS (Local press reports)

AUGUST 29TH

1809: On this day, Reading was visited by Joseph Lancaster, a Quaker, who had been invited to give a lecture at Mr Letchworth's house on his Plan for the Education of Poor Children. This had come as a result of the success of his ideas for providing education free of charge. Ten years earlier, in 1798, he had opened a small purpose-built school in Borough Road, Southwark, at a time when there was no free system of education. Hanging outside the school was a sign which announced: 'All who will may send their children and have them educated freely, and those who do not wish to have education for nothing, may pay for it if they please.' The school had grown rapidly and within a few years he was teaching over 1,000 pupils. Lancaster could not afford to pay any assistants, so he devised a plan using a monitorial system, under which a single master could oversee a class whilst older pupils, known as 'monitors', taught the younger ones. The system worked with military efficiency. The result of Lancaster's visit to Reading was the founding in 1810 of the British School in Reading's Southampton Street.

VC (Barnes-Phillips, D., *This is Our School*, Corridor Press, 2011)

AUGUST 30TH

1926: On this day, fire broke out at Caversham Park, then occupied by the Oratory School. No one was hurt, no boys being present in August, but the damage, which included the loss of over 150 beds, and a room panelled in silk and said to be alone worth £2,000, topped £25,000. The matron, awakened by the smell of burning, roused the headmaster and together they gathered and stacked outside as much furniture as they could. Five fire brigades attended the scene. Fortunately the recently erected chapel emerged unscathed. The BBC took over Caversham Park in 1942 for its overseas monitoring station. Currently the building also houses BBC Radio Berkshire.
VC (*Reading Mercury*)

———•—•———

1944: On this day, aged ninety-five, died John Owen Bowen, Reading's Borough Surveyor (1894-1923), who 'retired' at seventy-four but continued as 'consultant' until his death! It was he who upgraded late-Victorian and Edwardian Reading, and to him we owe many features which we still enjoy, such as Prospect Park, Kings Meadow, Thames-Side Promenade, and the green spaces of Tilehurst and Caversham. He improved Reading's water supply and road system and insisted that new buildings be equipped with adequate fire escapes. He deserves to be better remembered.
JRW (*Berkshire Chronicle/Reading Standard*)

AUGUST 31ST

1688: On this day, John Bunyan died following a visit to Reading. Born near Bedford in 1628, the son of a tinker, Bunyan is best known for his writings, especially the first part of *The Pilgrim's Progress*, which appeared in 1678. But he was also a prominent preacher in the Baptist cause and, as such, paid periodic visits to Reading. It is said that, in order to avoid recognition, he would travel through the town dressed as a waggoner; but on one occasion it is believed that the disguise slipped and he was briefly imprisoned in the old County Gaol in Castle Street, on the site of which St Mary's chapel now stands. He made his final visit in order to reconcile a father, a member of the Reading church, with his erring son, one Mark Whelham, who lived in Bedford. As a result of Bunyan's intervention 'the father was mollified, and his bowels yearned towards his returning son'. Mission accomplished, Bunyan preached to the congregation from a boathouse beside the Kennet, riding back to London the following day through driving rain in order to fulfil a preaching engagement. His drenching brought on the chill from which he died.

VC/JBD (Cousin, J., *A Short Biographical Dictionary of English literature*, 1910)

September 1st

1939: On this day, a Friday, the mass evacuation of some 25,000 adults and children from London to Reading commenced. The first batch arrived on an electric train from Vauxhall at 10.10 a.m. and found everything at the Southern Railway station in readiness to receive them. The evacuation programme continued during the weekend until the colossal task was finished with 1.5 million in total leaving the capital. The tremendous and varied influx of persons, including babies, schoolchildren, expectant mothers, hospital patients and others in need of refuge during the imminent war, called for almost superhuman endeavour on the part of the Reading officials and voluntary workers. Fleets of Corporation buses were utilised to convey children from the station to the schools which were used as distribution centres. Motorbuses, vans and lorries were adapted for use as ambulances, and buses and lorries were also requisitioned for the conveyance of the evacuees' luggage. Everything went well, thanks to the very detailed planning beforehand and to the many billeting officers who had secured accommodation. The whole exercise had come under the control of Mr Merriman, Chief Education Officer and Mr Winning, Welfare Officer, acting as his deputy.
SG (*Berkshire Chronicle*)

September 2nd

1756: On this day, John Rowell was registered at St Giles, Reading, as having died with a mortuary fee of 10s paid for his burial at High Wycombe. Three years earlier the *Reading Mercury* published his advertisement: 'John Rowell late of Wycombe, Bucks but now of Reading professor of the ancient art of staining glass having no son to succeed him, doth therefore for the encouragement and improvement of that curious art propose to teach same to any proper person for a reasonable consideration.' Born in London in 1689, Rowell settled early at High Wycombe where the family had lived; here he set up in business as a plumber, glazier and sundial maker. By the 1730s he was able to add stained-glass painter to his skills. In 1712 he married Mary Berry, by whom he had seven children. All predeceased him and Mary herself died in 1739. Rowell moved to London Street, Reading, in 1737. He was married a second time to Margaret House, who died in 1765 and is buried at Caversham. Rowell's work includes the *Adoration of the Shepherds* after Van Dyck, now at The Vyne, and a fragment depicting Aaron at Arborfield Church.
SG (Gold, S., *John Rowell*, 1965)

September 3rd

1808: On this day, Laurenthes Braag died – so reads the memorial stone on the outside wall of St Mary's Church, Reading. Born on the Caribbean island of St Croix in 1783, he was one of approximately 7,000 Danish prisoners of war held by the British during the Napoleonic Wars. During the period 1805-9 almost 900 prisoners from four different countries were on parole in Reading. Braag himself arrived in November 1807. The prisoners soon settled into English life and became part of the local community; many lodged locally and some even married Reading girls. Braag, who had been a merchant, was one of about six who died while on parole; the respect that he had gained for himself was such that his friends raised the memorial to him. It became almost illegible, but in 2009 Reading Civic Society raised money from subscribers for its restoration. There had been a second stone to Knud Fredericksen, but this is lost, probably broken during work to the south aisle. To mark the Golden Jubilee of George III, a general amnesty was granted to the 'Gentlemen Danes' but it came too late for Braag who had died a year earlier.

SG (Nixon, J., *The Gentlemen Danes*, Berkshire Old and New, 1993)

SEPTEMBER 4TH

1752: On this day, as on all the days from 3 to 13 September, nothing happened in Reading or anywhere else in England. These days simply did not exist, thanks to the change from the Julian to the Gregorian calendar.
AS (Holford-Stevens, L., *The History of Time*, OUP, 2005)

———— ◆ ————

1946: On this day, Reading Football Club ran up double figures in a league match for the only time in their history. In their first post-war home Division 3 South league game, they inflicted a 10–2 humiliation on Crystal Palace before a Wednesday night crowd of 8,000. The Biscuitmen took the lead through a Jackie Deverall centre which deceived the Palace keeper on a grey, windy evening, before debutant Vic Barney and Maurice Edelston added two further goals; but Palace pegged it back to 3–2 by half-time. Two minutes into the second half came the turning point, when Tony MacPhee was fouled and Edelston scored from the spot. With Palace losing heart, goals followed at regular intervals – four from MacPhee and one apiece from Deverall and hat-trick man Edelston. Three days later, Reading amazingly followed this feat with a 7–2 home win over Southend; MacPhee and Edelston once again grabbed hat-tricks.
NS (Local press reports)

September 5th

2012: On this day, students of Reading Blue Coat School returned after their holidays to a brand-new twenty-five-room humanities block, in addition to recently built science labs and a sixth form centre. What a contrast to what their predecessors found when the school opened in 1660! The will of Reading-born London merchant Richard Aldworth, in 1646, stipulated precisely that his legacy was to provide for 'twenty poore male children' who would board in the school to be founded in his name. Reading Corporation, charged with administering the will, were to provide '10 bedsteads for the 20 children with bolsters, sheets, blankets, coverlets …' and for each boy 'the sum of £6:13:4 for meat, drink and cloathing yearly and every year for ever'; but no building was provided for! Keen to avoid expense, the Corporation chose the vacated Talbot Inn at the corner of London Road and Silver Street. Here the school remained for nearly 200 years, until Brunswick House, Bath Road, was acquired in 1853. In 1947, a final move was made to spacious parklands at Sonning. On special occasions senior students still wear blue coats and yellow stockings, as specified in Aldworth's will.

PMS (Burgess, H., *History of Reading Blue Coat School*, 1977)

SEPTEMBER 6TH

1939: On this day, the first Wednesday of the Second World War, Reading's inhabitants were peacefully starting a new day when, at 7.30 a.m., the onset of war was brought home to them by the wailing of air-raid sirens sounding 'The Alert'. Townspeople going to work entered the nearest shelter and Civil Defence personnel and police stopped all traffic apart from Air Raid Precautions vehicles, while wardens wearing protective clothing and steel helmets emerged from their posts to deal with any emergency occasioned by enemy action. Most people early in the war were very jittery – air raids were a new experience and gas attacks were fully expected, hence the issue of gas masks to everyone. However, on this occasion the alert was a false alarm. The 'All Clear' sounded at 9 o'clock and folk scurried off to work. Local police, overwhelmed by nearly 1,000 telephone calls seeking information, requested through the local press that the public should in future refrain from asking questions and simply obey instructions given by wardens and other officials. Air-raid alerts proved extremely disruptive of life, not least the war effort, and it soon became usual not to take cover until absolutely necessary.

JRW (*Reading Standard*)

SEPTEMBER 7TH

1907: On this day, Ada Matilda Shrimpton, fifty-one, married William Giles, thirty-five, in Venice, thus uniting two inspirational artists who had met at the Reading School of Art in 1883 – when he was just a schoolboy and she a mature student. To what extent their paths crossed at this early stage is not known, but later it was their interest in the technique of wood-block printing in colour using the Japanese method that drew them together. Ada was born at Old Alresford in 1856, daughter of George Shrimpton and Elizabeth Blake, and educated at Queens College, London. After working as a governess, she moved to Reading in 1883, staying with a cousin, Eliza Hawkes, in Hamilton Road. While still a student in Reading, in February 1885 she gave a series of lectures on artistic anatomy. Later gaining a scholarship at the National Art Training School, South Kensington, she became known as a watercolourist and went to Paris to study oil painting, exhibiting at the Salon and at the Royal Academy. She exhibited over thirty works at the Society of Women Artists. Ada died on 3 February 1925 at the Eastern Avenue home of her sister, Mrs Elizabeth Warren, and is buried at Caversham Cemetery.
SG (*Reading Mercury*)

September 8th

1782: On this day, the traveller, John Byng, Viscount Torrington, rode into Reading, accompanied by 'a conversable farmer' he met on the way. 'On entering Reading, I bade adieu to my civil acquaintance and stay'ed two hours at an inn there, to send a letter and await the answer' before journeying on. On a later visit in 1787 Byng stayed at the Black Bear, complaining of the 'sour and weak punch' and damp sheets. **JBD** (Byng, J., *Rides Round Britain*, Folio Society, 1996)

———◆———

2011: On this day, David Walliams, forty-year-old comic writer and actor, reached Caversham Lock halfway through his 140-mile, eight-day Thames swim, which raised over £1 million for the charity Sport Relief. Walliams' journey began at Lechlade on 5 September; the following days saw him safely through Oxford and Wallingford until, as he neared Reading, normal aches and pains turned to vomiting and diarrhoea. (Although the Thames was 'biologically dead' fifty years ago, it is now home to 125 fish species – as well as bacteria such as E.coli and salmonella.) After recovering overnight at Reading, Walliams swam on determinedly, supported by his wife, cheering fans and celebrity friends including Lenny Henry, to finish at Westminster Bridge four days later. **PV** (National and local media)

September 9th

2009: On this day, Reading's Hobgoblin pub (Broad Street) chalked up the 6,000th different real ale served in the pub since it reopened in 1993. That works out at slightly more than one a day! Said to have been called the Cock until the mid-nineteenth century, the pub then operated for 150 years as the London Tavern, latterly in the Courage (formerly Simonds) estate. During the 1950s it was haunted by the Lemonade Man, who would sink eight pints of fizzy drink while watching TV in the bar. After some years of decline, it was then acquired by the Wychwood Brewery of Witney, Oxon, who the following year renamed it after its flagship beer. Landlady Katrina Leszczynska ordered a special brew as the 6,000th beer from local brewery Ascot Ales; this sold out in a matter of hours despite being of a fairly heavy strength for daytime drinking! No longer owned by Wychwood, the Hobgoblin was renamed the Alehouse in 2012 but continues with the tradition of serving up unusual and distinctive beers to Reading's drinking classes with the 7,000th currently on the horizon. By the time you read this it will almost certainly have arrived!

JBD (*Reading Evening Post*)

SEPTEMBER 10TH

1927: On this day occurred the funeral of Miss Matilda Knighton at St Peter's Church, Caversham, where her father had long been organist and choirmaster. Born in 1839, Matilda, along with her sister Rosa, ran Hemdean House School, a ladies' boarding establishment, which had been founded by her father in 1859. The school won an admirable reputation and Matilda continued there until 1926, only retiring because of failing health. She was described as 'a smiling, kindly old lady' and 'many thousands of girls all over England' are said to have been 'educated under her care'. For most of her time in charge, Matilda was the sole schoolmistress, with the help of various assistants and governesses. In the available census returns, pupils are listed from all over the United Kingdom, as well as from overseas – India, Ireland, South Africa, Egypt, Chile and Canada, to name but a few. Miss Knighton gave communion benches to St Peter's when the church was extended. There is also a Knighton memorial window in the Lady Chapel of the church, portraying St Peter holding a model of the church as it would have appeared in 1878.

VC (North, L., *Royal Reading's Colourful Past*, Cressrelles, 1979)

September 11th

1830: On this day, the *Berkshire Chronicle* reported a 'celebration of the proud triumph achieved by the Blue party in this borough', not marred by 'those vituperative and hostile traits which too often distinguish such festivals'. In 1830, Britain blazed with debate about electoral reform. At a time when Reading's electorate numbered only 1,200 from a population nearing 16,000, the Whig *Reading Mercury* fervently advocated reform, opposed by the Conservative *Chronicle*. Although one Reading MP, Charles Fysshe Palmer, was a Whig, the Tory Charles Russell now became Reading's other Member and his party was jubilant. At the subsequent 'Blue Dinner', Russell was honoured guest, in a hall 'hung with boughs, evergreens and flowers', decorated with banners and Russell's arms. 'The *tout ensemble* was splendid, and when lighted up had a brilliant and most imposing appearance.' Over 590 persons enjoyed the banquet, which included a baron of beef weighing 266lb (120kg). The leftovers were distributed to 250 Reading families – whether Tory supporters or the 'deserving poor' was not reported. Despite Russell's opposition, the 1832 Reform Act was passed, enfranchising millions and ending many abuses; the Whigs' celebration dinner at the Crown Inn duly followed. **PV** (*Berkshire Chronicle*/Phillips, D., *Story of Reading*, Countryside Books, 1990)

September 12th

1783: On this day, the thriving township of Reading in the state of Pennsylvania was incorporated as a borough. The English Quaker William Penn had founded Pennsylvania a century previously, as a haven of religious tolerance. In 1710, back in England, he came to Ruscombe, 5 miles from Reading, where he died in 1718. He probably attended the Friends Meeting House situated in Sims Court, off London Street. Reading, PA, owes its proud name not directly to Penn but to his son Thomas, who inherited William's American properties. Reviewing his inheritance, Thomas noticed one promising settlement on the Schuylkill River, which he developed, naming it 'Reading' in 1748. By 1752 it had achieved the status of county seat of 'Berkshire', becoming a city in 1847. Its present population is just over 88,000. The writer John Updike was born in Reading, and John Philip Sousa died there in 1932. England's Berkshire does not seem to have been a source of emigration to Pennsylvania on any large scale. However, emigrants' stories must lie behind Reading's transatlantic namesakes elsewhere, in Illinois, Iowa, Kansas, Maryland, Michigan, Nebraska, Ohio and Vermont. The connection of our English Reading to these places is yet to be uncovered.

PV (*Oxford Dictionary of National Biography*, OUP, 2004)

September 13th

1912: On this day, the council's Highways and Lighting Committee met and decided that 'the question of the desirableness of shortening the chains by which the drinking cups are attached to the public fountain at Whitley so as to prevent the cups from being dipped into the cattle trough at the foot of the fountain be referred to the Borough Surveyor for attention'.

AS (Council records)

1944: On this day, the actress Jacqueline Bisset was born in Weybridge. The daughter of a GP and lawyer turned housewife, she grew up in a 400-year-old cottage in the Tilehurst area of Reading. A fluent French speaker, Bisset took acting and ballet lessons and modelled fashions to pay for them. She made her screen debut in 1965, but her first speaking part came the following year in *Cul-de-sac*. Her many subsequent films and TV appearances include *Murder on the Orient Express*, *Casino Royale*, *Joan of Arc*, *Ally McBeal* and *Rizzoli and Isles*. She received the *Légion d'honneur* in 2010. In spite of several long-term romances, Jacqueline Bisset has never married, stating that caring for her chronically ill mother got in the way of personal relationships. She now divides her time between homes in England and Beverly Hills.

VC (*Hello!*)

SEPTEMBER 14TH

1538: On this day, the shrine of Our Lady of Caversham was desecrated. Thomas Cromwell, Henry VIII's Vicar-general, had sent Dr John London, a canon of Windsor and Warden of New College, Oxford, as Commissioner to ascertain the wealth of Reading Abbey and report on its conduct. London's report to Cromwell stated that Reading Abbey was well run and had an income of around £2,000 a year: 'the monks have a good lecture in scripture daily read in their Chapter House, both in English and Latin, to which is good resort and the Abbot is at it himself'. This placed it in the 'safe zone', as those religious houses with incomes of £200 per year or less were suppressed by Act of Parliament, and their properties passed to the King. On 14 September, Dr London wrote to Cromwell: 'Today I will go to Caversham, a mile from Reading, where is great pilgrimage, and send the image up to Your Lordship's place in London.' That image was the statue of Our Lady of Caversham, which was torn from its shrine, nailed inside a box, and sent up to London by barge. Reading Abbey survived for a further year.

VC (Phillips, D., *The Story of Reading*, Countryside Books, 1999)

SEPTEMBER 15TH

1937: On this day died Montague Wheeler. He was born in 1874, the son of Samuel Wheeler (1849-1913), a well-known local builder, surveyor and brick maker, founder of the Tilehurst Potteries, and grandson of another Samuel Wheeler, brickmaker of the Coley Kilns. Educated at Marlborough College and later Trinity Hall, Cambridge, Montague Wheeler declined to enter the family business but became articled to Edward Warren, an architect known to his father who had acted as his builder when constructing St John's Church, Caversham, in 1887/8. Edward Barclay Hoare also worked in the office of Warren and eventually, in 1898, the two formed a partnership which endured till the death of Wheeler in 1937, trading as Hoare & Wheeler. The firm had offices at 17 Friar Street, Reading and 63 Caversham Road, and designed St Mark's Church, Reading (1904), King Edward Buildings, Station Road (1903) as well as Wheeler's own residence known as 'Whitley Glebe' (*c.* 1900) in Glebe Road, Reading. His best-known work outside Reading was the Rudolf Steiner House, Park Road, NW1 for the Anthroposophical Society of which Wheeler was a member. His son, Samuel Dennis Wheeler-Carmichael, was also an architect.

SG (Gold, S., *Dictionary of Architects at Reading*, 1999)

SEPTEMBER 16TH

1953: On this day, several families in Reading and other local towns were rejoicing at the safe arrival in Southampton of the Royal Mail Lines' *SS Asturias*. This ship was repatriating 600 members of the British armed forces from war-torn Korea to the UK. Two of the returning men, Privates Clark and Marshall, hailed from Reading, and on arrival in Southampton the soldiers were greeted by the Band of the 1st Battalion Gloucester Regiment, before returning home to their families. The two men later shared with the local press their experiences of imprisonment. They described how they had been captured at the Battle of Imjin River in April 1951 and endured a twenty-one-day forced march in the inhospitable climate and difficult terrain of North Korea, relieved only by a couple of rest days and little food. When later they were held in prison camps they declared that the food was better but conditions were boring. Those who tried to escape suffered very harsh punishment by their captors. The young men were looking forward to being welcomed back to their old lives in Reading. In all, the Korean War claimed more than three million dead over a period of three years, of whom 686 were British.

JP (*Berkshire Chronicle*)

SEPTEMBER 17TH

1875: On this day, Edward Jackson opened the doors of his small gentlemen's outfitters shop at 6 High Street, Reading, starting the family-run department stores that continued for over 135 years – Jacksons. Edward was born to retailing! He would skip school to help in his parents' shop at Sherfield-on-Loddon. Aged only twenty-five, he decided to 'go it alone', specialising in menswear and boys' clothing. The company gradually expanded, first to a hardware department in Duke Street, and, finally, in the 1950s, to Henley and Camberley. By Edwardian times the firm's range included sports goods. Edward Jackson was elected Mayor of Reading in 1905 and died in 1928 aged seventy-eight. Soon, the increasing trade demanded a fleet of delivery vans. Jacksons survived the difficult war years and later became outfitters to many schools. In the 1960s expansion continued when the firm bought up the Saracen's Head pub, between the two High Street branches, and installed the Lamson pneumatic tube system to facilitate the handling of payments. The branches closed long ago but the high ceilings, display cabinets and interior fittings at Jackson's Corner represented a unique part of Reading's history. However, at the time of writing the future of Jacksons is in doubt.

JRS (Macey, T., *Jacksons: The Story of Reading's Oldest Family Owned Department Store*, 2009)

SEPTEMBER 18TH

2004: On this day, eighty-eight-year-old Mary Turner, a parishioner of St Luke's, Reading, died. Her father was killed in the Royal Flying Corps soon after her birth in Aldeburgh; her pilot brother, Godfrey, was a casualty of the Second World War. The family moved to Reading, Mary going to the Abbey School where she became Head Girl and Godfrey to Reading School. Mary began her life-long interest in youth work at Reading Girls Youth Club in Chain Street, later taking a training course in East London. In the late 1930s she worked with the Bermondsey Club but, after war was declared, she ran three community halls that housed 600 'Dockland' residents evacuated from the Blitz. Mary often spent nights with them under the shelter of London Bridge! She became leader of Poplar Youth Club where she once turned away two trouble-making lads whose names became notorious years later – the Kray twins. Later she became a deaconess; an overhanging church balcony protected her from a direct V2 hit during a service. Returning to Reading in 1958 to nurse her mother, she was appointed the Bishop's Lay Ministry Adviser at a time when three deaconesses covered 500 parishes. When she retired, aged seventy, her efforts had brought about a huge increase in the female diaconate.

JRS (*The Grapevine*, Parish Magazine)

September 19th

1908: On this day, the West Reading Adult School was opened at the junction of Gloucester Road with Kensington Road. The Society of Friends was active in the adult schools movement and organised several centres across the town at Church Street, Bridge Street, Norris Road, and at 63 Catherine Street; there was also a branch in Caversham. Catherine Street could take up to fifty students, but soon there was a need to expand and a new hall was built to accommodate 150. Robert Curtis, an experienced local builder, erected the new hall; glass and lighting were given free and the glazing and painting was undertaken by the members. There were classes at 9 a.m and 3.30 p.m on Sundays for men and women respectively. A directory at the time referred to the school as 'for social and biblical subjects democratic and undenominational'. Later additions included a social and slate club and lectures but, as the years passed, these activities waned and eventually ceased. The premises continued to be available for community activities. Battle School, opposite, utilised the hall in the 1960s and '70s as an overflow classroom. Today it is used by a multicultural playgroup.
SG (Anon, A brief history of the Gloucester Road Adult School and Centre/*Reading Standard*, 1908)

September 20th

1934: On this day, for the first time, Reading Corporation Transport bus tickets were printed on a plain paper roll from a TIM ticket machine. This had a telephone dial on top which the conductor used to select the correct fare and the ticket was issued by turning a handle. Previously, before the TIMs arrived, conductors carried a ticket rack with pads of ready-printed tickets of different values, which were inserted in a punch the conductor wore on a strap round his neck, together with his money satchel.

JRW (Reading Corporation Transport records)

———— ◆ ————

1943: On this day, an auction was held at the Central Liberal Club, Reading, in conjunction with a charity billiards and snooker exhibition. Some items were donated by No.10 Downing Street, including an oil painting of Winston Churchill which fetched £10, together with two of his cigars which went for £2 10s. All proceeds were in aid of the Duke of Gloucester's Red Cross POW Fund. The billiards exhibition was between women's champion Joyce Gardner of Gloucester and Arthur Goundrill (Northampton), the one-armed champion. Miss Gardner won 185–85, then teamed up with Goundrill for a snooker match against top local players Ballard and Newman – and lost.

NS (Local press reports)

SEPTEMBER 21ST

1927: On this day, the chapels at the Henley Road Cemetery, designed by Gerald Berkeley Wills, were consecrated. Fifty-two years later the *Berkshire Chronicle* of 4 May 1979 carried the following report:

> The architect who designed the Reading Crematorium has had his dying wish granted. Mr Gerald Berkeley Wills had a soft spot for the Reading building and requested he be buried there. He died in another building he designed, Marlow Cottage Hospital, and last week he was cremated at the Reading Crematorium. Aged 96 Mr Berkeley Wills designed many public buildings including a number of public houses in the Reading area as well as numerous country houses.

A pupil and later assistant to Sir Reginald Blomfield, Wills opened his own office at 7 Stone Buildings, Lincoln's Inn, in 1909 and shortly afterwards an office at Marlow where he remained till his death. The public houses mentioned in the newspaper report, not all of which survive, are the Alfred's Head, Butchers Arms, Marquess of Granby, The Pond House, The Roundabout and the Tudor Arms, mostly for Wethered & Sons of Marlow. He also designed Harpsden Village Hall and Kensal Green Crematorium. He was elected ARIBA in 1908 and a Fellow in 1924.

SG (Royal Institute of British Architects records)

SEPTEMBER 22ND

1802: On this day, Reading's famous Michaelmas Cheese Fair was held, the *Mercury* reporting that 'a vast quantity of cheese was pitched for sale'. From medieval times, around St Michael's feast-day, the Cheese Fair far surpassed Reading's February, May and July cattle fairs. This fair also 'pitched' hops and cloth, and St Laurence's church-walk was a venue for hiring male and female servants. Outgrowing Fisher's Row, adjoining the Market Place, it occupied the Forbury by 1697. Roundabouts, swings, peep-shows, animals and pickpockets invariably enlivened the scene. In 1820, young James Sherman, newly arrived in Reading, gained his reputation as a preacher when he denounced the Fair's worldly excesses. Cheese traded reached 1,200 tons by 1795, probably its high point. Coates described 'many thousand tons of cheese, annually brought from the dairy counties and sold in the Forbery', and noted that 'The tract of Canal now opened facilitates the exportation of cheese, the great staple of North Wiltshire'. Carriage by canal cost three times less than over land but, even so, the Fair slowly declined, down to 700 tons in 1836. The railway, offering direct access to London's wholesalers, dealt the final death-blow, and Michaelmas Cheese Fair expired in 1869.

PV (Coates, C., *History and Antiquities of Reading*, 1802/ *Reading Mercury*)

September 23rd

1560: On this day, Queen Elizabeth I gave the town what has been called 'The Magna Carta of Reading'. Although not the borough's first Charter, it authorised much greater self-government, under a Mayor, nine head-burgesses and twelve secondary burgesses, whose powers and responsibilities were comprehensively defined. The Mayor would appoint constables and watchmen, and, *ex officio*, act as a JP. The Corporation would maintain the Counter, a prison for felons awaiting trial and those convicted; and monitor weights and measures used in selling bread, ale, wine, fish and spices. Perceiving Reading's 'decayed state', the Queen transferred to the Corporation much property formerly owned by religious houses; it would henceforth enjoy the fines from local courts and tolls from the ancient St Philip and St James fairs, from two new fairs and the weekly market. In return, the Corporation had to repair the bridges, nineteen of which were termed 'very ruinous', and to this end Elizabeth granted wood and stone – thirty oak trees from Whitley royal manor and 200 loads from Reading Abbey's ruins. This Charter also defined the borough boundaries, which remained unchanged until the nineteenth century.

PV (Coates, C., *History and Antiquities of Reading*, 1802)

September 24th

1898: On this day, club rugby came to town as Berkshire Wanderers RFC, now Reading RFC, played their first ever game at the County Cricket ground, Kensington Road. Admission was 3*d*, enclosure 6*d*, but ladies were admitted free. The opposition was a London XV, and the local press reported that 'no such galaxy of talent had ever been seen on a Rugby Football field in the district'. The Wanderers side, which won 19–6, was by no means lacking in star players, including four internationals, full back Field, centre Leslie-Jones, fly-half Rotherham and forward Jacob, in their line-up. The match was refereed by RFU secretary G. Rowland-Hill, and the *Reading Observer* confirmed that further games had been arranged against Redhill & Reigate, Surbiton, Portsmouth and 'other good clubs'. The first meeting of the Berkshire Wanderers had been held only a week earlier at Kensington Road when RFU president Roger Walker was elected in a similar capacity at the new club. Vice-presidents included George Palmer MP and other local figures such as the headmasters of Wellington College and Reading School. Oozing ambition, Mr D.H. Evans suggested a match should be arranged with Llanelly and offered to use his influence to set up the fixture.

NS (*Reading Observer* and other local newspapers)

SEPTEMBER 25TH

1967: On this day, a Board of Enquiry was convened to investigate the allegations of inhumane treatment at Reading Borstal by members of the staff. These had been published in the *People* newspaper on 17 September under the headline: 'Brutality at Borstal'. Among the many complaints it was alleged that 'officers had slapped, even beaten, recalcitrant prisoners and that others had been forced into baths of near-scalding water. Verbal abuse was constant, and complaints to the Board of Visitors went unheeded'. The prison authorities, uncharacteristically, acted quickly and within a week had set up the five-man Board of Enquiry to look into the matter. The Board was thorough in its investigations, with both officers and prisoners called to give evidence. In March 1968 James Callaghan, Home Secretary, reported to Parliament that there was substance to the allegations, and that a pattern of behaviour had grown up over time among some of the officers, who believed that discipline could be imposed by force rather than by personality and example. The future Prime Minister informed the house that, although the malpractices had ceased, the Borstal was to close and the establishment revert to its former rôle as a prison. This was put into effect on 14 January 1969.

VC (Southerton, P., *Reading Gaol by Reading Town*, Alan Sutton, 1993)

September 26th

1964: On this day, a Saturday, one of Reading's trolleybuses, suitably decorated with white ribbon, acted as wedding transport for a newly married couple. David and Jenny Embery tied the knot at West Reading Methodist Church in Oxford Road and were conveyed, together with a bus-load of their wedding guests, to the Upper Deck in Duke Street. Because of the layout of Reading's trolleybus overhead wiring, this required a trip beyond Duke Street, along Mill Lane and round the depot to turn round, so that the entourage could leave the vehicle in Duke Street in safety on the correct side of the road! Although extensively reported in the following day's Sunday papers, this was not the first occasion that a Reading trolleybus was so used. On 4 December 1943 one was used to convey a wedding party from the church of St Mary-the-Virgin in the Butts to the reception at the Caversham Bridge Hotel, adjacent to the Promenade terminus. In the wartime conditions prevailing at the time, in particular petrol rationing, putting a trolleybus to such use was not so much a novelty as a necessity. The vehicle was actually hired by councillor Bennet Palmer, Chairman of the Transport Committee – for 'ten bob' (50p)!

JRW (Hall, D.A., *Reading Trolleybuses*, Trolleybooks, 1991)

SEPTEMBER 27TH

1859: On this day died John James Tagg, aged fifty-seven, proprietor of Reading's Bear Inn for some thirty years. He was probably born at the old inn, which had been acquired in 1801 by his father, James, formerly cook to Viscount Palmerston, father of the future Prime Minister. James rebuilt the inn and it became a popular venue for parties, as in 1814 when 'the birthday of Mr Pitt was celebrated … by a humorous and respectable meeting of gentlemen of this town' and 1830 when a grand dinner marked the retirement of Dr Valpy from Reading School. John James took over in around 1827 and, during his tenure, the Bear operated its own brewery. Its fortunes declined with the demise of the coaching era. In 1897 it was acquired by Simonds and, in 1938, landlord Bert Rex called last orders for the last time.

JBD (Darter, W., *Reminiscences of Reading by an Octogenarian*, 1888/Dearing, J., *Reading Pubs*, The History Press, 2009)

———◆———

1994: On this day opened the first Reading Beer Festival sponsored by the Campaign for Real Ale, held at the Trade Union Club in Chatham Street. The theme 'Beer Round Berkshire' highlighted the fact that no traditional beer was brewed in the modern county.

JBD (Personal records)

SEPTEMBER 28TH

1961: On this day, 350 citizens attended a meeting at the Town Hall, summoned by Eric Knell, Bishop of Reading. Following speeches by the Bishop, the Mayor, John Betjeman and Sir John Wolfenden, Vice-Chancellor of the university, preparations were made towards the formation of the town's Civic Society. In December the Bishop reported progress. The executive committee had just held its first meeting at which three sub-committees were formed, dealing with public relations, the streets of Reading (including the proposed ring road) and the rivers.

> A programme of monthly meetings to stimulate interest among our members is being drawn up … I ought perhaps to make it clear that we are not a Reading Complaints Society and are not anxious to receive letters from people complaining of this and that which offends them. We are out to save what is worth saving of our old buildings, to see what can be done in cleaning up our streets, festooned as they are … with wires and signs and poor advertisements and choked with traffic, and to keep a watchful eye on whatever is proposed in the way of 'development'.

The Society has waged many campaigns over its first half century, notably saving the Town Hall, Mansion House and the Polish church (formerly St John's).
AS (*Reading Mercury*)

SEPTEMBER 29TH

1953: On this day, the Biro Pen Manufacturing Company, which had been producing the very first ball point pens in premises on Woodley Aerodrome near Reading, went into liquidation. This news was formally announced in the *London Gazette* on 6 October and led to large-scale redundancies in the local area, hitting its mainly female workforce hard. The concept of a ball point pen had been successfully developed by the Hungarian Laszlo Josef Biro, from an American idea, and he patented the design in 1943. F.G. Miles, plane designer and innovator, based in Woodley, recognised the potential and entered into partnership with an American company in 1944, to market and produce the pens, the first of which retailed at 55s (£2.75). By mid-1947 the company had earned between £100,000 and £150,000, but a dispute over faulty refills led to a loss of £64,000 within a few months. The company later returned to profitability and at its peak produced tens of millions of biros. However, a final dispute between the marketing and the production wings of the joint venture resulted in the company being placed into liquidation and production moving to Theale, west of Reading.

JP (*London Gazette*/Temple, J.C., *Wings over Woodley*, Aston, 1987)

September 30th

1728: On this day, John Watts was for the second time sworn in as Mayor of Reading, Justice of the Peace, and 'Clark of the Markett'. The vicar of St Mary's, the Revd Francis Fox, preached an excellent sermon before the Mayor and aldermen that day, suitable to the occasion. After the business of the court was ended 'about one of the clock', those present sat down to dinner, and spent the rest of the day in conversation until they finally 'departed in good order'.

VC (Burton, K. (Ed.), *Memorandums of John Watts, Esq. Mayor of Reading*, 1950)

———•◆•———

1907: On this day, the Palace Theatre was opened in Cheapside opposite McIlroy's store. The theatre, designed to seat 1,460, had high-quality upholstered seats while the auditorium was lit by a gold electric chandelier with matching circle and gallery lights. The management was said to be well satisfied with demand for admission at both houses on the opening Monday night. Apparently the best turn of that first evening was a troupe of lady acrobats, while others included a musical novelty act by the Three Phydoras, some amazing card and coin tricks by the Card King, and a comedian named Rowland Hill.

NS (Local press reports)

OCTOBER 1st

1927: On this day, Frederick Stokes, the first England rugby captain, opened the new Old Redingensians RFC headquarters at Emmer Green. The 19.5-acre site provided room for two pitches, a cricket square and grazing by livestock. Stokes, a seventy-seven-year-old, performed the ceremony before OR's 3–0 victory over Thames Valley. In 1871, Stokes had accepted the challenge to play Scotland at Edinburgh, skippering a team of twenty which was beaten in a match of fifty minutes each way. **NS** (Local newspapers)

—— • ——

2011: On this day, temperature records were shattered as high pressure to the east brought in warm southerly winds from North Africa and Spain. The mercury rose to over 29°C (84°F) in Reading, higher than had been recorded in early autumn in the last 100 years! Swimming gear was taken out of drawers where it had languished over a miserable summer, barbecues were wheeled out of garages, and Reading basked in temperatures normally associated with the Mediterranean! Hundreds flocked to Forbury Gardens, enticed by the aromas of freshly baked bread and spiced curry, on the occasion of the first Town Meal, served up by Food4Families, a Lottery-funded project designed at encouraging all to 'grow your own'. **JRS** (*Reading Chronicle*/Reading University Climatological Station)

OCTOBER 2ND

1929: On this day, the inquest opened at Reading's Coroner's Court on local tobacconist Alfred Oliver, who had been murdered in his Cross Street shop. Witnesses claimed that the American actor Philip Yale Drew, on tour with his company in Reading, had been seen near the shop at the time of death. The inquest ended up being a virtual trial of the actor, even though no formal charge of murder had been made against him. The jury eventually issued a verdict of 'Murder by person or persons unknown', which effectively meant that Drew was a free man. He addressed an adoring crowd of well-wishers from the balcony of the Great Western Hotel immediately after his ordeal had ended. By this time, the people of Reading were very much on his side, especially the womenfolk, who gave him a rapturous reception on hearing the news. Their support of Drew caused criticism in the national press, which considered their behaviour unseemly. The incident started a downhill slide into obscurity for Drew, an alcoholic. He was unable to cash in on the fame that the murder had brought him and died eleven years later at the age of sixty. It was rumoured that he ended his days as a London newspaper vendor.

NS (Gaute, J. & Odell, R., *The Murderers' Who's Who*, Harrap, 1979)

OCTOBER 3RD

1907: On this day, the pupils of the British School in Southampton Street, Reading, transferred to their newly built replacement school in Basingstoke Road – the George Palmer School (named after Reading's MP, businessman and philanthropist). One hundred and forty-five children transferred and forty-seven came from other schools. Two Education Committee members – Miss E. Sutton and Mr W. Thatcher – visited the school in the first week. As well as previous staff coming from Southampton Street, Miss Osman (headteacher) and the Misses Gibbs, Fabry, Killford, West and Wellman, there was one new teacher, Miss Davis. Any furniture from the Southampton Street School that could be salvaged was to be refurbished by the Clerk of Works Department for use by the new school, and a wheelbarrow and extension ladder were supplied for its caretaker.
VC (Barnes-Phillips, Daphne, *This is Our School*, Corridor Press, 2011)

———◆———

1957: On this day, a special passenger train carrying railway enthusiasts traversed the Coley branch line in Reading. The line was built during 1905-10 purely for freight. Part of the route is now a footpath from Rose Kiln Lane to Southcote; a short length of rail survives near the old Maltings on Fobney Street.
AS (*Great Western Railway Journal No. 74*, spring 2010)

OCTOBER 4TH

1869: On this day, Lewis Carroll, author of *Alice's Adventures in Wonderland,* photographed Maud and Isobel Standen at their parents' house in Reading. He had met the family in the Forbury Gardens while waiting for a train connection; both girls remained friends of Carroll for many years.

AS (Cohen, M. (Ed.), *Lewis Carroll: Interviews and Recollections*, 1989)

———•✦•———

1901: On this day, Martin Hope Sutton died. Born in 1815, he suffered ill health throughout his life. Working in the family firm of corn factors from thirteen years old, he started at the bottom, in the warehouse and counting-house. Sutton's love of botany was discouraged by his father, John. When he was banned from dealing in seeds during working hours, he did so in his spare time. Eventually, the enterprise known as Suttons Seeds flourished, and Martin was recommended as seedsman to Queen Victoria. Although appointed a JP, he declined to become involved in most other civic duties of the town. Sutton was twice-married; his first wife and their two children died, but his second marriage was long and happy, producing nine children. His religious faith was strong and he gave much support to numerous evangelical and missionary causes.

VC (Earley Local History Group, *Suttons Seeds: A History*, 2006)

OCTOBER 5TH

1975: On this day, Kate Elizabeth Winslet, actress, was born in Reading. Kate is the second of four children born to Roger and Sally Winslet; hers was a family of actors, who lived their lives on a shoestring. Her grandparents, Oliver and Linda Bridges, ran Reading Repertory Theatre. Both of Kate's sisters have also been bitten by the acting bug, but her brother decided to stay out of the 'family business'. She has, to date, two Golden Globes to her name and an Academy Award (Oscar), after becoming the youngest person to accrue six Academy Award nominations. Kate has starred in a string of blockbuster films and guest rôles in television series. She made her film debut in 1994 in *Heavenly Creatures.* Possibly her most famous films since then have been *Titanic*, *The Reader* and *Revolutionary Road*. Thrice married, she divides her time between homes in England and the USA. Kate's parents continue to live in Reading, where Sally is especially famous for her prowess at onion-pickling, demonstrated at the Retreat public house's annual contest. Roger has made a name for himself as a musical performer, notably with the group Bidgie Reef and the Gas.
VC (*The Sun*)

OCTOBER 6TH

1864: On this day, Arthur Purey Cust, president of the Reading Philharmonic Society, wrote to the Mayor:

> We beg to offer for the acceptance of yourself and the Corporation this Organ which has been erected by public Subscription and which we trust will prove not only a suitable Ornament for this restored and beautified Town Hall, but also the cause of much pleasure to all classes of the Inhabitants of Reading and the neighbourhood. As Stewards of the funds placed in our charge, we have endeavoured to fulfil the trust imposed in us by committing the work to a Gentleman whose reputation as an Organ Builder is second to none and who having already provided one beautiful instrument for this Town was quite competent we felt assured to provide another … We believe that, when completed, the Organ of Reading Town Hall will bear comparison with any other in the Kingdom.

The Father Willis organ was installed at first in the 1785 building, now known as the Victoria Hall; the other instrument referred to is in the Reading Minster of St Mary the Virgin. **AS** (Marr, P. (Ed.), *The Organ in Reading Town Hall*, Berkshire Organists' Association, 1982/*Berkshire Chronicle*)

OCTOBER 7TH

1573: On this day, William Laud was born in Broad Street, Reading, the son of a clothier. He was educated at Reading School and St John's College, Oxford, and in 1611 he became president of his college. In 1621 he was appointed Bishop of St David's in Wales, then Bishop of London in 1628. Becoming Archbishop of Canterbury in 1633, he zealously promoted the Church of England, showing a marked distaste for the Puritan party but at the same time opposing Roman Catholicism. Laud's closeness to King Charles I meant that he was a sure target for the Long Parliament when it met in 1640. After a travesty of a trial that did not begin until 1643, when Laud had already been held prisoner for thirty months, Parliament sentenced him to death. His property was taken from him and his goods sold. At the age of seventy-one, he died on the block by the executioner's axe, at the Tower of London on 10 January 1645. For Reading, Laud gained a new Charter from the King; he subsidised an increased salary for the headmaster of his old school, unknotted some of the problems that beset Kendrick's Charity, and left an inheritance that survives to this day as Archbishop Laud's Charity.

VC/KCB (Childs, W., *The Story of the Town of Reading,* 1905)

OCTOBER 8TH

1913: On this day, George William Palmer died. He was born in Reading in 1851, eldest son of George Palmer and his wife, Elizabeth Sarah (*née* Meatyard). In 1879 he married Eleanor Barrett. From 1874, George William was a partner in Huntley & Palmers biscuit company, after joining the firm at the age of sixteen as an unpaid clerk. A member of the Reform, National Liberal and Devonshire Clubs, George William served as Justice of the Peace for Berkshire and Reading. He became a member of Reading Council in 1882 and was Mayor in 1889-90. It was during his term as Mayor that his father announced that he was giving Palmer Park to the town. In 1892 George William Palmer became Liberal MP for Reading, winning the seat from Charles Townshend Murdoch, but Murdoch retook the seat at the 1895 general election, which brought the Tories back to power. Palmer regained his seat in the 1898 by-election and remained MP until he resigned in 1904, succeeded by Rufus Isaacs (later Lord Reading). In the early 1900s he presented Reading University College with a £50,000 endowment fund for new classrooms, laboratories and other facilities at its London Road site. His country estate was Marlston House in Bucklebury, west of Reading.

VC (*Who's Who,* 1914)

OCTOBER 9TH

1746: On this day, a General Thanksgiving was proclaimed for 'the glorious Victory obtained by his Royal Highness, the Duke of Cumberland, near Culloden House, April 16th 1746'. In Reading, this triumph was celebrated in the singing of a new hymn for the occasion by the Baptist minister, Daniel Turner:

> Accept the Praise – thy People own,
> And guard Thyself the British Throne;
> Then George shall live – Nor Bourbon dare,
> With Britons wage intestine War.

A native of St Albans and a former schoolmaster, Turner had come to Reading in 1741, at the age of thirty-one. The Reading Baptists, then meeting in Church Street near St Giles', were a somewhat strife-ridden body. Although Turner added eighteen members during his eight years, he had to deal with disciplinary problems as well as suffering the loss of his wife. In 1748 he moved to Abingdon, where he exercised an effective ministry till the end of his life in 1798. His hymns, some showing more merit than the Culloden verses, were published in 1748. He also published prose works, including *An Abstract of English Grammar and Rhetoric* at the age of thirteen and in 1758 *A Compendium of Social Religion*.
JBD (Payne, E., *The Baptists of Berkshire*, Carey Kingsgate, 1951)

OCTOBER 10TH

1860: On this day Rufus Isaacs was born, later to become MP for Reading, 1904-13; Lord Chief Justice, 1913-20; and Viceroy of India, 1921-6. He was elevated to the peerage in 1917 as the first Earl, and then Marquess of Reading in 1926. He died in 1935. Foxhill in Whiteknights Park had been his residence during his period in Reading. The sculptor, Charles Sargeant Jagger (1885-1934), was commissioned in 1928 to create a statue of Lord Reading, for erection at Government House, New Delhi, with other former Viceroys of India. However, after India gained independence in 1948, imperial statues like this were no longer wanted and many were put into storage. This prompted the Dowager Lady Reading to secure her late husband's statue for Reading. The Indian government later offered it as a gift, and it eventually reached Reading in 1969. It was then stored at Yeomanry House, while a suitable site was sought; in all, nineteen were considered. The Viceroy's statue, showing him in his robes as a Privy Councillor, was finally erected in the King George V Memorial Gardens, Eldon Square, and unveiled by his grandson, the 3rd Marquess, on 8 July 1971 in the presence of all Isaacs' living descendants.
SG ('Reading Statues, Monuments and Memorials', Libraries pamphlet/*Evening Post*)

OCTOBER IITH

1946: On this day began the trial of airman Eric Pocock, for the murder of Constance Lillian Boothby. In uniform, but without cap, collar and tie, Pocock had approached a police constable in Friar Street, and confessed he had just strangled a woman at 54 Friar Street. He was arrested and his story investigated. At first it seemed a false confession, as all doors and windows of the premises were locked; then the constable shone his torch into a room behind the shop and saw a woman's legs. After forcing entry to the premises, the body of Mrs Boothby was found, dressed only in underwear, with her other clothes neatly piled on a table. Pocock's missing clothes were also found, with a note from 'Connie'. It appeared that she had sought release from her marriage to Edward Boothby, but he had refused. As they could not be together Connie and Pocock had entered into a suicide pact with her being strangled and him stabbed. Evidently one was successful and the other not. Pocock was found guilty of murder, with a recommendation for mercy. However, the law was explicit: Pocock was condemned to death, although his sentence was commuted to life imprisonment later that year.

VC (Eddleston, J., *Foul Deeds and Suspicious Deaths in Reading*, Wharncliffe, 2009)

OCTOBER 12TH

1975: On this day, after over twenty years of discussion, there came to fruition a co-ordination arrangement between the two major bus undertakings which operated in Reading. Back in 1915, when British Automobile Traction, the predecessors of Thames Valley Traction (from 1972 part of Alder Valley), had begun bus operations, Reading Corporation operated only electric trams. Accordingly, BAT arranged to charge 'protective' fares within the borough to avoid loss of revenue to the Corporation – who greatly prized this arrangement. The co-ordination settlement required the Corporation to give this up, with Alder Valley buses henceforth able to carry passengers within the borough at the Corporation's lower fares. In return, however, Alder Valley transferred to the Corporation all its Woodley services, a fairly lucrative section of its network, together with its part of the jointly operated service to Long Lane. While the ordinary person might perceive the change as of little consequence, Reading Transport had effectively consolidated its operating area to embrace Greater Reading, leaving Alder Valley to operate in the remaining towns it had long served, together with connecting trunk routes. Alder Valley, then part of the National Bus Company, was subsequently split up and privatised in the 1980s.

JRW (Bus Fare journal)

OCTOBER 13TH

1827: On this day, the *Berkshire Chronicle* reported a 'daring robbery' at The Oracle, Minster Street. Hearing noises from McFarlane's first-floor silk-manufactory, the watchman called for help. Two men were caught, and stolen cash and lengths of silk found in their possession. They had also burgled Messrs Douglas' silk-mills at The Oracle. Silk-weaving was recorded in Reading since 1640. Later, 'Octogenarian' noted a silk-manufactory at the Kennet end of London Street, which was demolished in the formation of Queens Road, and also rooms in The Oracle occupied by silk-weavers and pin-makers. In 1818 Deely, silk-manufacturer of East Street, who was moving to London, advertised for sale 'the implements of trade' – bobbins, winding-engine, warping-mills and much else. 'Octogenarian' also describes 'a silk-manufactory of many years' standing' next to the Abbey Arch, 'but it became useless in consequence of legislation in Huskisson's time'. (This refers to William Huskisson, who pursued Free Trade policies during his time as president of the Board of Trade from 1823-27.) In 1841 Messrs Baylis were said to be erecting an extensive silk-manufactory in Kings Road, but the industry seems not to have survived in Reading beyond the nineteenth century.
PV (*Berkshire Chronicle*/*Reading Mercury*/Darter, W., *Reminiscences of Reading by an Octogenarian*, 1888)

OCTOBER 14TH

1933: On this day Dr Deissman, a German academic working in London and a firm supporter of Hitler's policies, came to Reading to address a meeting of the Reading and District Free Church Council. His aim was to explain the anti-Semitic policies in Germany which had attracted much international criticism. According to him Hitler was 'a man of courage and action', who had been forced to take severe measures to relieve the sufferings of the German people. Deissman claimed that Jews had prospered during the period after the First World War, when the rest of the population was suffering; other Jews with Bolshevik and Communist tendencies had also arrived in Germany from Eastern Europe. So dangerous was their influence deemed to be that it was thought necessary to take stringent measures against them. Whilst Dr Deissman agreed that there might be some suffering amongst a few Jews, he felt that some critical reports from Germany were exaggerated. After questions, the council expressed their thanks to him for his speech, their sympathy for the sufferings of the people and good wishes for the country's prosperity in the future, whilst remaining unconvinced by his rhetoric.

JP (*Berkshire Chronicle*)

OCTOBER 15TH

1792: On this day, the *Reading Mercury* carried an appeal for funds to support the 'Distressed French Clergy' – Catholic priests fleeing to England to escape the French Revolution. The revolutionaries opposed not only the King and aristocracy supporting him, but also that great upholder of the 'status quo', the Roman Catholic Church. Around five thousand *émigré* clergy reached England, and several hundred found welcome in Reading. The first arrivals were housed in a Hosier Street tenement but later comers were accommodated in the King's Arms, Castle Hill, a former coaching inn, which was home to over 300 priests by 1800. In 1801, Napoleon's Concordat with the Papacy allowed them back to France. Most left, but some preferred to remain and continue their ministry to a growing Catholic congregation. The most prominent was Father Longuet (*see* February 13th), who in 1812 built the first public Catholic chapel since the Reformation. Not until 1820 did the first English-born Catholic priest, Fr Francis Bowland, arrive in Reading, to build on the foundations of Roman Catholic revival which the French refugee priests had laid. Thus it was that, by a strange turn of fate, Roman Catholicism in Reading owes much to the French Revolution.

PMS (*Reading Mercury*/Bellenger, D., *The French Exiled Clergy in Reading in the British Isles after 1789*, Downside Abbey, 1986)

OCTOBER 16TH

1987: On this day came the onset of the memorable 'hurricane' in the evening. BBC Weatherman Michael Fish later said that a woman had phoned to ask if there was a hurricane on the way, but she had been assured: there was no hurricane! However, that night the country suffered serious wind damage, particularly the south of England. In Reading, power lines and thirty trees came down; in Caversham two families escaped when a tree crashed through their roofs. Shinfield mourned the death of its 'oldest inhabitant' – a Cedar dating from Tudor times which fell victim to the winds. Indeed, the storm caused the worst damage to trees yet recorded in the area, and rivalled in violence the 1703 storm recorded by Daniel Defoe. Although the 1987 winds were 'of hurricane force', this was no true hurricane, which thrives over very warm seas and gives extensive torrential rain as well as winds up to 150mph! Learning from its forecasting and communication shortcomings, the Meteorological Office set up a Press Office to ensure closer media contact in the future.

JRS (Meteorological Office forecasts and Action Reports/ Currie, I., Davison, M. & Ogley, R., *The Berkshire Weather Book*, Froglets, 1994)

OCTOBER 17TH

1900: On this day, a series of accidents befell Reading inhabitants. The *Reading Mercury* reported: 'Chatham Street residents were alarmed by a loud report ... a gas-pipe in the footway opposite the Prince of Wales public house had exploded. A small portion of the ground was torn up, and the scullery at the inn was slightly damaged. Fortunately, no-one was injured.' Elsewhere in Reading:

A boy named Joseph Woodham, aged 11, who lived ... in Elgar Road, met his death under sad circumstances. He went to school (in Dorothy Street) in his usual good health. Whilst exercising, about 11.30am, on the horizontal ladder, which is only 6½ feet from the ground, he fell and struck his head ... It being apparent that he was badly injured, his mother and Dr Guilding were sent for ... Dr Guilding found that the unfortunate boy had sustained fracture of the skull and he was immediately conveyed to hospital. Despite every attention, the lad died on Friday morning [19th October]. An inquest is to be held.

At 9.30 p.m., Albert Gilham sustained facial injuries when he was thrown from his cart in Bath Road. Albert's horse had taken fright, collided with a cab and come to a standstill. The cab-driver received a hand injury. Not a good day in town!
VC (*Reading Mercury*)

OCTOBER 18TH

1886: On this day, the celebrated poet, designer and Socialist firebrand, William Morris, gave a lecture in Reading; his theme was 'The Coming Epoch', and his audience a radical debating society meeting at the British Workman, a temperance coffee-house in Abbey Square. Morris had become famous for his Pre-Raphaelite romances and designs for domestic furnishings, fabrics and wallpaper. More recently he had espoused Socialism of a modified Marxist variety, with a strongly Utopian flavour, which he advanced through the Socialist League that he formed in 1885. A version of Morris's lecture was later published in *Signs of Change* as 'The Dawn of the New Epoch'. Here Morris argued:

> The new order of things says ... why have masters at all? Let us be fellows working in the harmony of association for the common good ... This ideal and hope of a new society founded on industrial peace and forethought, bearing with it its own ethics, aiming at a newer and higher life for all men, has received the general name of Socialism, and it is my firm belief that it is destined to supersede the old order of things ... and to be the next step in the progress of humanity.

JBD (LeMire, E., *Unpublished Lectures of William Morris*, 1969/Morris, W., *Signs of Change*, 1988)

OCTOBER 19TH

1897: On this day, the final phase of Reading's Municipal Buildings was completed: the New Art Gallery and Reading Rooms were opened, at the corner of Blagrave Street and Valpy Street, a site previously occupied by the County Treasurer's office. The final buildings were erected by his brothers George and Samuel in memory of W.I. Palmer, a generous benefactor to Reading. William Roland Howell, of local architects Cooper and Howell, designed them to blend with the adjacent buildings. An attractive feature is the moulded terracotta frieze created by the Reading and London sculptor William Charles May (1853-1934). Its panels draw on four appropriate themes: Panel 1 (Ancient Britain) – a smith, a child, a hunter, a warrior and bulldog, a Briton making flint instruments and a druid; Panel 2 (Roman Life) – blacksmith making weapons, potters at work, digging clay, architectural mason and a sculptor; Panel 3 (Literature) – representing Tennyson, Shakespeare, Burns, Milton, Chaucer, Homer and Dante; Panel 4 (Science) – Maxim with his Maxim gun, female figures symbolising science and chemistry, Nansen the explorer and Edison with his phone. May did not, however, create the isolated panel on the Concert Hall building representing Henry I founding Reading Abbey; this was the work of Charles Pinker in 1888.

SG (*Berkshire Chronicle*)

OCTOBER 20TH

1911: On this day, the poet Wilfred Owen aged eighteen, came to the Reading area as a lay assistant to the Vicar of Dunsden. This was not a happy experience for Owen, causing him some loss of faith. While at Dunsden he enrolled for classes at Reading University College. He wrote to his mother, Susan, in April 1912: 'I went into Reading with the iron-clenched purpose of bearding the College Tutorial Secretary in his den. After a long wait, I saw him, and settled to take only Botany classes, this term: 2 hrs on Tues! 3 hrs on Wed!! 1 hour on Thurs. (afternoon). This is grand.' These studies stood Owen in good stead five years later when, convalescing at Craiglockhart Hospital, he gave a lecture on the subject, 'Do plants think?' To Susan Owen he reported it a huge success: 'My laborious escapes from Dunsden Vicarage to Reading College have been well crowned tonight.' Towards the end of his time at Dunsden, the vicar went off to Bournemouth, leaving Owen to find someone to take Sunday evening service: 'I had infinite labour to find a 'clergy'…Went to about nine people in Reading about it, walking from 2.15 till nearly 10 pm.' He finally left his position in February 1913.

JBD (Bell, J. (Ed.), *Wilfred Owen, Selected Letters*, OUP, 1985)

OCTOBER 21ST

1933: On this day, a special Ladies Luncheon was held at Reading Aero Club in the Woodley area of Reading. The hostesses of this event included Mrs Blossom Miles (wife of F.G. Miles, and an aircraft designer in her own right), Mrs Handley-Page (wife of the eponymous designer), Mrs Powis and Mrs Heelas (owners of the department store in Reading). There were about a hundred guests, all of whom were women pilots in the British flying club movement. The ladies flew in, and Mrs Gabrielle Patterson of Lympne won the punctuality prize of £5, as she had arrived within a minute of the deadline of 12.45 p.m. Mrs Patterson had only that morning taken delivery of her Hawk aeroplane. This two-seater Hawk aircraft was a new product that year, designed by Miles and his wife under the trade name of Miles Aeroplane Company and built in the Phillips Powis aircraft factory at Woodley. Made of wood, with folding wings for storage, it cost £395, cruised at approximately 90mph and achieved 23mpg! After the luncheon the ladies enjoyed a show of the latest designs for the fashion-conscious aviatrix.

JP (Temple, J., *Wings over Woodley*, Aston, 1987/*Berkshire Chronicle*)

OCTOBER 22ND

2007: On this day, local pop band The Hoosiers released their first album, entitled *The Trick to Life,* which climbed to number one in the charts and eventually achieved double platinum. Drummer Al Sharland from Bracknell and singer/guitarist, Irwin Sparkes from Reading came up with the unusual band name while on a road trip through America. In 2011 they returned to the Reading area to play at Sharland's old school and also at Waingels College, Woodley. The Hoosiers are not the only band with connections to Reading. Back in April 1960, John Lennon and Paul McCartney, billed as 'The Nerk Twins', performed at the Fox and Hounds in Caversham to a grand audience of three and then went on to serve behind the bar! It was to be their only outing as a duo, as weeks later they became known as The Beatles. David Graham, son of a local publican, achieved fame as a member of the Four Pennies, whose single 'Juliet' reached number one in 1964. The 'Tubular Bells' star Mike Oldfield was born in Reading in 1953 and attended Leighton Park School until his early teens. He also played at local folk venues, before his family moved to Essex.
VC (*Daily Mail*)

OCTOBER 23RD

1923: On this day Reading Bridge officially opened, to relieve the overloaded Caversham Bridge. It featured an elegant single-span of 600ft (185m) and wide carriageways. Its use of ferro-concrete was a radical innovation; before the opening, a spectacular procession of steam-rollers crossed the bridge to demonstrate its strength! Passageways below the roadway allowed walkers along the Thames' banks, while barge-horses passed beneath on a walkway extended from the bank on piles. As Reading Bridge settled into use, the demand to upgrade Caversham Bridge became vocal. A timber bridge, renovated time and again, had stood here since at least 1231. After seven centuries an unhappy hybrid replaced it: a stone bridge from the Reading bank joining a wooden bridge at mid-river. Caversham village being in Oxfordshire, Reading Council refused to underwrite all its maintenance or improvement costs. Finally Reading and Oxfordshire agreed to pay jointly for a modern bridge, which opened in 1869. But this utilitarian cast-iron structure was so ugly that Reading declined to honour it with a formal opening. After another half-century, the eyesore yielded place to the Caversham Bridge we see today. Also constructed in ferro-concrete, with parapet-walls of Aberdeen granite, it cost £70,000, and was ceremonially opened by Edward, Prince of Wales, in June 1926.

PV (Phillips, D., *The Story of Reading,* Countryside Books, 1999)

OCTOBER 24TH

1824: On this day, the *Reading Mercury* announced: 'In answer to questions that have been put to us by several correspondents respecting the legality of roasting coffee, we have ascertained that there is no Act of Parliament which forbids the roasting of coffee by private persons for their own consumption.'
AS (*Reading Mercury*)

———•◆•———

1843: On this day, much-needed public rooms in London Street, Reading, were officially opened, followed by an inaugural dinner. It provided a long-needed venue for such activities as lectures, concerts and dinners. At the inauguration, beautiful prints of the building by William Ford Poulton (1822-1900) were on sale. Charles Dickens was invited to attend, but other business prevented him. The building's main user was the Mechanics Institute, founded nearly twenty years earlier to organise classes and lectures for Reading's artisans. The Institute had failed at one point but then reopened in these new premises. By 1860 the Institute closed, and the Primitive Methodists began their occupation, lasting eighty years. The building later became home to the Everyman Theatre, *Reading Standard* newspaper offices, a civil engineers' office and finally Great Expectations pub and hotel. The bold Ionic portico is London Street's dominant architectural feature, designed by William Brown (1809-65).
SG (*Reading Mercury*)

OCTOBER 25TH

1879: On this day, a football match between London Pilgrims and Reading, at Reading Cricket Ground, was stopped after fifteen minutes when Reading's captain, Henry Rogers, collapsed. A doctor from the crowd attended him but he died within minutes of an epileptic fit, aged just twenty-five. The game was abandoned and all games before Christmas cancelled out of respect. Rogers had come to Reading from Leamington Spa seven years previously for a position with architects Brown and Albury, and promptly joined Reading's newly formed amateur side, playing in their first game. From 1873-7 Rogers studied at Reading School of Art, and in 1876 *Building News* published his architectural drawings of Kenilworth and Thatcham churches. He was buried at Leamington Spa, with many of his colleagues attending the funeral.
SG (Gold, S., *Dictionary of Architects at Reading*, 1999/ *Berkshire Chronicle*)

———•◆•———

1968: On this day, Enoch Powell MP addressed 500 Reading University students in defence of his controversial views on immigration. Powell kept calm despite dropping his portable microphone and knocking his watch off the lectern. The meeting ended in a good-natured spirit, and press reports suggested that there were more cheers than boos from the audience.
JBD (Heffer, S., *Like the Roman*, Weidenfeld & Nicolson, 1998)

OCTOBER 26TH

1842: On this day, the foundation stone of the Episcopal chapel at the new Reading Cemetery was laid with grand masonic honours, after a public procession from the town. Fortunately it was a fine day; although bad weather the day before had deterred some travelling from a distance, many Reading inhabitants attended. The route was 'thronged with well-dressed persons' while the windows of several houses were crowded with ladies. A dinner was held in the evening with celebratory toasts to the Cemetery Company solicitor, Mr Richards. At this period a Parliamentary Act was required to establish a cemetery and, with some opposition from the clergy, it had not been a straightforward legal procedure.
PSm (*Illustrated London News*)

———— • • ————

1955: On this day, the Queen Mother opened Reading Technical College. The presentations included an iced cake model of the college, accurate in every detail! The master cake-maker, from Huntley & Palmers, Jack Bogart, had worked on many 'important' cakes, particularly that for the 1947 wedding of Princess Elizabeth and the Duke of Edinburgh, on which the Icing Department worked continuously for three weeks. (*See* November 20th.) Others included those for Princess Anne and Mark Phillips (1973) and Prince Charles and Lady Diana Spencer (1981).
JRS (*Reading Museum Royal Panel,* 2012)

OCTOBER 27TH

1928: On this day, the *Berkshire Chronicle*, under the heading 'Remarkable Tribute from all Classes', devoted several columns to the funeral of Sir George Stewart Abram, an eminent and much loved citizen of Reading. St Luke's Church was packed. As well as family and friends, the Mayor and Corporation were present, with representatives of the university, the Royal Berkshire Hospital, and many other institutions and societies which Sir George had supported. His wide interests had run from duties as senior physician at the hospital and as a borough councillor for thirty-one years to service as Mayor, JP and Chief Magistrate. He was also governor of several schools, a member of the Court of Reading University and a devoted supporter of charitable causes. As a keen amateur sportsman, he played rugby and tennis at a high level; a capable actor, he helped establish the annual dramatic performances in the Abbey ruins. As Sir George lay on his deathbed on the evening of 23 October, a meeting of the Town Council voted that he should be made a Freeman of the Borough. The presentation was made at his bedside without delay by the Mayor and he signed the Roll at 8 p.m. Five hours later the new Freeman died. **PMS** (*Berkshire Chronicle*)

OCTOBER 28TH

1896: On this day, Arthur Silver died, at the age of forty-three. In spite of his relative youthfulness he had been one of the most influential designers of fabrics, wallpaper, textiles and floor coverings of the day. In 1880 he had formed the famous Silver Studio, a worthy contemporary of Morris and Co., which was to dominate the market by supplying designs to Liberty's, Warners, Sandersons and Lines for their own ranges. Arthur was born in Reading in 1853, the son of James Silver of Duke Street, Reading, an upholsterer and cabinet maker. He became a pupil of the Reading School of Art from 1869-72 under Charles Havell. When he left, he joined the studios of H.W. Batley, a well-established London designer of carpets and fabrics, remaining with him until he opened his own studio. In 1878 he married Isabella Walenn by whom he had two sons, Rex and Harry, who continued the business. Silver Studio, which was renowned for its distinctive art nouveau style, eventually closed in 1963, when the remaining stock, design books, and archive (including Arthur's student drawings from the Reading School of Art) were transferred to Middlesex University.

SG (Turner, M. & Hoskins, L., *Silver Studio of Design*, Webb & Bower, 1988)

OCTOBER 29TH

2011: On this day, Reading Old Boys' Lodge became the first Masonic Lodge to meet in the Borough of Reading for a number of years, when it celebrated its first hundred years with a centenary meeting. The ceremony took place in Big School, the fine main hall of Reading School, which was the centrepiece of the design by the school's architect, Alfred Waterhouse. The Old Boys' Lodge had met in Big School from its inception until November 1990, when it moved to the Berkshire Masonic Centre at Sindlesham; the school permitted it to return to its roots for this auspicious anniversary. The day also saw the installation of the Worshipful Master of the Lodge for the ensuing year and, although the Lodge is no longer confined to Reading School men, the felicitous choice to embark on the next century was an old boy of the school, His Honour Judge Simon Oliver. When the Lodge was consecrated 100 years earlier, in October 1911, a banquet was held in Big School presided over by the first Master of the Lodge, B. St J. Warren-Hastings OR. Among the founder members was the headmaster of Reading School, Revd W. Charles Eppstein DD.

KCB (Reading School Archives)

OCTOBER 30TH

1876: On this day, the new clock and carillon, installed in the tower of the new Reading Municipal Buildings, were ceremonially inaugurated. Designed by Alfred Waterhouse, the mechanisms were manufactured by Gillett & Bland at their steam clock factory in Croydon. The time is shown on four 6ft illuminated dials glazed with opal glass. The hour was struck on the tenor bell, and the quarters chimed on four bells similar to those at Westminster Palace. The carillon played a fresh tune every day for twenty-eight days. The total cost was £700, all paid for by public subscription. The Mayoress performed the opening ceremony by touching an electric switch to set off the chimes. When the tunes followed, this part of the ceremony became an embarrassing disaster: the bells could not be heard in the Town Hall nor could they be heard very much outside. It was generally agreed that the bells were too small and that £400 more should have been spent. One wit referred to 'this baker's dozen of inharmonious tin kettles'. The clock and carillon were stopped and the bells labelled an utter failure. The carillon was sold but fortunately the clock itself is still in situ and in working order.

SG (*Berkshire Chronicle*/North, L., *Reading Chronicle*, 1978)

OCTOBER 31ST

1900: On this day, the Reading Hebrew Congregation's Synagogue was opened in Goldsmid Road. Designed by local architect William George Lewton, in a Moorish style, the building cost £2,300. A stone bearing the date 5661, which in the Hebrew calendar coincides with the year 1900, surmounts the main entrance. The opening was the culmination of years of hard work by the town's small Jewish community. Fourteen years before, a Hebrew congregation had been founded with thirteen members and little money, at the house of Israel Ehrenberg in Derby Street. At that time some forty Jewish families lived in Reading, meeting for worship in each other's houses, mostly along Oxford Road. The family of the late MP for Reading, Sir Francis Goldsmid, gave generously towards the cost of the new synagogue, and Junction Road on which it stood was renamed Goldsmid Road in his honour. Goldsmid was also England's first Jewish barrister and Queen's Counsel.
SD (North, L., *Reading Chronicle*, 1980)

1901: On this day, Reading County Borough purchased the one-route horse tramway (barracks to cemetery) owned by Reading Tramways Company Ltd., after much dispute and arbitration concerning its value, and formed Reading Corporation Tramways.
JRW (Reading Transport 75th Anniversary Brochure, 1976)

November 1st

1930: On this day, the first exhibition of the Reading Guild of Artists opened at the Municipal Art Gallery. The Mayor welcomed the large gathering and said that much of the credit for the success of the exhibition was due to Mr W. Smallcombe, the Curator of the Museum. After the closure in 1908 of the Berkshire Art Society, there had been little encouragement or exhibition space for local artists. The university Art Department was confined to academic life and the Art Studios were a private venture. The president of the new Guild, Allen Seaby, stressed that it was being founded to meet the insistent demand on the part of art workers in the district. Local artists exhibiting in this year were H.A. Barkas, Mark Symons, Harold Yates, Alfred Rawlings and Margaret Bradley. In 2005, a large exhibition was held at the Art Gallery to celebrate seventy-five years of the Guild, and five years later the eightieth anniversary was celebrated. Other famous names associated with the Guild over the years include Robert Gillmor, Marcus and Gilbert Adams, Herbert Beecroft, Gilbert Spencer (Stanley Spencer's brother), Alan Caiger Smith, and Eric Stanford.

SG (*Berkshire Chronicle*/Watson, E., *History of the Reading Guild of Artists 1930-1980*, 1980)

NOVEMBER 2ND

1910: On this day, what is now Reading Golf Club was opened as Caversham and South Oxfordshire Golf Club. It was unable to assume the name of the town because a Reading Golf Club was already in existence in Lower Tilehurst. The opening ceremony was performed by local MP Valentine Fleming, father of author Ian Fleming of 'James Bond' fame. The cost of the clubhouse was £350 and the laying out of the course £750. In its early stages it comprised just twelve holes, which had taken only six months to prepare. One of the most eminent golfers of the era, James Braid, designed the course, located at Emmer Green, apparently at a fee of only 25 guineas. Braid, who won the Open five times, had been responsible for many other courses in the British Isles, including Troon and Gleneagles. Further work on the course was undertaken by another famous golf architect, Harry Colt. His work included both courses at Wentworth, besides redesigns of Muirfield and Hoylake and the nearby courses at Calcot Park and Goring & Streatley.
NS (Tierney, M., *The Story of the First Hundred Years of Reading Golf Club*, 2009)

NOVEMBER 3RD

1794: On this day, Richard Dewell, a brickmaker at Mr Sharman's brick-kilns in Reading, was accidentally killed. He had been working in a chalk-well, and was coming up to take his dinner, but as he approached the top of the shaft, the spindle of the wheel broke, sending him down to the bottom, nearly 60ft below. His neck was broken, and he was otherwise much bruised.

AS (*Reading Mercury*)

———◆·◆———

1968: On this day, Reading bade a final farewell to its trolleybus system after thirty-two years' operation. Using electricity rather than imported oil fuels, trolleybuses were an enormous boon during the Second World War, when Reading's population multiplied as the town was considered safe for evacuee children and businesses. Trolleybuses were discontinued for several reasons: the vast post-war increase in road traffic; new motorway routes which prompted Reading's adoption of one-way traffic schemes; the wearing out of the power distribution system; and the government subsidies which provided for diesel but not electricity. Many fought to retain the popular trolleybuses, which received an outstanding send-off and are still fondly remembered. Enthusiasts preserved no fewer than six, which can be seen still working at the Trolleybus Museum at Sandtoft, North Lincolnshire.

JRW (Hall, D., *Reading Trolleybuses,* Trolleybooks, 1991)

NOVEMBER 4TH

1975: On this day, the Opening Session of the Council of the European Centre for Medium Range Weather Forecasts (ECMWF) was held. The Centre, an independent organisation sited on Reading's Shinfield Road, was established in recognition of the need to pool the scientific and technical resources of Europe's meteorological services and institutions for the production of medium range (ten to fifteen days ahead) weather forecasts, which would, it was expected, bring both economic and social benefits. The Centre employs about 160 staff and seventy consultants from thirty-four member and cooperating states (mostly European but including Israel and Morocco). As well as medium range weather forecasts, staff prepare monthly, seasonal, ocean wave and other forecasts. The wealth of information, backed by research, is used worldwide to predict extreme weather events and climate change. Probably the greatest achievement so far has been the accurate prediction – seven days before it happened – of Hurricane Sandy's landfall on the east coast of the USA in November 2012. The Centre monitors worldwide weather around the clock, all day, every day; so there is no truth at all – as mischievous wags have been known to relate – that ECMWF stands for: 'Early Closing, Mondays, Wednesdays and Fridays'!

JRS (Report of the Opening Session of the ECMWF Council, November 1975)

NOVEMBER 5TH

1910: On this day, Guy Fawkes Night proved particularly spectacular in Tilehurst, Reading. A serious fire broke out at Tilehurst Potteries' Kew Kiln, which caused damage worth around £3,000 and temporarily threw many men out of work. The blaze broke out at about 8 p.m. and at first went unnoticed since residents thought it was just another bonfire. However, it was spotted as something out of the ordinary by the daughter of a Mr Casey, who lived in nearby cottages. The damage to the premises could have been far worse, but a ready water supply was available direct from Tilehurst Water Company. As there was no wind, the fire did not spread to a new kiln nearby. The County Fire Brigade was soon on the scene after a telephone call from the owner. Pangbourne and Englefield brigades also attended, but their assistance was not required.
NS (Local press reports)

———— • ◆ • ————

1995: On this day, Tony Walsh from the Reading League won the British Isles Open Bar Billiards Championship in Jersey. He was the first Reading victor since Dave Harris in 1986. Bernie McCluskey was another Reading winner in 1985 and 2000, by which time the competition was restyled as 'World Championship'.
JBD (All-England Bar Billiards Association records)

NOVEMBER 6TH

1886: On this day, a letter appeared in the *Berkshire Chronicle*, signed by one Arthur Englefield, from which the following is an extract:

> Sir, I was present last Friday at the distribution of prizes to the successful students of the Reading Science and Art Schools, and was in no slight degree astonished at the remarks of the Chairman (John Walter) in reference to art. Mr Walter stated that if there was to be a falling off of students he would rather see it occur in the art section than in the science section and he gave his reason as 'that the study of science was profitable to the individual and a source of wealth to the nation, whereas the only good of art was to enable people to paint pictures and one only had to go to exhibitions to learn the amount of trash produced.

The writer further regretted that 'one who is, I suppose, a leading man in your town, is not ashamed to give tongue to views so narrow, and upon an occasion when he might with more grace have said something helpful and encouraging' rather 'than the fact that the inhabitants here are apathetic in regard to the institution for the good in their midst'.
SG (*Berkshire Chronicle*)

NOVEMBER 7TH

2000: On this day, HRH Princess Anne opened The Oracle shopping centre. The cold, damp, weather did not deter the hundreds of shoppers awaiting the Princess Royal's arrival. The River Kennet was wider than planned as it had burst its man-made banks and climbed the steps towards the shopping complex. The Lord Lieutenant of the Royal County of Berkshire, Philip Wroughton, welcomed the Princess and introduced her to the waiting dignitaries. She was led up the escalators to a purple ribbon, which she cut to mark the opening of Phase Three of The Oracle. After stopping to chat to some of The Oracle's staff, various Shopmobility users, shop managers, and carers and youngsters from the Lilyput [*sic*] crèche, she then walked along the flooded Riverside area to the glass Rotunda where the inscribed 'O' sculpture was waiting to be unveiled. The 2.2m-high stainless-steel structure had been moved up a few steps because its original site was now under water following the persistent rains. The town let its hair down later in the evening with a Fire Spectacular on the Oracle Riverside, featuring a host of street entertainers followed by a firework, laser and music extravaganza. The Princess's previous connection with Reading related to a speeding offence on the M4.

AS/VC (*Reading Evening Post*)

NOVEMBER 8TH

1830: On this day, Albin Roberts Burt announced in the *Reading Mercury* his arrival in Reading, 'where he intends to stay working as a portrait painter, miniaturist and drawing master'. Born in London in 1783, Burt had as a young man been something of an itinerant painter and his advertisements can be found in many other towns. However, he had resided for nearly twenty years in Chester before moving to Reading, where he remained until his death in 1842. At first he took rooms in London Street, later moving permanently to Conduit Crescent (now part of Whitley Street). His parents were Harry Burt and Mary Roberts, who hailed from Hawarden. Mrs Burt is said to have brought Emma Hart, later Lady Hamilton, with her to London. Albin's eldest son, Henry Wellington Burt, though only sixteen in 1830, was the master at the Drawing Academy for young beginners, and later settled in New Zealand. His daughter, Emma Hamilton Burt, married John White, a school master, artist and pupil of Albin. They were the parents of Sydney Victor White, the well-known photographer. The Museum of Reading has a good collection of portraits of local characters painted by Albin Roberts Burt, and the National Portrait Gallery holds several more of his portraits.
SG (*Oxford Dictionary of National Biography*, OUP, 2004)

NOVEMBER 9TH

1822: On this day, William Cobbett visited Reading on one of his famous 'Rural Rides'. Leaving Egham 'at day-break in a hazy frost' he breakfasted at Binfield and finally by 'a road as smooth as a die, a real stock-jobber's road' reached Reading by 11 a.m. It seems that the purpose of Cobbett's visit was to address (or in his own words, 'harangue') a meeting of 300 farmers at the Ship Inn in Duke Street. Unlike some visitors to Reading, Cobbett was delighted by all he met: 'I have seldom seen a number of persons assembled together, whose approbation I valued more than that of the company of this day … Their kindness to me is nothing compared with the sense and spirit which they appear to possess.' However, Cobbett was a driven man and rode off west the following day.
JBD (Cobbett, W., *Rural Rides*, J.M. Dent, 1932)

❖

2012: On this day, the ninth Pride of Reading Awards were presented, hosted by Reading's own Chris Tarrant. Past Award recipients include Liz Longhurst (campaigner for a ban on violent internet porn) and PC Lee Umpleby (who saved three lives in two separate incidents). He had also been one of Reading's Olympic Torch bearers in July.
VC (*GetReading*)

NOVEMBER 10TH

1817: On this day, the *Reading Mercury* reported on the first use of gas for lighting in Reading:

> On November 3rd, the spacious and elegant billiards room, news room and library in this town, were lighted with gas for the first time. The public are indebted to Reading's leading Gentlemen for introducing this admirable invention to their notice. We hope the hint thus given will be taken advantage of by a general adoption of the plant throughout this large and populous Borough, which will add greatly to its beauty, comfort, and convenience.

VC (*Reading Mercury*)

———◆———

1981: On this day, the normally uneventful life of Sherman Road in the Katesgrove district of Reading was disturbed when Mrs Edith Dearing drew back her bedroom curtains to discover a nearly full-grown cygnet in her front garden. The bird was injured: a metallic object rather like a curtain ring through its beak was preventing it from being able to eat. Police and swan-uppers were alerted; the former held up the traffic on Pell Street while the swan was escorted back towards the River Kennet. Eventually the RSPCA were able to remove the ring and the bird was released back into the river later in the day.
JBD (*Reading Chronicle*/author's diary)

NOVEMBER 11TH

1918: On this day, internationally known as Armistice Day (signifying 'laying down of arms') the First World War came to an end. The date is marked annually in Reading, as elsewhere, by remembrance ceremonies paying tribute to those who gave their lives. After 1945, the date came to commemorate those who fell in both World Wars. Reading's most celebrated hero was Trooper Frederick William Owen Potts VC, who was born in 1892 in Edgehill Street, Reading. He first demonstrated his courage in 1913, when he saved a boy from drowning in the Thames. The following year, war broke out. Potts (a Reservist) mobilised with the Berkshire Yeomanry and was in Egypt by 1915. They moved thence to Gallipoli, where Potts achieved fame through another heroic act. On 21 August, the Yeomanry assaulted Hill 70; Potts, although injured in his thigh and under continuous machine-gun fire, stayed for over forty-eight hours tending a wounded comrade – another Reading man – eventually dragging him 600 yards on a shovel, back to safety. For this selfless act, he received the Victoria Cross. After the war, Potts ran a tailor's shop in Reading. He died on 3 November 1943 and is laid to rest in Reading Crematorium.
VC (Snelling, S., *VCs of the First World War – Gallipoli*, Sutton Publishing, 1995)

NOVEMBER 12TH

1812: On this day, Henry Briant, architect, was born. In the 1830s he and his brother, Nathaniel, moved to Reading and established an architectural practice at 7 High Street. In this decade they purchased plots of land along Kings Road, erecting many substantial residences whose façades were faced with Bath sandstone, transported via the recently extended Kennet and Avon Canal. They were also responsible for many houses on nearby Eldon Road and Square. In 1836 Henry Briant submitted two plans – one in the Grecian, another in the Gothic style – to the competition for the design of Royal Berkshire Hospital. The former was chosen by the assessor, eminent architect George Basevi, who awarded Briant £50. Briant's architectural career was brief, however, since at thirty-one he was ordained, serving curacies in Cheshire. He died in Manchester in 1884.

SD (Gold, S., *Biographical Dictionary of Architects at Reading*, 1999)

———— •◆• ————

1978: On this day, the death of Lucy Gmiterek was reported, amid strong rumours that the cause had been 'instantaneous human combustion'. Experts were baffled by the lack of damage to the rest of the basement room in which she was found, burnt to a cinder in her chair. The mystery remains to this day.

VC (*Reading Chronicle*)

NOVEMBER 13TH

1836: On this day, in Cambridge, the death occurred of the Revd Charles Simeon, fifty-four years vicar of Holy Trinity Church in that city and one of the leading evangelicals of his generation. Simeon had been born in Reading in 1759, at an address in the Forbury. Two of his brothers, John and Edward, distinguished themselves in the fields of politics (as the town's MP) and banking. Charles inherited a large sum on Edward's death in 1815, investing the bulk of it in his religious activities. Although his life work was centred on Cambridge, where he had been a student, he continued to keep an eye on events in Reading. He preached the funeral sermon of William Bromley Cadogan in 1797, and a few months before his death had to turn down an invitation to preach at the service celebrating the return of the Castle Street congregation to the established church as St Mary's Episcopal Chapel. Like many a prophet, however, he was 'without honour in his own country'. In the words of Darter, one of the 'jocular members of the Corporation' said that 'a greater than he has about this same time departed this life, viz. the Duke's horse, Copenhagen, which carried the Duke at Waterloo'.

JBD (Darter, W., *Reminiscences of Reading by an Octogenarian*, 1888/Simeon, C., *Memoirs*, 1847)

November 14th

1539: On this day, Abbot Hugh Faringdon was executed in Reading for high treason, supposedly for financing northern rebels. Of obscure birth, he was a native of Faringdon in West Berkshire. He was a friend of Arthur Plantagenet, Lord Lisle, a natural son of King Edward IV, and received his stepson, James Basset, to be educated in the Abbey School under his supervision. In 1520, Faringdon was elected to be Abbot of Reading Abbey, and shortly thereafter King Henry VIII visited. The King and Faringdon appear to have been on good terms, exchanging gifts, and the abbot even supplied books that might help Henry to justify his views on matrimonial law. Faringdon sat in Parliament from 1523-39, as was the custom for a mitred abbot. In 1530 he signed his name on a letter to the Pope, along with other spiritual and temporal lords, pointing out the evils likely to result from delaying the divorce desired by the King. In 1536 he signed the Articles of Faith passed by Convocation at Henry's wish, which virtually acknowledged the royal supremacy. He was present in the House of Lords at the passing of the Act for the Suppression of the Greater Monasteries in 1539.

VC (*Dictionary of National Biography 1885-1900*)

NOVEMBER 15TH

1913: On this day, Caversham came to a halt for the funeral of Sergeant J.S. Perry, which was held with full military honours at Caversham Cemetery, in the presence of many people. Perry had been invalided out of the Army at the close of the South African (or Boer) War of 1899-1902 and on his return to Caversham was appointed porter at the Caversham Free Library. Sergeant Perry was a member of the Caversham and Reading Veterans' Association, and many of his comrades assisted in the sad rites.

Meeting opposite the Free Library, they marched in a body to Paardeberg Cottage, Blenheim Road, Caversham (where Perry had died), taking with them a gun carriage on which the coffin, draped with a Union Jack, was reverently placed. At 3 p.m. the funeral procession started for the cemetery, the band of the Veterans' Association playing the Dead March from *Saul* en route. Behind the coffin came three carriages containing the chief mourners, including his widow, daughter, two sisters and a brother-in-law. From the cemetery chapel, the coffin was borne to the grave by six colour-sergeants of the Coldstream Guards. Three volleys were fired at the graveside and the 'Last Post' sounded.

VC (*Reading Standard*)

NOVEMBER 16TH

1272: On this day, King Henry III died. The great-great-grandson of Henry I, founder of Reading Abbey, he is said to have been the most frequent royal visitor to Reading, often staying three or four times a year for weeks at a time. At twenty, in 1227, he celebrated Christmastide here, with masses, banquets and jousting. However, as a cultured, religious man, he was ill-equipped to handle contemporary problems like fractious barons and Welsh and Scottish conflicts, and quarrels with France continued despite his marriage to Eleanor of Provence in 1235. In 1243 the Abbey donated 100 marks towards Henry's costs of 'going into Gascony'; there were several such ventures, to underpin the Plantagenet possessions, now reduced to Gascony alone. Reading claimed his intervention in 1253, when his important Charter granted privileges to merchants disputing the abbot's control of trade. His handicapped daughter, Katherine, was allegedly cared for at Swallowfield Manor before she died in 1258. Abbey records of that year show Henry's further attempts to raise funds from Reading, and he participated in 1259 at the Abbey's Courts of Justice. Again in 1263, it was at Reading that he chose to convene Parliament.

PV (Hurry, J., *Reading Abbey*, 1901/Slade, C., *The Town of Reading and its Abbey*, MRM, 2001)

NOVEMBER 17TH

1946: On this day an unusual ceremony took place, as Reading's new Mayor, Phoebe Cusden, chose to hold her 'Mayor's Sunday' at the Friends' Meeting House in Church Street. The councillors robed in the Olympia Ballroom in nearby London Street and then marched to the Meeting House, followed by the chief officers of the borough, walking two by two. The Librarian and the Chief Coroner were followed by the Deputy Town Clerk and Museum Curator, and after them came the Water and Electrical Engineers and finally, in splendid isolation, the Food Executive Officer. Phoebe had expressed the hope that 'the very strangeness of the service may serve a useful function' but the thoughts of the guests as they sat in silence for an hour are not recorded. Phoebe Cusden (1887-1981) was a long-serving Labour member of Reading Council from 1931 to 1949, and one of the area's first female magistrates. On the national and international scene she was a tireless campaigner for women's rights, peace, nursery education and later nuclear disarmament. The most lasting achievement of her Mayoralty was the link with the war-ravaged German city of Düsseldorf, which was born of her deep compassion for the victims of war, even those who were perceived as the enemy.

JBD (Stout, A., *A Bigness of Heart*, Reading Düsseldorf Association, 1997)

NOVEMBER 18TH

1338: On this day, Edward III gave orders to John de Flete, Keeper of the London Royal Mint, to make dies for coins to be minted at Reading Abbey. Henry I's Foundation Charter of 1125 had given the Abbey the right to a mint, and some later charters confirmed this. No evidence survives that coins were in fact minted at this earlier period, and none have been found. (According to Hurry, Aethelred II, 'the Unready', 978-1016, had a mint at Reading, but no Reading-made Saxon coins appear to have survived.) Edward now ordained that Reading was to receive dies for pennies, half-pence and farthings. This was perhaps no gesture for raising Reading Abbey's prestige, but a strategy connected with the parlous state of royal finances. Only in June 1338, Edward had pressured the Abbey to lend him gold plate and other treasures (valued then at £200); and now the cost of the coin-dies was laid on the abbot. The coins from these dies were coins of the kingdom, not simply for local circulation. Incorporating the Abbey's scallop-shell symbol in its design, one – of 1339 – was recently unearthed by a detectorist.

PV (Doran, J., *The History and Antiquities of the Town and Borough of Reading in Berkshire*, 1835; Hurry, J., *Reading Abbey*, 1901)

NOVEMBER 19TH

1940: On this day, the sale took place at the Masonic Hall, Greyfriars Road, Reading, of fifty-two lots of the property of the late Mrs Ann Gundry. The items sold, from the Gundry & Co. brewery in nearby Goring, comprised nine fully licensed pubs, sixteen beerhouses, four off-licences and the brewery itself. Much of the property was acquired by fellow-brewers Nicholson's of Maidenhead and Brakspear's of Henley, with the latter taking eighteen of the pubs. Most of the estate was in and around Goring but included the Albion Tavern in Alfred Street, Reading. The brewery itself is believed to have closed following the sale, and the equipment was no doubt recycled elsewhere. Ann was a member of the Pittman family who had operated the brewery from the 1840s. Her husband, Thomas Gundry, was a native of Reading and brewer until his death in 1928. Ann continued as principal brewer and became very popular with her customers when she absorbed a penny increase in the price of beer! She died in 1933, leaving her business, valued at £77,479, in trust for five years, then to be sold with an option of purchase resting with her great-nephew, William. He chose not to exercise his right, hence the 1940 sale. **JBD** (Brown, M., *Oxon Brews*, Brewery History Society, 2004)

NOVEMBER 20TH

1976: On this day, three crossbars collapsed in separate football games at Palmer Park, Reading – two causing injuries. The Reading Combination League clash between Hillbury and Basildon was abandoned after twenty minutes when the crossbar fell on Basildon goalkeeper Dickie Baldwin, who was rushed to Battle Hospital with concussion and detained overnight. The second incident occurred before the start of the Combination Reserve Cup tie involving Reading GPO and Henley YMCA, while the same strange event happened during a Reading and District League encounter between PO Telephone Reserves and Reading NALGO. In the last, a PO Telephone player suffered head wounds. The Parks Department claimed that, although the park-keeper at Palmer Park was away that Saturday, his second-in-command – a capable man – had checked all the goals. It was suggested that, in future, the woodwork should be checked by the referees before each game – thus preventing headaches of a different kind for both players and council.
NS (Local newspapers)

1947: On this day, Princess Elizabeth and the Duke of Edinburgh were married. For the occasion, Huntley & Palmers' Master Cake Maker baked a cake that was originally designed to weigh 400lb but was reduced to 195lb on 'austerity' instructions from Buckingham Palace.
JRS (Reading Museum, Royal Panel, 2012)

NOVEMBER 21ST

1817: On this day, Thomas Sowdon, Mayor, launched the idea of illuminating Reading by gas. Prompted by 'many persons of respectability', he called a public meeting to discuss providing gas lamps in Market Place and adjacent streets. For decades previously, residents were required to hang lamps before their houses. By 1811 this was a municipal responsibility, with 218 lamps in use. But in London the Westminster Gas-Light and Coke Company was making 'town gas' practicable. Reading quickly followed, with the establishment of the Reading Gas Company. Mayor Sowdon's initiative culminated on Bonfire Night in 1819 with the town-centre lighted by gas for the first time, although financial prudence ruled out public lighting during the summer months. Castle Street Chapel marked its jubilee in 1822 by installing gas lighting, claiming to be the first public building lit by gas. Discontent at the low level of street lighting – blamed for causing coach accidents – arose in the 1830s. The rival Reading Union Gas Company, formed in 1835, offered cheaper supplies and by 1837 the reduced prices permitted the use of a third of the lamps throughout the year. Gas lighting extended to Caversham Bridge in 1843, and to outer Reading areas gradually over subsequent years.

PV (Childs, W., *The Town of Reading During the Early part of the Nineteenth Century*, 1910/*Reading Mercury*)

NOVEMBER 22ND

1802: On this day, the Reading Dispensary – the oldest of our charitable healthcare institutions – was opened, founded by three local doctors to give poor patients treatment and advice; it pre-existed both the Eye Infirmary (1826) and the Royal Berkshire Hospital (1839). Supported mostly by private donations, and directed by a succession of volunteers, the Dispensary operated from Chain Lane, facing St Mary's churchyard. Its services grew steadily. In 1814 vaccine inoculations were offered gratis, and action taken against parents publicly exposing 'children who have the small-pox upon them'. By 1832 Dispensary patients numbered nearly 18,000; by 1837-8 there were many more as railway construction came closer to Reading (although soon the new hospital assumed responsibility for the 'navvies'). Dental care was added in 1903. The Dispensary premises were rebuilt as an 'Italianate palazzo' in 1848. Although listed Grade II by English Heritage, the 'palazzo' disappeared during 1980s extensions to Heelas' department store. While the National Health Service assumed its 'hands-on' medical function, the charity survives into its third century as the Reading Dispensary Trust. Its modest offices in Wokingham Road now provide grants and support to the sick and handicapped in cases not treated by the NHS.

PV (Dear, W., *History of Reading Dispensary*, 1983)

NOVEMBER 23RD

1954: On this day, Ross James Brawn was born in Manchester. At the age of eleven he moved with his family to Reading, where his father had found employment. Brawn became interested in engineering, often visiting motor sport venues as a boy. He attended Reading School from 1966-71 and then trained as an engineer, specialising in instrumentation, at the Atomic Energy Research Establishment at Harwell, near Didcot. Brawn's motor sports career began in 1976, when he joined March Engineering in Bicester, as a milling machine operator. In 1978 he moved to Frank Williams' team, making rapid progress. Stints with other motor sports teams followed. In 1991, he became technical director at Benetton's Formula One team, helping them win the World Drivers Championship in 1994 and 1995, and the World Constructors Championship in the latter year. In 1996, Brawn followed Michael Schumacher to Ferrari, where he won acclaim for his racing strategies. Leaving Ferrari in 2006, he joined Honda; but when in 2008 Honda withdrew from the F1 Championships, Brawn's future looked in danger. However, by March 2009 he had completed a 100 per cent buy-out of the Honda team. Six months later the Brawn GP team was bought out by Mercedes-Benz, although initially Brawn retained a substantial shareholding. In 2010, he was awarded an OBE for services to motor sports.

VC (*Daily Telegraph*)

NOVEMBER 24TH

1930: On this day, Kenneth Frank Barrington was born in Reading, the son of Percy and Winifred Barrington. At the time his father was a batman in the Royal Berkshire Regiment, stationed at the Brock Barracks in Oxford Road, Reading. Educated at Wilson and Katesgrove schools, Ken Barrington played cricket for his native minor county, Berkshire, before finding his way in 1953 into the Surrey side. During sixteen years as a first-class cricketer, Barrington scored 31,714 runs at an average of 45.63; this included seventy-six centuries. He was not called up for England till 1959 but from then until his retirement in 1968 he turned out eighty-two times for his country, scoring 6,806 runs (average 58.67), and making twenty centuries. His highest test score of 256 was in 1964 against Australia and took a total of eleven hours and twenty-five minutes. Barrington's painstaking performances sometimes evoked comment of the 'Borington' variety in the tabloid press but his figures speak for themselves. He was also a useful leg-break bowler with 273 wickets, 29 in tests. He died in 1981, from a heart attack, while assistant manager of the England team then touring the West Indies.

JBD (Martin-Jenkins, C., *Complete Who's Who of Test Cricketers*, Orbis, 1980)

NOVEMBER 25TH

1872: On this day, members of the Japanese Embassy arrived at Reading on the train from London, at about 11 a.m. They were on a fact-finding tour, having been invited to visit the Huntley & Palmers biscuit factory and also view a display of Suttons' show vegetables. Despite pouring rain, a large crowd had assembled to see them arrive, but may have been disappointed to find that the visitors were not, as hoped, clad in oriental garb, but 'dressed in ordinary English costume and even wearing high, uncomfortable English black hats'. The Mayor and Corporation, in their official robes, formally welcomed the visitors at Reading station. A newspaper report describes the party as 'looking highly intelligent with a polite and gentlemanly bearing, creating a very favourable impression'. During the tour of the factory, the visitors watched processes involving the making of various biscuits including 'crisp gingerbread nuts, arrowroots, nic-nacs, etc.', and also Christmas and bridal cakes. After this they drove to The Royal Berkshire Seed Establishment, entering via the new premises in the Market Place, specially decorated with flags for the occasion, to see the display and the vast seed-packing room. A grand luncheon at the Town Hall was served in style, speeches were made and toasts drunk.

PSm (*Reading Mercury*)

NOVEMBER 26TH

1757: On this day died Samuel Watlington, aged sixty-seven years; he lies buried at St Giles' Church, Reading, with his wife, Esther. Watlington, a cloth maker by trade, was twice Mayor of Reading. In 1688, he built for himself a fine residence, Watlington House, at Orts Meadow, then on the edge of town. It has panelled rooms, a graceful staircase and a spacious garden with a fine boundary wall of flint and brick under English Heritage protection; the wall materials probably came from the nearby Abbey ruins. During the early 1800s, Watlington House was occupied by one Captain Purvis of the Berkshire Militia, whose ghost is said to haunt it. From 1877 it was home to Kendrick Girls' School, which was founded by Reading Corporation using the endowments of John Kendrick. The school moved to a new building on London Road in 1927. The popular artist Beryl Cook (1926-2008) was a pupil there in the 1940s; one of her paintings records a classroom incident. In 1929, the demolition of Watlington House was under consideration; however, it was saved by a public appeal. Today, it is home to the Mills Archive Trust (*see* August 17th) and is also available for occasional use by local charities.

SD (Dormer, E., *Watlington House,* 1929)

NOVEMBER 27TH

1878: On this day was opened the 'Iron Church' of St Luke's within St Giles' Parish. The service, at which Canon Randall, Rector of Sandhurst, preached, was preceded by a tea given by the Mayor and Mayoress, Mr and Mrs H. Bilson Blandy. Inclement weather meant that only 250 of the 350 invitees could come. The Iron Church cost £967 19s, much of the money being provided by Mr Blandy. It soon became clear that this church was inadequate to serve a growing population, and the foundation stone of a new St Luke's, laid by Mr Blandy on 27 June 1882, was duly consecrated by the Bishop of Oxford. The new church was 'erected to meet the spiritual needs of a rapidly expanding neighbourhood, the large area known as Redlands Estate, many people being employed at the Biscuit Factory'. The red-brick church, seating 530, was designed by J. Piers St Aubyn, who also designed All Saints' and directed the restoration of St Giles'. Its arcades are supported on columns of Combe Down stone. The roof was 'entirely framed and put together without the use of iron, every part secured by stout oak pins'. The 'sanctus' bell turret is still clearly visible from many parts of the parish.

JRS (The St Luke's Church Jubilee Year Book, 1933)

November 28th

1953: On this day, the *Berkshire Chronicle* reported on a double commemoration by the Polish community in Reading: for Remembrance Day and for the anniversary of Poland's Declaration of Independence after more than 150 years of domination by foreign powers. Services were held for Lutherans in St Laurence's Church and for Catholics in St James', Forbury. A wreath was laid at the War Memorial before lunch in the Great Western Hotel. Later, a concert took place in the Town Hall, at which the Chopin Choir sang, and Poles from the resettlement camps in nearby Checkendon and Nettlebed performed national dances and music.
JP (*Berkshire Chronicle*)

———•◆•———

2009: On this day, following a night of strong winds that had battered Reading, residents described what they called a 'mini-tornado' which ripped off roofs and destroyed a wall behind St Anne's Primary School in Caversham. Also in Caversham, a chimney fell through a roof, a 25m tree was blown onto a summerhouse and garden furniture was scattered. Such tornadoes are not unusual in Britain and 'minor' damage occurs most years. They are a far cry from the monster tornadoes of 'Tornado Alley' in southern USA, which annually wreak untold damage.
JRS (Currie, I., Davison, M. & Ogle, R., *The Berkshire Weather Book*, Froglets, 1994)

NOVEMBER 29TH

1911: On this day, Reading gained an exciting new facility for fitness and fun. The occasion was the eagerly awaited opening of the Arthur Hill Memorial Baths in Kings Road. The plaque still displayed at the Baths recalls that they were erected by the family of Arthur Hill, Mayor of Reading 1883-7 (*see* February 16th). Hill was a great benefactor to Reading, responsible for modernising its out-dated municipal finances, master-minding improvements in libraries and museums, and acquiring (with his own money) the Bayeux Tapestry replica that he then donated to Reading Museum – where it is still a prized exhibit. Another of Reading's great benefactors, Dr Jamieson Hurry and his wife, one of Hill's daughters, presented the site. The opening of the Baths was celebrated with a grand swimming gala attended by such worthies as Mayor J.W. Martin and the famous Octavia Hill, Arthur Hill's half-sister. The evening's star was PC Hobson, who received a life-saving award, and dived from the top board to swim a length of the pool in full police uniform! Now with a gym and spinning cycles, the Baths still serve local residents – but diving is no longer allowed, in or out of uniform!

PV (Vaughan, P., *The Arthur Hill Memorial Baths*, 2011)

NOVEMBER 30TH

1850: On this day, the *Berkshire Chronicle* recorded the opening of the Reading Cattle Market. The market was designed by the Reading architect John Berry Clacy, who was later to design other notable buildings in the town, including the Corn Exchange, the Assize Courts and the Freemasons Hall. This edifice, it was agreed, was 'no architectural gem, but the arrangement and detail showed considerable ingenuity. The south west corner is filled with stalls for 150 bullocks, a sheep market for up to 2000 sheep, a calf shed for 150 calves and pens for 500 pigs'. The whole structure had taken only eight weeks to complete, and when fully organised Reading would boast the most convenient and best arranged cattle market in existence, 'as the defects of those which have recently been erected have been carefully studied and avoided'. It was further proposed to erect a shed for the dealers' convenience in wet weather; space was reserved for future requirements. There were three entrances: two in Great Knollys Street, the other in Caversham Road. The market still stands today, but has hosted no livestock sales for many years. Instead, there are periodic auctions, a Farmers' Market, and occasional sales of plant and equipment, livestock, and classic and vintage carriages.
SG (*Berkshire Chronicle*)

DECEMBER 1ST

1135: On this day, King Henry I, founder of Reading Abbey, died in Normandy, reputedly as a result of eating too many lampreys. The historian, William of Malmesbury, described him as a 'brawny, fleshy man … heavy to sleep and frequent to snore'. Henry's court immediately made preparations for the funeral. His embalmed body was sewn into a bull's hide and carried to Cherbourg, whence it was shipped to England. The ship and its escort reached Gravesend in the Thames estuary on the 12th, where it remained while the organisation of the funeral was completed. The King's remains began their final journey up the Thames to Reading the following day. The records of the funeral expenses show that nothing was spared to ensure that the King's corpse was brought home with due ceremony. The offices for the dead were sung during the river journey by monks from Reading Abbey who had travelled to meet the ship. Each psalm sung or office recited earned them 12s, paid into the Abbey's coffers by the King's treasurer. The funeral at the Abbey was attended by the great and good, who gathered to see Henry's sarcophagus lowered into the tomb prepared for him before the altar.

VC (Wykes, A., *Reading: A Biography*, Macmillan, 1970)

DECEMBER 2ND

1793: On this day, the poet Samuel Taylor Coleridge, then aged twenty-one and heavily in debt, enlisted as a volunteer private in the 25th Light Dragoons in return for a bounty of six and a half guineas. Two days later he found himself at the regimental headquarters in Reading, after a route march from London. Having given his name as Silas Tomkyn Comberbache, he was issued with leather breeches, stable jacket, riding boots and carbine, and set to the task of mucking out the stables. While in Reading, Coleridge was billeted at the Bear Inn, where he wrote love-letters on behalf of his illiterate comrades. That he was not quite what he seemed is said to have been discovered either when he corrected a Greek quotation from Euripides made by one of the officers or when in desperation he inscribed some Latin verse by Boethius on the wall above his harness peg. This very raw recruit proved entirely unfit for cavalry duties and after basic training he was transferred to Henley as a medical orderly. Eventually, after four months in the ranks, Coleridge's discharge was negotiated by members of his family at a cost of around forty guineas (approximately £800 at current values).
JBD (Holmes, R., *Coleridge: Early Visions*, Hodder & Stoughton, 1989)

December 3rd

650: On this day, the death of St Birinus is observed by Roman Catholics. Born about 600, Birinus came to Reading while on a mission to England ordered by Pope Honorius I. After meeting Cynegils, King of Wessex, he received permission to preach to the pagans of Berkshire, and succeeded in converting the local tribe, the Redingas, who eventually gave their name to Reading. Birinus founded a cathedral at Dorchester-on-Thames, as well as – tradition has it – St Mary's in Reading. His shrine at Dorchester became a centre of pilgrimage after his death.

PV (*Encyclopaedia Britannica*)

1902: On this day, Prince Christian of Schleswig-Holstein unveiled the statue of King Edward VII presented to the town by Martin John Sutton as a permanent memorial of the Coronation. The bronze statue, 9ft in height on a 12ft pedestal, was the work of George Wade. Erected on an island facing Reading station, it shows Edward in three different rôles: as king with crown, orb and sceptre; as head of the army in Field Marshal's uniform; and as head of government in Parliamentary robes. The occasion also provided a fitting opportunity of presenting the Freedom of the Borough to Sutton himself and to George William Palmer, two of Reading's leading citizens.

SG (*Reading Standard*)

DECEMBER 4TH

1872: On this day, the foundation stone was laid for the Wesleyan Methodist Church in Queens Road, Reading. The ceremony commenced at 2.30 p.m. with the singing of a hymn composed for the occasion by the Revd G. Penman, the church's first minister; a bottle containing documents and other articles was then placed under the first memorial stone. The founding of this church was the culmination of a revival of Methodism in Reading. After the death of John Wesley in 1791, the Methodist cause in the town had declined and by 1804 it had ceased to be represented. In 1815, following pioneer work by George Banwell and James Shoar of the Wesleyan Home Missionary Department, the Revd John Waterhouse was appointed to Reading and a great revival followed. The congregation soon outgrew the chapel off Church Street, with the result that a new church was needed. Once a site was identified beside Queens Road, a London Methodist minister, Revd J.P. Johnson, was commissioned to produce a design, with local architect, Joseph Morris, supervising the building work. It was completed in 1872 at a cost of £7,000, including the site. In 1899, a manse, designed by Joseph Morris, was built next to the church.

SD (Centenary Souvenir Brochure, 1973)

DECEMBER 5TH

1923: On this day Reading was in the last throes of the parliamentary election campaign that brought to power the first Labour government, albeit one with a minority sustained by Liberal support. On 6 December, Reading electors voted in their first Labour MP, Dr Somerville Hastings, displacing the sitting Tory, Edward Cadogan. Hastings, a specialist in ear, nose and throat treatment, was forty-five at the time of his election; he lost the seat at the next election a year later. He also held Reading from 1929-31 and later served as MP for Barking, from 1945-59. He died in Reading in 1967.

JBD (*Oxford Dictionary of National Biography*, OUP, 2004)

———— • ◆ • ————

1943: On this day, Elm Park, Reading, was the venue for a showdown between two American Football teams – the Sky Trains and the Screaming Eagles. The match was organised to mark the start of Anglo-American Week in the town. Cheerleaders at the event included four specially trained Reading girls: Mary and Margaret Shrimpton, Roma Child and Jacqueline Simpson, who were all volunteer workers for the American Red Cross. The encounter between two American Forces teams raised £156 for the Red Cross POW Fund, with a special allotment to Reading YMCA Hostel Fund.

NS (Local press reports)

DECEMBER 6TH

1919: On this day, a wet Saturday, Reading Corporation Tramways tried something new – the operation of motorbuses. After electric trams had been introduced in 1903, the borough had grown, taking in both Tilehurst and Caversham in 1911. These areas had hitherto remained unserved by passenger transport, mainly because the First World War intervened. Initially, two double-deck and two single-deck motor omnibuses were put into service. With bodywork built in the undertaking's own workshops on ex-War Department AEC chassis, they were finished originally in a grey livery relieved with crimson. In order to avoid competition with the trams, the route chosen was somewhat circuitous, connecting Caversham Heights to the Plough at Tilehurst via Caversham Bridge, Stations, Town Centre, Tilehurst Road, Norcot Road, and School Road. Since their running costs were higher than those of the trams and they carried far fewer passengers, the buses operated to a different fare scale. For many years the operating cost of each and every route was meticulously recorded to monitor its profitability. Municipally run motorbuses are still with us, but modern buses are huge compared with those with which the operation commenced – open-topped, solid-tyred, high-floored and powered by wheezing petrol engines.
JRW (*Reading Standard*)

DECEMBER 7TH

1754: On this day Dr Richard Valpy, the eldest son of Richard and Catherine Valpy, was born in Jersey. His early education took place in Normandy, Southampton and Guildford. Valpy then went on to Pembroke College, Oxford, graduating in 1776. After taking orders in 1777, he became second master of Bury St Edmunds School. In 1781 he was appointed headmaster at Reading School, which was then in a depressed state. Under his guidance for over fifty years, the School reached the highest standard yet achieved. From his own pocket, he built a house for boarders, who had previously been lodged in the town. He also added a large Master's house. Among his famous pupils was Sir Thomas Noon Talfourd. Believing that education should be funded by fees rather than charity, Valpy changed Reading School from a free school. He had the reputation of being a strict disciplinarian, an attribute that gave him the nickname 'Dr Whackerback'. Valpy was also well-known as a preacher, and during his time at Reading School he became a Doctor of Divinity and served as Vicar of Stradishall, Suffolk. He died in Kensington on 28 March 1836.

VC (*Dictionary of National Biography 1885-1900*/Oakes, J. & Parsons, M., *Reading School*, DSM, 2005)

DECEMBER 8TH

1903: On this day, the Revd Dr Thomas Stokoe DD died. He was appointed headmaster of Reading School in 1871, the first to preside in the present buildings in Erleigh Road, where the school had moved after centuries in the Forbury precincts. Dr Stokoe increased numbers to near 300, achieved high standards and displayed great energy in promoting the school. However, he resigned in despair in 1877, after becoming embroiled in controversy. 'Though he was always scrupulously loyal to Reading and to Reading boys, there was a party in the town that did not understand him,' wrote Joseph Wells, Warden of Wadham. In essence the town would not accept the need for increased fees nor appreciate that boarding income subsidised day boys' fees. Although he died in Lincolnshire, Stokoe was buried next to his wife in Sonning churchyard. There is a stained-glass window to his memory in the School Chapel 'erected by some of his old boys'.
KCB (Reading School records)

1999: On this day protestors, including a Father Christmas, gathered outside the 200-year-old Greyhound pub in Mount Pleasant, Reading, to oppose its destruction by developers – but all to no avail. In the New Year, the bulldozers moved in.
JBD (*Reading Chronicle*)

DECEMBER 9TH

1688: On this day, during the 'Glorious Revolution', John Westmorland, a Reading clothier, was sent to Newbury on behalf of the town to request help from the Count of Nassau. It was alleged that Irish troops, stationed in Reading, who were loyal to King James II, had 'threatened to murther and plunder' the townspeople. Westmorland's action led to the Battle of Reading, more correctly described as a skirmish, which took place the following day. The Irish, who had taken up their position in St Mary's churchyard and also around the Market Place, were routed by 'the Dutch with two hundred and eighty horse and dragoons'. As Daniel Defoe described the event: 'The [Irish] troops being numerous made two or three regular discharges; but finding themselves charged in the rear by the other Dutchmen, who had by this time entered Broad Street, they not knowing the strength, or weakness of their enemy, presently broke, and fled by all ways possible.' At a later period, John Westmorland served as postmaster of Reading from 1716 at a salary of £30 per year. He died in 1723 at the age of sixty-two.

JBD (Defoe, D., *A Tour Through the Whole Island of Great Britain*, 1724-27)

DECEMBER 10TH

1960: On this day Kenneth Charles Branagh, actor, director and writer, was born in Belfast. The middle of three children born to William and Frances, he moved with them to Reading at the age of nine, to escape the troubles brewing in Ulster. Branagh attended Meadway School where he was attracted to sports and journalism and had his first starring rôle, as Toad, in *Toad of Toad Hall*. His call to a stage career was confirmed at the age of fifteen by seeing Derek Jacobi as *Hamlet*. He honed his acting skills at Reading's Progress Theatre, with which he maintains close links to this day. He attended the Central School for Speech and Drama, before moving on to RADA. From there, Branagh landed a second lead rôle in a West End play. His subsequent career has seen him act in and direct numerous films and television shows. He has particularly specialised in Shakespeare, whose *Midsummer Night's Dream*, *Hamlet*, and *Henry V* are among Branagh's triumphs on stage and screen. The rôle of Professor Gilderoy Lockhart in the Harry Potter films brought him to a younger generation, while *Wallander* is his best-known television part. For services to drama and to Northern Ireland, he was knighted in 2012.

VC (*Daily Telegraph*/Kenneth Branagh website)

DECEMBER 11TH

1974: On this day, the Reading and Mid-Berkshire branch of the Campaign for Real Ale (CAMRA) was founded at 'a meeting to test support' held at the Hope and Anchor, Wokingham. Estimates of the numbers present have differed but ran well into three figures. CAMRA was then itself only three years old but has since grown into a major campaigning organisation with over 100,000 members. Originally the Reading branch encompassed a wide area including Wokingham, Bracknell and Ascot, but since 2001 has been confined to Reading and its immediate surroundings.

———— ◆ ————

2009: On this day, CAMRA members met at the Eldon Arms in Reading to celebrate thirty-five years' campaigning in and around the town. They included at least two survivors from the inaugural meeting. The occasion coincided with the thirty-fifth anniversary of Brian and Ann Mackie running the pub, an event recognised by the brewers, Wadworth of Devizes, with a special commemorative brew, 35 Years Porter. In addition, CAMRA presented the couple with a framed certificate recording their sterling efforts in campaigning for real ale over that period, including many entries in the *Good Beer Guide*. And – a great 'real pub' tradition – sausages were served!
JBD (Personal diaries)

DECEMBER 12TH

1898: On this day, the Berkshire Art Society, which had been formed a few months earlier, held its first annual exhibition in Reading's newly extended Corporation Art Gallery. The exhibition, which was opened by Lord Wantage, displayed some 249 excellent pictures. Such was the interest aroused that between two and four o'clock about a thousand people flocked to view the exhibition. The objects of the Society were to encourage artists and amateurs residing in Berkshire and foster of a greater interest in art in the public at large. G.D. Leslie RA was the president, and other well-known members included the Royal Academicians Alfred Waterhouse and E.J. Gregory. Twenty members came from Reading town itself. The Society flourished for about ten years but in 1907 they were turned out of the Town Hall following allegations that the holding of an exhibition there had damaged the walls. It found a new home at the YMCA, but did not long survive the move.
SG (*Berkshire Chronicle*/Berkshire Art Society catalogue, 1898)

———— • ◆ • ————

1963: On this day, the Rolling Stones played at the Town Hall for a £200 fee. The contract stipulated that 'a piano and microphone equipment' were to be provided.
AS (Local press reports)

DECEMBER 13TH

1713: On this day, a future Reading doctor, physician to King George III, was born in Twyford, Berkshire. He was Anthony Addington, Oxford graduate in medicine, who came to Reading in 1745 to practise at 73 London Street, where his house still stands (now bearing a memorial plaque). In the same year he married Mary Hiley, daughter of the headmaster of Reading School. To provide for the treatment of the mentally ill, in whom he had a particular interest, Addington built special accommodation next-door to his London Street house. Among his general patients was Henley solicitor Richard Blandy, poisoned by arsenic in 1752. Addington was 'expert witness' in the trial, at which Blandy's daughter Mary was found guilty of the murder and sentenced to death. Addington turned to the study of scurvy and submitted serious proposals to the Admiralty for saving sailors from this killer disease. In London from 1754, he became Fellow of the College of Physicians, with patients including Lord Chatham and later King George III, who suffered bouts of insanity. His treatment was deemed beneficial – indeed, George outlived him by thirty years! Addington later retired to Reading, where he tended poor patients at no charge, dying there in 1790. His son, Henry, became Prime Minister and a founder of the Royal Berkshire Hospital.

PV (*Dictionary of National Biography 1885-1900*)

DECEMBER 14TH

1931: On this day, while visiting Reading Aero Club, flying ace Douglas Bader attempted low-flying aerobatics over Woodley Airfield. He had previously received, and ignored, cautions over his daredevil stunts. At the time, he was preparing to fly for his squadron in the Hendon Air Show and was hoping to achieve a second consecutive win. All pilots had been warned not to fly lower than 50ft but, in spite of this, Bader's left wingtip touched the ground and he crashed. He was taken to the Royal Berkshire Hospital where the eminent surgeon, J. Leonard Joyce, amputated both his legs. In his logbook Bader recorded: 'Crashed slow rolling near the ground. Bad show' – underlined three times! After a long convalescence Bader was fitted with artificial legs, but was not permitted to rejoin the RAF until 1939. Flying over Northern France in August 1941, his plane was downed and he was captured by the Germans. The RAF were allowed to parachute in an artificial leg to replace the one lost when he bailed out. Because of his frequent escape attempts he was imprisoned in Colditz until the end of the war. Knighted for his services to the disabled in 1976, he died in 1982.

JP (Temple, J., *Wings over Woodley*, 1987)

DECEMBER 15TH

1943: On this day the Ministry of Aircraft Production placed a contract with Miles Aircraft in Reading to research and produce a plane capable of flying at supersonic speed. The design team worked strenuously in conditions of the utmost secrecy and after three years of intense effort the aircraft, code-named the M52, had reached an advanced stage. The mock-ups were complete, two prototypes were well underway, and the first flight was expected in the summer of 1946. In February, however, the Director-General of Scientific Research passed on to the team the devastating news that all work was to be suspended. Technical considerations derived from German research on a similar project, and fear that test flights could place the lives of pilots at risk, were put forward to support this announcement, even though it was known that pilots, including ex-Luftwaffe pilots, were more than willing to participate. The Ministry of Aircraft Production also ordered that all technical data should be handed over to Bell Aircraft in America and thus Britain lost its chance. During its twenty-seven years of service, the Anglo-French Concorde flew daily over that part of Reading where the original work had taken place.

JP (Temple, J., *Wings over Woodley*, 1987)

DECEMBER 16TH

1787: On this day, Mary Russell Mitford, the celebrated novelist and chronicler, was born in Aylesford, Hampshire. She was the only daughter of a country doctor who had married into money. Mary had a comfortable childhood; the family lived for some years in London Road, Reading, and from there she went to boarding school in London. Mary's first venture into a literary career was with poetry, which showed promise of what was to come. It led to friendships with her contemporaries, Elizabeth Barrett Browning becoming a lifelong friend. After her father squandered all the family wealth, they moved to a cottage in Three Mile Cross, just outside Reading. It was this village that became the source for 'Our Village', an account of life and experience in a small village, first serialised in *The Lady's Journal*, then published as a book. This became Mary's best-known work, although she wrote other books, including *Belford Regis* (based on the town of Reading – *see* February 25th). Ill-health forced Mary to give up writing and Queen Victoria contributed to a private fund set up to supplement her Civil List Pension. She died on 10 January 1855 in Swallowfield, only a few miles from the village that made her famous.

VC (Mitford, Mary Russell, *Our Village*, Sidgwick & Jackson, 1986)

DECEMBER 17TH

2009: On this day, heavy snowfalls brought Reading to a standstill and turned Forbury Square and Broad Street into fairytale scenes. Reading University Climatological Station recorded the biggest snowfall since December 1987. With major roads gridlocked, the Royal Berkshire Hospital warned highly pregnant women to contact emergency services rather than risk venturing out by car. Even so, paramedics had to battle through deep snow to deliver 'an early Christmas present' – christened 'Snowflake' – to one Whitley couple! The hazardous conditions brought widespread early closures for schools, no doubt to the delight of the children. The traffic chaos in Bath Road, Liebenrood Road and Caversham was dramatically captured in YouTube footage. Vehicles were abandoned on the slopes of Caversham and their drivers given refuge in the local Methodist church. Stranded shoppers were invited into a Morrisons store to enjoy hot meals. In Alexandra Road, water-main replacement was delayed for three weeks. Local youths used the metal 'Road Closed' signs as toboggans, with the result that a number of cars, the occasional bus and even an articulated lorry slid ignominiously while trying to negotiate blocked roads. Further snowfalls followed, stretching into February 2010.

JRS (*Reading Post*/Reading University Climatological Station data)

DECEMBER 18TH

1817: On this day, William Blandy, the Reading alderman, drowned at 'the Katesgrove bathing-house'. He went, as usual, to bathe alone, and it was supposed that he experienced cramp, and was unable to save himself. As Chief Magistrate for Reading, he had shown firmness and integrity; as a man, great philanthropy and beneficence; and exemplary charity as a Christian. His social virtues and friendly disposition made his loss deeply lamented, and his memory long and much revered. He was sixty-two years old.

VC (*Hampshire Chronicle*)

———◆———

1886: On this day, in Forbury Gardens, Reading, the Lion was unveiled to commemorate the 328 soldiers of the 66th Royal Berkshire Regiment killed in the Afghan Campaign of 1879-80, chiefly at the Battle of Maiwand. Sculptor George Simonds had taken five years over the work, making twelve models before the design was finally settled. He spent many months at London Zoological Gardens making detailed studies of lions; the popular tale that the legs of the sculpture were misplaced and Simonds committed suicide as a result is unfounded. The cost of the Maiwand Lion was £900, out of a subscription of £1,088, with the surplus funding a stained-glass window at St Mary's Church.

SG (Stacpoole-Ryding, R.J., *Maiwand*, The History Press, 2008)

DECEMBER 19TH

1863: On this day, the *Berkshire Chronicle* reported that the medallists at the Royal Academy included Charles Barber, who was awarded a Silver medal for drawing from the antique. The indication of his great talent had been discovered by Charles Havell, headmaster of the Reading School of Art, who strongly advised him to pursue his studies in London. Charles Burton Barber was born in Great Yarmouth in 1845. He came to Reading when he was about seven or eight, with his father, Charles senior, an upholsterer by trade. The father almost immediately involved himself with local affairs, becoming secretary to the Mechanics Institute; when it closed he was made secretary to the newly formed Reading School of Art. Charles junior was destined to become one of the most popular artists of his day, eventually succeeding Landseer as a favourite of Queen Victoria. She commissioned a number of paintings from him; one of them, showing the Queen with her ghillie, John Brown, recently changed hands for £145,000. Much of his work portrays dogs and pretty children, and he also worked on artwork for *The Graphic* and Pears Soap. His successful career was cut short, however, as he died in 1894 aged forty-nine. Two of his works are kept by the Museum of Reading.
SG (*Berkshire Chronicle*)

DECEMBER 20TH

1887: On this day, the Harrinson Memorial Cross was unveiled in the churchyard of St Mary's, Reading. It was erected as a token of the respect that the parish held for Isaac Harrinson, a wealthy medical practitioner and parishioner. His largesse had included the restoration of the church (particularly the north aisle), the enlargement of the organ, the removal of run-down cottages bordering the churchyard, and the general tidying-up of the St Mary's Butts area, making way for the new Jubilee Fountain that had been erected a few months earlier. Harrinson also made a £1,000 donation towards the construction of the new municipal buildings. The Memorial Cross, which is 14ft in diameter at the base and rises to 20ft, takes the form of a traditional pre-Reformation churchyard cross, decorated with the arms of Harrinson, the arms of Reading and those of the Oxford and Salisbury Dioceses. A design competition had been held, won by Spencer Slingsby Stallwood, with the masonry and carving undertaken by Wheeler Brothers. Harrinson came to Reading in 1839 from Bardsey in Yorkshire, becoming a partner with Dr George May and marrying Ellen May, his relative. He died in his seventy-ninth year on 26 June 1888, just over six months after the unveiling of his memorial.
SG (*Reading Observer*)

DECEMBER 21ST

1633: On this day Lodowick Bowyer was set in Reading Market Place pillory, after accusing Archbishop William Laud of treason on 11 September 1633. He had claimed that Laud had been in communication with the Pope, and was subsequently arrested by the King. The Mayor of Reading doggedly pursued Bowyer until he was sent to London, and taken before the Court of Star Chamber. This day, 21 December, was a Saturday, market day, and the Mayor and Corporation, constables, other officers, town and country-folk all assembled in Market Place to see Bowyer set in the pillory. His ears were nailed to the wooden frame, and a paper fixed to his head detailing his offence. He was forced to read out loud a confession of his guilt, and was then left there as a target for those who wished to throw stones or filth at him, until he was deemed to have served his punishment. The full sentence ordered by the Star Chamber comprised: a £3,000 fine; three stints in the pillory (two in London, as well as the one in Reading); whipping; branding on the face with R for rogue and L for liar; and finally imprisonment for life.

VC (Childs, W., *The Story of the Town of Reading*, 1905)

DECEMBER 22ND

1971: On this day the final section of the M4 motorway, comprising some 50 miles, was opened. The road's London and Welsh ends had been completed years before, but the only link in between them was the A4 that ran, as it still does, through Reading town. Ever-increasing volumes of traffic, including all manner of commercial vehicles, had made the A4 a nightmare for residents. A 1970 survey had counted 30,000 cars travelling daily between Reading and Maidenhead on a road with capacity for only 13,000. Government minister Michael (now Lord) Heseltine officially opened the completed motorway, congratulating all involved in its planning and construction. It would greatly shorten travelling-time to his South Wales home, he observed; he then drove off in his red Jaguar to Cardiff, where he presented greetings to the Lord Mayor from the Lord Mayor of London. For ill-prepared drivers surprised that the M4 had no services between Heston and the Severn Bridge, the AA announced an increase in motorway patrols carrying emergency supplies of petrol and water. Some residents soon expressed concern about increased traffic (from Oxfordshire) over Caversham Bridge, but those living beside the Bath Road route gave warm approval.

PV (Hunter, J., *A History of Berkshire*, Phillimore, 1995/ *Reading Chronicle*)

DECEMBER 23RD

1851: On this day Charles Dickens, as a leading member of the once famous Amateur Company of the Guild of Literature and Art, was in Reading taking lead rôles in performances of a farce and a comedy at the New Hall, Reading. The comedy, *Not So Bad As We Seem* by Sir Edward Bulwer Lytton, had been performed for Queen Victoria and Prince Albert in May of this year. The performance was one of a series taking place in London and on tour around the country in aid of indigent artists and authors. Dickens proved an admirable actor, in the rôle of Lord Wilmot. Other notables in the casts were: Wilkie Collins, Douglas Jerrold, John Forster, Mark Lemon, John Tenniel, Charles Knight and R.H. Horne. This was not the only time that Dickens came to Reading for literary purposes. He returned in December 1854 as the newly elected president of the Literary, Scientific and Mechanics' Institution in London Street, to give a dramatic reading of his *Christmas Carol* to a large and enthusiastic audience. A further visit by 'The Inimitable' Dickens came in November 1858, when he gave readings from *Dombey and Son* and the trial scene from *The Pickwick Papers*.

VC (Cooper, J., *Some Worthies of Reading,* 1923)

December 24th

1763: On this day, the *Reading Mercury* recorded the following event: 'This morning, as Mr. John Weller, limner [portrait painter] of this town was lighting his fire he was seized with a fit of apoplexy, and expired immediately.' John Man mentions Weller as one of the town's worthies and cites an epitaph by Richard Cole with the following opening lines:

> If thou can'st yet, lamented shade, attend
> The heartfelt sorrows of a faithful friend
> Accept the humble homage of a lay,
> The only tribute that the muse can play,
> In blameless confidence who dares impart
> By songs sincere and dictates of the heart.
> Friend of thy fame, but more a friend of truth
> Thou once kind guide of my unstable youth.

There are three known works by Weller: a self-portrait, and portraits of John Rowell, the stained glass-painter, and the Revd Dr Henry Stebbing, Chancellor of Sarum. Another, an oil of the Revd William Reeves, vicar of St Mary's, Reading, has also been ascribed to him and is now in the Museum of Reading.
SG (Man, J., *History and Antiquities of Reading*, 1816)

DECEMBER 25TH

1345: On this day, King Edward III was at Reading for Christmas, celebrating at the Abbey with feasting and a great tournament. Henry III (his great-grandfather) had also kept his Christmas at the Abbey in 1217 (probably the first king to do so). Numerous English monarchs have visited Reading, at various seasons: Richard II in 1389, Henry IV in 1483, Edward VI in 1552, Mary Tudor in 1554, while Elizabeth I came on six occasions, on one of which she gave the town a portrait of herself, now on show at Reading Museum. When Reading was in Royalist hands during the Civil War, Charles I is said to have had his headquarters at Coley Park. After the Restoration, Charles II made a formal visit, during which he and his Queen were received by the Mayor in the Orts Road, and presented with a bag of gold. A relatively recent visit was that of Queen Elizabeth II in 1989 – to open the then new railway station (now again under re-construction).
PMS (*Berkshire Chronicle*)

———— ◆ ————

1908: On this day, Reading Winter Bathers held their Annual Breakfast at Phillips' Restaurant, Duke Street, at 8.45 a.m. sharp. A. Watson, Chairman, and J. Eighteen, Vice-Chairman, presided.
AS (Clark, G., *Down By The River*, Two Rivers, 2009)

DECEMBER 26TH

1962: On this day, the snows began that were to freeze the ground until early March 1963. After a freezing Christmas night the snow set in later on Boxing Day with some 10cm (4in) recorded at the Reading University Climatological Station. The icy roads took their toll when a newly married man was killed in a collision on Bath Road. Families were hit when 2,500 workers were laid off, and ten times that number had to go part time. The Thames froze at Reading, as it had many times during earlier centuries, and channels for navigation had to be kept clear by the Thames Conservancy. Animals and birds suffered too – swans had to be rescued by the RSPCA from frozen ponds and lakes. Reading's local papers reported on the vast sums of money that had been used for snow clearance both of roads and railway lines, and there were endless arguments over the Local Authority's response to gritting as well as whether the Meteorological Office had given adequate warnings. As the new year began, fresh snowfalls were carried into deep drifts by a biting wind. All in all, this proved to be the coldest winter period since the mid-eighteenth century.

JRS (Currie, I., Davison, M. & Ogley, R., *The Berkshire Weather Book*, Froglets, 1994)

DECEMBER 27TH

1830: On this day, the 'Swing Trials' took place in Reading. Among those charged was William Winterbourne, who stood trial in a temporary dock erected in the Town Hall before the Special Assize. During November a crowd of between 200 and 500 mainly agricultural labourers had visited towns and villages in West Berkshire, making demands for food and drink and money, and destroying threshing machines along with machinery in an iron foundry; this culminated in negotiations with Hungerford Magistrates for increased wages. A chase through the country led by MP Charles Dundas and Lord Craven, described as a 'good day's sport', led to the capture of the farm workers, who were delivered into military custody. William Oakley, Alfred Darling and William Winterbourne were sentenced to death, which was commuted to transportation for life for the first two as a result of petitions and representations. On 11 January, however, Winterbourne was executed on the west wall of Reading Gaol. His body was brought from Reading by the Vicar of Kintbury, the Revd F.C. Fowle, and buried in St Mary's churchyard, with a gravestone in the name of 'William Smith' aged thirty-three. *The Times* concluded: 'Life had not dealt so tenderly with him for death at last to hold much bitterness.'

KJ (Fox, N., *From Berkshire to Botany Bay*, 1996)

December 28th

1918: On this day the post-war Parliamentary Election for Reading was won by Leslie Orme-Wilson (Conservative) with 15,204 votes. T.G. Morris (Labour) polled 8,410, F. Thoresby (Liberal) 3,143 and L.E. Quelch (Socialist) 1,462. Earlier that year, on 16 April, Lorenzo 'Len' Edward Quelch, as secretary of Reading Trades Council, had convened the meeting which formed Reading Labour Party. When the Social Democratic Federation, Britain's first Marxist Party, split in 1916, Len Quelch with his brother Harry had joined the pro-war faction, the National Socialist Party, whose executive, he claimed, had refused to allow him to withdraw his nomination in 1918. The other part of the split Federation, the British Socialist Party, which had nominated Morris, was – according to Quelch – infiltrated by pacifists and Bolsheviks. Although he had been elected councillor for Reading's Minster Ward in May 1914 as a Socialist, and subsequently became alderman, it is likely that by standing as an independent Socialist against the official Labour candidate, Quelch was denied a wider political career. He died in 1937 at the age of seventy-five. In the 1890s he had lived in Addington Road, where in recent years a children's playground was opened in his memory.

KJ (Quelch, L., *An Old-Fashioned Socialist,* 1992/Bellamy, J., *Dictionary of Labour Biography,* 1987)

DECEMBER 29TH

1946: On this day, Marianne Evelyn Faithfull was born in Hampstead to Major Robert Faithfull, a British military officer and professor of psychology, and Eva von Sacher-Masoch, Baroness Erisso. From the age of six, she grew up in Milman Road, Reading, living with her alcoholic and now divorced mother in much reduced circumstances. Her girlhood was further marred by bouts of tuberculosis. As a student at St Joseph's Convent School in Reading, Marianne joined the Progress Theatre's student group. She began her music career in 1964, landing her first gigs as a folk music performer in coffee houses. At eighteen, she married artist John Dunbar, with whom she had a son, Nicholas, but John's heroin addiction led to their splitting up. In 1966 there followed a highly publicised romance with three Rolling Stones, including Mick Jagger, which was to last five years. In the succeeding decades, Marianne Faithfull has bounced back from almost every setback imaginable, including her own heavy drinking, late pregnancy miscarriage, heroin and cocaine addiction, attempted suicide, sleeping rough in Soho, and breast cancer in 2006. She forged herself a new successful career as a singer and songwriter, which still endures, as is evident from recent records and performances with Jarvis Cocker, Nick Cave and P.J. Harvey.
VC (*Daily Mail*)

DECEMBER 30TH

1624: On this day died John Kendrick, a highly successful cloth-merchant. A Reading School alumnus and son of Reading's Mayor, Kendrick had made his fortune in London, trading with the Netherlands. Reading Corporation received a huge bequest of £7,500, with which to buy 'a fair plot of ground' and build 'a strong house of brick, fit for setting the poor to work therein … in the trades of clothing … and dyeing, or otherwise'. After this house of industry, called 'The Oracle', was built in Minster Street, Reading's cloth trade unfortunately began its long decline. The Oracle became a run-down warren of tenements and workshops where the indigent were occupied in such ventures as the weaving of 'galoons, satin and ribands' and the manufacture of sail-cloth, rope and pins. Accusations of mismanagement eventually led to the Lord Chancellor's judgement in 1843 that the Corporation had been negligent in administering the Kendrick Trusts. By 1850, The Oracle, with its grandiose gateway flanked by Ionic columns, had been sold and converted to other commercial uses; but its name survives in that of Reading's newest shopping centre. Kendrick's benevolence lived on in the foundation of Kendrick Girls' School, which still owns his impressive portrait, salvaged from the old Oracle.

PV (Childs, W., *Town of Reading in the Early Nineteenth Century*, 1910)

DECEMBER 31ST

1929: On this day, the future England cricket captain, Peter Barker Howard May, was born in Reading. Often considered the finest post-war English batsman, May showed promise as a schoolboy at Charterhouse and subsequently during his three years at Cambridge and national service in the Royal Navy. He made his debut for Surrey in 1950, captaining the side from 1957 until 1962. He scored a century on his test debut against South Africa in 1951 and was a key figure two years later when England finally overcame the Australians to regain the Ashes. In a total of twenty-one tests against the old enemy, he scored 1,566 runs at an average of 46, including three centuries. However, perhaps his greatest innings was against the West Indies in 1957 when he made his highest score of 285 not out in a fourth wicket partnership of 411 with Cowdrey. As captain he was less successful, losing the Ashes in 1958/9 and failing to regain them in 1961. Thereafter, he played no further test cricket and in 1963 retired from the first-class game. Altogether May hit eighty-five centuries, thirteen in tests, and scored 27,592 runs, 4,537 for England. He died in 1994 from a brain tumour.

JBD (Martin-Jenkins, C., *Complete Who's Who of Test Cricketers*, Orbis, 1980)